The Life and Death
of John Price

The Honourable Sir John Vincent William Barry has been a judge of the Supreme Court of Victoria since January 1947. Born in June 1903, he was admitted as a barrister in 1926, and was appointed a King's Counsel in Victoria in 1942 and in New South Wales in 1946. Chairman of the Department of Criminology at the University of Melbourne since it was established in 1951, and of the Parole Board of Victoria since its inception in 1957, he has studied criminology and penology in U.S.A. and in Europe. He was leader of the Australian delegation at the 1st and 2nd United Nations Congresses for the Prevention of Crime and the Treatment of Offenders held, respectively, in Geneva in 1955 and in London in 1960. He is the author of *Alexander Maconochie of Norfolk Island* (Oxford University Press, Melbourne, 1958) and, in collaboration, of *An Introduction to Criminal Law in Australia* (Macmillan, London, 1948), as well as of numerous articles in legal and other journals.

John Price

From a portrait, about 1853
By courtesy of the Royal Society of Tasmania

The Life and Death of John Price

A STUDY OF THE EXERCISE OF NAKED POWER

THE HONOURABLE MR JUSTICE

JOHN VINCENT BARRY

MELBOURNE UNIVERSITY PRESS

LONDON AND NEW YORK: CAMBRIDGE UNIVERSITY PRESS

First published 1964

Printed and bound in Australia by
Melbourne University Press, Parkville N.2, Victoria

Registered in Australia for transmission
by post as a book

Text set in 11 point Fairfield type

There must be power, either that of governments, or that of anarchic adventurers. There must even be naked power, so long as there are rebels against governments, or even ordinary criminals. But if human life is to be, for the mass of mankind, anything better than a dull misery punctuated with moments of sharp horror, there must be as little naked power as possible.

Bertrand Russell, *Power* (1938)

PREFACE

It was on the persuasion of a dear friend, the late Robert Hanlon, that I undertook research for this study. He had assembled an extensive collection of Australiana, and was deeply interested in the convict system. He lamented the absence of a reliable biography of John Price, and he thought I could supply the omission. At the time of his death on 27 October 1959, a good deal of material had been gathered by our combined researches, and thereafter, as happens when one is interested in a subject, this grew by constant and sometimes unexpected additions. Regard for my friend's memory, and a feeling it would be a pity if the material were not collated in a form suitable for publication, induced me to write this study. To me, however, Price has more than an historical or legendary significance. I have long been fascinated and disturbed by human cruelty (a pleonasm, for cruelty is uniquely a human characteristic), and in the concluding chapter I have tried to set down my puzzled reflections on the enigma of this aspect of man's nature in the hope that some more penetrating mind will take up an enquiry that is of supreme importance to mankind.

My obligations for assistance I have received are extensive. My first acknowledgments are, of course, to the State Libraries of Victoria and of Tasmania, and the Public and Mitchell Libraries of New South Wales, whose principals, Mr John Feely, Mr B. W. Wray, and Mr G. D. Richardson, and the Deputy Mitchell Librarian, Mrs Marjorie Hancock, and their staffs, have been consistently helpful. My indebtedness to Mr P. V. Garrett, Chief Research Officer of the State Library of Victoria, calls for special mention; it is a pleasure to record my appreciation of his friendship and my admiration for his erudition and efficiency and unfailing courtesy. His assistant, Miss Patricia Reynolds, has also earned my special gratitude.

Many friends have given me help in various ways when I sought it. Mr Ian McLaren and Mr Ivo Hammett have lent me, generously and trustingly, rare items from their own libraries. Dr W. E. L. Crowther of Hobart, and his son, Dr William Crowther, and Dr Eric Cunningham Dax have read some chapters and given me the benefit of their comments. Mr Karl von Stieglitz answered my enquiries promptly and sent me a rubbing of the inscription on the salver presented to Price and preserved at Entally, Launceston. Mr Wilson Evans made available his extensive knowledge of the early days of Williamstown, and a long letter from Lt-Col. R. C. R. Price, D.S.O., O.B.E.; Mr Eric Cook furnished me with material he has collected about the Victorian hulks, and Dr Mary Kent Hughes provided me with a copy of Dr John Singleton's autobiography, long out of print. Mr D. T. Jones, formerly of the Penal and now of the Crown Law Department, obtained for me information and documents from the early penal records of Victoria. Mrs Nicholas and Mrs Jaggs lent me, for copying, the address presented to John Price's widow by the penal staff of Victoria. A brother judge, the Hon. Mr Justice A. D. G. Adam, gave me the benefit of his examination of Sir Rose Price's will, and Mrs Mary Trott brought to my notice Price's correspondence with the Quaker missionary, George Washington Walker.

Without the assistance of my associate, Mr James H. Edwards, and of Miss J. L. Carruthers and Mrs R. A. Patching, who prepared the typescript, this work could never have reached the stage of publication, and I am happy to record my appreciation of their help.

When I sought to separate fact from fancy concerning Henry Beresford Garrett, whose account of John Price is described in an appendix to this study, Mr John P. Kennedy's help was invaluable. He lent me the transcripts he made of Garrett's manuscripts containing 'The Demon' and the 'portraits' of Colonel Champ, Price's successor, and George Duncan, superintendent of Pentridge Stockade, and later also Inspector-General of Penal Establishments. Mr Kennedy supplied me with information, too, about the circumstances under which the manuscripts came into his possession so that he was able to copy them. The facts concerning Garrett's criminal convictions in Victoria and in New

Zealand have been established through the kindness of my friends, Mr Arthur Payne, Prothonotary of the Supreme Court of Victoria, and Dr J. L. Robson, Secretary of Justice, New Zealand.

I acknowledge, too, my debt to the Royal Historical Society of Victoria for lending me the manuscript regulations for the Victorian hulks.

JOHN V. BARRY

Judges' Chambers
Supreme Court
Melbourne
May 1964

CONTENTS

ILLUSTRATIONS

J. V. Barry, *The Life and Death of John Price*

ERRATA
p.   2, 1.24.   For 1734, read 1739.
p.   4, 1.33.   For 1826, read 1836.
p. 11, 1.30.   For Pendari, read Pindari.
p. 40, 1.37.   For State, read Colony.
p. 65, 1.28.   For State, read Colony.
p. 77, 1.20.   For: Each hut was, read: The huts were.
p.151, 1.18.   For guilt, read guilty.
p.186, 1.55.   For 1935, read 1953.

Chapter One

BACKGROUND

The *Strathisla*, a ship of 332 tons, arrived at Hobart Town on Wednesday, 26 May 1836. She had put out from Liverpool on 19 January, and the passage had taken just over eighteen weeks.[1] Among her seventeen passengers was a powerfully-built man of twenty-seven, reddish-haired and ruddy-complexioned, whose urbane manner concealed a tigerish nature. He was John Giles Price, and his name was destined to live on as a synonym for harshness when legend itself had forgotten most other despots of the convict system.

Born on 20 October 1808, John Price was the son of Sir Rose Price, of Trengwainton, Cornwall. Rose Price's marriage in 1798 with Elizabeth, youngest daughter of Charles Lambart of Beau Parc, County of Meath, was prolific, yielding six sons and eight daughters. John was the fourth son. His mother, who had married when she was sixteen, died on 2 December 1826, aged forty-four, when John was eighteen. Sir Rose loved her dearly; when he died it was found that his will directed that he be buried beside her, with a locket of her hair around his neck, and 'the fine hair that was taken from her head at her death beside me in my coffin, as testimonies of the love I bore her.' It was the second time that year that death had struck the family; the eldest son, Rose Lambart, died at Holding's Hotel, Dover Street, London, on 16 January, when he was twenty-six. He had married Catherine, countess dowager of Desart, not quite two years before. Sir Rose survived his wife by seven years; born on 21 November 1768, he died at Trengwainton on 29 September 1834, in his sixty-sixth year.[2]

John Price's family background is important for an understanding of his haughty nature, and the autocratic personality of his father for an appreciation of the son's strangely complex character. The Prices traced their descent from Caradoc Vreichvras,

1

Prince between the Wye and the Severn. It was, however, through Francis Price that this branch of the family became wealthy. Francis was an army captain and a member of the expedition that set out on Christmas Day, 1654, under a direction from Cromwell 'to assault the Spaniard in the West Indies'. Admiral (later Sir) William Penn (1621-70)[3] was general-at-sea and commander-in-chief of the expedition, whose forces comprised the fleet, a regiment of seamen, and a body of troops, commanded by General Robert Venables. The enterprise was only indifferently successful, but Jamaica was captured in May 1655, and Francis Price settled on the island. He married Sarah Booth, who bore him a daughter and three sons. The daughter, Elizabeth, married Francis Rose, of Rose Hall, the finest of the old Jamaican houses. The considerable Jamaican estates owned by the Rose family devolved upon Elizabeth's brother, Charles (d. 1730), whose son and grandson both figured prominently and creditably in the affairs of Jamaica. The son, the first Sir Charles, known as 'The Patriot' for his public benefactions, his political independence, and his services in the parliament of Jamaica, was created a baronet in 1768. He died in 1772. His son, also Sir Charles, was similar in character to his father and, like him, became Speaker of the House of Assembly of Jamaica. He died in 1788 without children, and the baronetcy expired.[4] The family estates devolved upon John (d. 1734), youngest son of the first baronet, and his only son, John (1738-97), was the father of Rose Price, also an only son. Thus, by the accidents of descent and the effect of testamentary dispositions, Rose Price, father of John Giles Price, was a man of fortune, owning great estates in Jamaica. An eccentric of choleric disposition, his wealth enabled him to give free play to his idiosyncracies. In 1814 he was appointed Sheriff of Cornwall. Shortly after, on 27 December 1814, he was created a baronet, as a reward, it is said,[5] for his refusal as sheriff to convene a public meeting to consider 'the claims of the Roman Catholics'. His crest embodied a dragon's head holding in the mouth a hand, dropping blood, and some have seen in it a portent of the violent death that overtook his son John.[6]

Sir Rose Price was a man of imperious temperament. He was soundly educated at Penzance Grammar School and at Harrow, and at Magdalene College, Oxford; and afterwards he spent three years in Jamaica. On his return to England he lived, in progressive magnificence, in houses at Trevailor, at Chun(or Chyoone)-in-Paul, and at Kenegie-in-Gulval. When he was living at Chun he conceived the idea of building a residence at Tredavo-in-Paul suited to his taste for splendour. The site was exposed to the east wind, however, and to gain protection, he set about the erection of an immense mound. It still remains. Forming two sides of a square, it is about twenty feet high and twelve feet wide at the top, and nearly a quarter of a mile long. At first known locally as the 'great wall of China', it was soon dubbed 'Price's folly'. Abandoning that project but becoming more grandiose, he set about the construction of an enormous mansion on an estate which he bought at Trengwainton. The surrounding granite hills were planted with fir trees; the drives were lined with laurels; and, set within an estate of 773 acres, the mansion was surrounded by 70 acres of plantations and shrubberies. In a valley three large ponds were constructed for trout-fishing and the breeding of wild duck, and he built the first ice-house the locality had known. He was not content only to improve and beautify his own estates; his passion for ordered beauty extended to the parish of Madron, and he saw to it that the roads were drained and improved, and new roads opened.

Even according to early nineteenth century ostentation Sir Rose's mode of living was impressive in its extravagance. He had his own pack of hounds, and his own brewery on the estate, where every caller was welcome to a horn of ale. When he drove out, it was in a carriage with four servants in livery and powdered wigs. Attending the church at Madron with his beautiful wife and fourteen handsome children, walking two by two, he sat with his family in special pews. But though his scale of living was splendid, the children were dressed simply, and were subject to his autocratic rule. His imperious personality made itself felt not only within his family circle but also in many useful aspects of the life of the neighbourhood. The first president of the Public Library of Penzance, he was also president of the Penzance branch of the Society for Promoting Christian Knowledge. Never one to shirk controversy, he was tenacious in the assertion of his views. When he found, in 1824, that he could no longer accept the doctrine of the Trinity, and expressed himself in favour of the Unitarian form of worship, he was accused of heresy and had to resign the latter presidency.[7]

His second son, Charles Dutton, was apparently something of a ne'er-do-well, and ultimately his father rejected him completely. The quarrel must have been bitter beyond reconciliation and his will, executed on 9 April 1831, recorded it for posterity. It contained a provision,

I hereby give and bequeath unto my now eldest son Charles Dutton Price the sum of one shilling which is more than his base and unnatural conduct towards me and my family deserves but I will add my hope that though he may for a time persist in the career of vice and infamy which now mark his conduct he may die a penitent sinner in the strict sense of the doctrine of our Blessed Redeemer.

His unrelenting attitude to this son (who succeeded to the baronetcy but died at the age of seventy-two without progeny) was further revealed by a stipulation that his daughter Agnes should forfeit an annuity of £100 immediately she had any 'personal intercourse' with Charles Dutton. His will disclosed, too, that he must have been haunted by a dread of being buried alive. After expressing his desire to be buried in the handsome mausoleum he had erected in the churchyard at Madron, he went on to direct 'that the lid of my coffin may not be nailed or screwed down for four days next after my death nor until putrescence shall in the opinion of a medical man have taken place'. Although he had lived magnificently, he desired no extravagant obsequies; his will stipulated that his funeral should be 'conducted without pomp or parade and with as little expense as possible'.

John entered Brasenose College on 21 May 1827,[8] but there is no record that he took a degree, and nothing is now known of his time there or how he was occupied until he left England for Van Diemen's Land in January 1826, except that, on his own statement, he went a good deal among the labouring classes.[9] There is a family tradition that Sir Rose Price's will was challenged by John, though according to another (and more probable) version[10] it was the son Charles Dutton who did so. Whatever the truth may have been, the dispute did not reach the courts. Probate of the will was granted by the Prerogative Court of Canterbury on 24 November 1834, and the records disclose no contentious proceedings either before or after the grant of probate.[11]

The will was elaborate in its provisions.[12] The four executors named were Sir Rose Price's brother-in-law, Earl Talbot, his wife's cousin, Lord Sherborne, and Earl Talbot's sons, Henry Viscount Ingestre and the Hon. John Talbot. Schedules to the will listed 237 negroes, male, female and children, as the testator's property at one time or another between 1797 and 1830, and his lands were extensive; but the affairs of the estate were gravely involved. Trengwainton had to go, and was sold in November 1835. Despite the expectations he must have entertained from the display of wealth to which he had been accustomed all his life, it was clear to John that his share of the estate would be relatively small, and that enjoyment of it might be long delayed. The scheme of the will was complicated, but his main interest was a one-tenth share, with three brothers and six sisters, in a fund of £30,000. Before even that share became available, however, the fund had to provide a marriage portion for one sister and an annuity of £100 for another, but his interest might, in time, have been worth £2,500. Another provision entitled him to £1,400 out of a fund of £9,000 to be raised out of the father's residuary estate for distribution among four sons in unequal proportions, but enjoyment of this sum was, of course, contingent on the satisfactory winding-up of the estate. John was then in his late twenties, adventurously inclined, physically very powerful and active, and singularly clever with his hands.[13] The prospect of becoming a gentleman farmer in Van Diemen's Land was attractive, particularly as the undertaking would not require a great deal of capital, and he decided to leave England. The trustees of his father's estate made him a substantial advance (said to have been £1,000)[14] and, armed with an official letter written at the behest of his uncle, Earl Talbot, to Colonel George Arthur, Lieutenant-Governor of Van Diemen's Land, in January 1836 he sailed for Hobart. Though doubtless he did not intend it, the break was final. Twice at least he planned to return to his native land. It was his destiny never to do so, but to meet a violent death and gain a permanent place in the legends of the convict system in Australia.

Chapter Two

SETTLER AND MAGISTRATE, VAN DIEMEN'S LAND, 1836-1846

I *Hobart Town*

When John Price stepped ashore at Sullivan's Cove it is unlikely that he thought of the words of Bishop Heber's hymn, 'every prospect pleases, and only man is vile', but they were fairly applicable in 1836 to Hobart Town. It was the capital and administrative centre in an island whose function, in the eyes of the English and local authorities, was primarily that of a penal colony. The natural surroundings of Hobart were then, as they are now, surpassingly lovely. Flanked north and east by the broad sweep of the Derwent River as it joins the sea, it is set among the hills that rise in stages on the west bank of the river. On the west, too, Mount Wellington broods majestically over the city, and to the south Mount Nelson stands guard.

Lieutenant-Governor David Collins arrived at the Derwent in February 1804, after abandoning Port Phillip as unfit for settlement,[1] prematurely, as events were to show. Dispatched for the purpose of forestalling the French, the unlucky Lieutenant John Bowen had preceded him in charge of an odd band of forty-nine colonizers,* and had established a settlement at Risdon Cove, on the east bank of the Derwent. He named the new settlement Hobart Town, after Lord Hobart, then the Secretary of State for the Colonies. Bowen's human material was poor (Collins eventually shipped them back to Sydney), but he him-

---

*Bowen's first 'General Statement of the Inhabitants of His Majesty's Settlement on Van Dieman's [*sic*] Land', 27 September 1803, gave the 'number of souls in the settlement' as forty-nine, including Bowen, a surgeon, a storekeeper, a lance-serjeant, seven privates, and (with the military) three women and one child above two years old; twenty-one male and three female convicts; one man and two women; three male settlers and two women, and two children above two years old (*H.R.A.*, III. i. 200). Within two months of the landing, the total had increased to over one hundred persons (ibid., p. xxiii).

self does not seem to have been of the stuff of which successful colonizers are made. Collins considered Risdon Cove unsuitable, and five days after his arrival moved his company to 'a plain well calculated in every degree for a settlement' (as the Rev. Robert Knopwood described it) about five miles below Risdon but on the opposite side of the water.[2] Thus Hobart Town was founded, so to be known until 1 January 1881, when 'Town' was dropped from the name.

In 1811 Governor Lachlan Macquarie visited Van Diemen's Land from Sydney and examined the settlements at Hobart Town and Launceston. His orderly mind was offended by 'the irregularity of the buildings and the inattention to any established plan in the formation of the town'. These he determined to remedy by laying down a master plan for Hobart Town and prescribing building regulations, and he gave its main streets the names they still bear.[3]

In 1812 the arrangement was ended whereby the island had two administrations, one at Port Dalrymple and the other at Hobart Town, and Hobart Town became the seat of government for Van Diemen's Land.[4] Collins died suddenly in 1810. He was succeeded as Lieutenant-Governor by 'Mad Tom' Davey, and despite Davey's defects as an administrator, the colony began to develop. Its progress continued under the able and urbane William Sorell, who replaced Davey in 1817, and who was himself recalled in 1824.

II *Arthur's System*

Colonel George Arthur became Lieutenant-Governor in 1824, bringing his considerable talents and unremitting energy as a colonial administrator to the prompt and sweeping reorganization of the whole governmental structure. For twelve years he controlled the destiny of Van Diemen's Land and the fate of its residents, bond and free, white and black, with a relentless efficiency and a singleness of purpose that brought order and at least a veneer of conventional morality to a restive community sadly in need of them. When Price arrived in 1836 bearing a letter of introduction to the Lieutenant-Governor from R. W. Hay, the Under-Secretary for the Colonies, written at the request of

Price's uncle, Earl Talbot,* Arthur's long administration was drawing to a close. Begun on 12 May 1824, it ended on 30 October 1836, and Arthur left the island the next day amid the rejoicing of his numerous critics.[5] It had been highly successful in many ways, but the colony could no longer be preserved as an insular gaol, and resentment among colonists of Arthur's authoritarian rule was sufficiently widespread to require a change. However, the benefits from his administration were manifest and undoubted. The population had increased from about 12,000 (5,938 convicts and 6,209 free inhabitants) in 1824 to over 43,000 in 1836 (17,611 convicts and 25,914 free inhabitants). Land under cultivation had more than doubled, from 35,000 to 90,000 acres. Imports had increased from £62,000 to £584,000, and exports from £14,500 to £320,000.[6] Essential community features were established in the shape of roads, mail and banking services, and religious and educational facilities. The menace of the bushrangers was largely ended; grave crimes against person or property had decreased; and the penal system functioned efficiently on a basis of certain, though degrading, severity. Arthur's penal philosophy and his methods of carrying it into effect at Port Arthur are well exemplified in his *Standing Instructions for the Regulation of the Penal Settlement on Tasman's Peninsula*. They are dated 25 January 1833, and are reproduced as an appendix in this study because they reveal, as no amount of comment can, the spirit of the convict system. The key passage is:

It is distinctly to be kept in view by the Commandant and the several public officers employed on Tasman's Peninsula, that the design of this Establishment, is the severe punishment of the vicious part of the community, as the means of deterring others from the commission of crime, as well as the reformation of the criminals themselves; and to this end, the most unceasing labour is to be exacted from the convicts, and the most harassing vigilance over them is to be observed, together with such a minute system of classification as may be best calculated to develop their characters, habits, and dispositions.

*On 3 June 1836 Arthur wrote to Hay, acknowledging receipt of his letter of 2 November 1835, and stating 'Mr. Price presented to me your letter, from which as well as from himself, I learnt that his object in emigrating to this Colony was with the view of becoming a permanent settler—and I beg to assure you that I shall have much pleasure in affording him the full benefit of my advice and services' (G.O. 33/32).

Arthur's administration, though, had the great merit of predictability, achieved by his insistence on implicit obedience from
his officials. Subservience, too, was expected:

he preferred military men as government servants, and advanced
his nephews to important positions, and for this reason also he got
rid of men like his first attorney-general, Gellibrand, who showed an
independent spirit. The results of this exacting requirement were the
creation of a distinct official class, much snobbery and sycophancy on
the part of the patronized, and consequently enmity to the government on the part of the less favoured.[7]

But the price exacted from the community in human misery and
the loss, even by citizens, of the satisfactions of free and un-
supervised association was too high for human endurance, and
even before Arthur's departure it was clear the rigid system
could not long survive.

III *Gentleman Farmer*

John Price would have found himself in sympathy with
Arthur's attitude. His own temperament was haughty and authoritarian, and he valued the efficiency and predictability of a
totalitarian system above the intangible benefits of a free society.
Indeed, it is plain that in his later career as a government official
he was greatly influenced by what he learned from Arthur's
methods, and he used them (and in particular the system of
spying and delation) when he exercised naked power within the
penal system. But these times were still ahead of him; he had
come to Van Diemen's Land as a gentleman farmer, and his first
years there were thus employed. He obtained a land grant of
1,280 acres and established a farm in the Huon River district,
near the present site of the town of Franklin. There was a proposal, in 1850, that his land should be proclaimed a township and
called 'Priceville', but the Lieutenant-Governor, Sir William
Denison, preferred 'Franklin'.[8] In 1838 it was the only settled
farm in the area. An oft-repeated story is that Lady Franklin
bought it later, and divided it into allotments which she made
available to settlers, but Price still owned the land in 1854 and
had fifteen convicts working on it.[9]

Although he did not confine himself for long to farming,
Price had advantages from the start; years later, in the course of

his evidence before a Select Committee of the Legislative Assembly of Victoria in January 1857, he mentioned his arrival in Van Diemen's Land.

In the year 1836 I arrived in the Colony of Van Diemen's Land, where I was a settler, and had an introduction to the principal superintendent of convicts, who placed me in a position to obtain servants, under the convict assignment system, of a better class than generally fell to settlers newly arrived in the Colony.[10]

Price was soon on friendly terms with the officials who dominated the life of the colony. He found no difficulty in getting labour; during 1839, after he became Muster Master, and was farming at Restdown (or Risdon) the Board of Assignment granted him thirteen convicts. He made the most of his advantages. Highly competent in pursuits requiring mechanical skill and practical knowledge, his farm at Risdon was said to be 'well worthy of inspection of all who are desirous of seeing a regular English establishment, in the highest order and managed in the best style'.[11] And it is clear from his evidence in 1857 (which is the most complete exposition of his ideas upon convict discipline that is available) that criminals and their ways and their cant language fascinated him. It has been claimed by his anonymous biographer that during his farming days he displayed 'extraordinary sagacity and aptitude in capturing bushrangers',[12] and although no details have been discovered to substantiate the claim, it is not improbable. Price was young, of great physical strength and endurance, and expeditions in search of outlaws, with their physical hardships and spice of danger, would have been a welcome relief from the boredom of farming.

Arthur's successor, Sir John Franklin, arrived to take up his duties as Lieutenant-Governor in January 1837. Sir John Franklin was amiable and easily approachable, in character and bearing the opposite of the cold and haughty Arthur, and his charming and intrepid wife was highly intelligent, warmly generous in her impulses, and ever eager to raise the cultural standards of the colony. Her gallant husband adored her, and she was believed, probably rightly, to exert great influence over him, but they were poor politicians and the very excellence of their qualities completely unfitted them for the unpleasant intrigues and bitter feuds of official Hobart Town. The story of Franklin's conflict with

John Montagu, the Colonial Secretary, and his unjust recall is among the most unsavoury episodes in a society that has known many.[13] Price became friendly with the Franklins and the members of their household, and was a welcome visitor at Government House. In 1838, after an illness, Lady Franklin went to convalesce at Price's cottage at Risdon. Four escaped convicts had taken to 'bushranging', and one night Price came to his guest as she lay upon a sofa, telling her that the bushrangers were a few miles away and were expected to attack the house within a few hours. In a letter Lady Franklin described the sequel:

My reply instantly was 'There's your boat, can't we cross over instantly to Hobart Town?' 'Will you do so?' said he, fearing from my state of weakness and the alarm I should feel in crossing the sea several miles in a little boat at night, that this was one of the last resources I should adopt. Any alarm on that score did not enter my head; I thought only of the horrors of the bush-rangers, and of not being off in time . . . We left two people in the house with arms, and orders to bar up every inlet, and then pushed off with Mr. Price and his boy from the little creek where his boat was moored between two closing hills, from which the bush-rangers, if there, might have fired down upon us and easily brought us to again. Presently we were in open sea, for a beautiful breeze was blowing most favourably. A sail was put up, a sharp look out was kept for anything we might perchance run foul of, and in about twenty minutes we landed safely at the wharf at Hobart Town.[14]

IV *Muster Master and Magistrate*

Among the vice-regal household were Franklin's daughter Eleanor, and his nieces, Sophia Cracroft, daughter of his sister Isabella, and Mary Franklin, daughter of his third brother, James. James Franklin served with distinction in the Pendari War, and as a major of cavalry was Assistant-Quartermaster-General of the Bengal Army; he died, aged fifty-one, in England in August 1834.[15] Arrogantly aware of his established English background, John Price was already a figure of significance in the class-conscious and obsequious society of Hobart Town. Eligible husbands (and, for that matter, eligible brides) were few, and Price, handsome, dandified, and well-connected, was regarded as a proper suitor for Mary Franklin. They were married on 12 June 1838, when he was in his twenty-ninth year, and Mary was about twenty-four.[16]

Price must by then have found that farming did not occupy his energies fully or, perhaps, satisfy his taste for power, for in the following year, on 2 January 1839, Franklin appointed him Muster Master in the Convict Department, in place of W. T. N. Champ, who had been appointed chairman of the commission for investigating land titles, known generally as the Caveat Board.[17] Price was the last man to hold the position, for it was discontinued in October 1843. The position of Muster Master was combined with that of Assistant Police Magistrate and is described in Lieutenant-Governor Arthur's memorandum, dated February 1828, setting out the scheme to be covered by the Police Regulations for the Nine Districts of Van Diemen's Land:

The Muster Master. This officer will reside in Hobart Town, and be attached to the office of the Chief Police Magistrate, and will perform the duties detailed by the Superintendent of Police, in his letter to the Colonial Secretary of March 27, 1827, and, under the direction of the Chief Police Magistrate, he will be responsible for the most regular and careful Registry of any transaction connected with the Police of the Territory.[18]

Price had been outside the bitter controversy over the convict system which disrupted Franklin's administration in his first year as Lieutenant-Governor. It was precipitated by Franklin's private secretary, Captain Alexander Maconochie, R.N., K.H., whose report on prison discipline was strongly critical of the system. Only Captain Cheyne, Director-General of Roads and Bridges, agreed with Maconochie; Arthur's nephew, Captain Matthew Forster, who had been Chief Police Magistrate since 1832, Josiah Spode, the Principal Superintendent of Convicts, the Colonial Secretary, John Montagu, and the Military Commandant, Major Ryan, ranged themselves against him.[19] Price knew Maconochie well; 'a better-hearted man never existed but he formed too high an estimate of human nature', he told the Select Committee of the Legislative Assembly in 1857,[20] but his and Maconochie's ideas of convict discipline were poles apart. Forster, Price's official superior, was Montagu's friend, but when the conflict between Franklin and Montagu resulted finally in the latter's suspension, there is nothing to suggest that his friendship with the Franklins was impaired or that he lost the regard of his official superiors. Indeed, it was Price who brought to the Lieutenant-

Governor the news of the arrival of his successor, the ill-fated Sir John Eardley Eardley-Wilmot. The Colonial Office had not notified Franklin officially that he was recalled and a successor appointed. The vessel carrying the new Governor had put into Port Arthur by mistake, and a constable had been sent to Hobart where he gave the news to Price.[21]

The salary of the Muster Master was £400 a year, but Price lived in style and did his share of entertaining visitors to Hobart. A description of a visit of H.M.S. *Fly* to Hobart is revealing:

Mr. Price, a police magistrate who had a handsome villa on the opposite shore near the mouth of the Derwent, was especially generous, entertaining the middies to dinner and starting them on an opossum shooting expedition which lasted the whole night. He provided for them as a guide an old opossum hunter of whom he gave a brief history. The opossum hunter in question was originally a hardened old sheep stealer. He was consequently transported to Van Diemen's Land, and, escaping, set up as a bushranger. So skilful was he in evading pursuit that Mr. Price had men on his tracks for weeks without avail. Eventually Mr. Price himself headed a party fully determined to bring him in dead or alive. At last he was captured, and Mr. Price assured his listeners that he had not at that moment a more faithful or honest servant under his command. An all-night opossum hunt was arranged under the old hunter's supervision and in the morning Mr. Price left his bed purposely to invite the party to hot coffee and a break of day breakfast and insisted on seeing his guests safely on board in one of his own boats.[22]

With his appointment as Muster Master Price had found his life's work. He had no professional training in the law, but a lively intelligence and a capacity for quick decision stood him in good stead. His duties gave him enormous powers over convicts. He had to see to the posting of the convict registers, recording the personal descriptions, trades, connections, former modes of life, crimes and sentences of convicts, and the particulars supplied from British gaols. The parchment 'characters' were his responsibility, as were, too, the registers of free and conditional pardons, the triplicates of tickets-of-leave, certificates of freedom, and the registration of changes of address. He had to examine all convicts on their arrival in Van Diemen's Land, and to ensure their physical appearance and previous histories were recorded. It was, too, the Muster Master's duty to supply without delay any information about a convict that any government department required.[23] He soon won the approval of his superior, Chief Police Magistrate Matthew Forster, who endorsed Price's application for an increase in salary in October 1842, 'I do not know how Mr. Price's place could be filled so well as by himself'.[24] In support of his application Price claimed that when he was appointed in 1839 his cases involved convicts, but they were now mainly concerned with free individuals; 'frequently even in the most trifling cases the parties are attended by counsel on both sides. Indeed I may say I have the whole weight of the Colonial Bar against me ready to take advantage of any inadvertence on my part'. His application was successful, and his salary was raised to £500 a year. In the same year Lieutenant-Governor Franklin appointed him a member of the Board for the Distribution of Convict Servants on Wages, informing Lord Stanley, Secretary of State for the Colonies, that Price had rendered himself 'nearly indispensable'. This additional position carried an extra salary of £100 a year. In March 1844 he was appointed a Coroner.[25]

Price's methods were frequently autocratic, and sometimes they resulted in litigation in which he was a defendant. In May 1840 Thomas MacDowell, the editor of the *Hobart Town Courier,* and John Moses, a publican, complained that he had wrongly convicted an assigned servant named Turner, and had treated their evidence with contempt. When the Lieutenant-Governor referred the complaint to him, Price justified his conduct. His explanation was accepted then,[26] as it was so often in the years to follow. But juries were not so complaisant. He was a defendant in 1843, when two brothers named Drum sued him for false imprisonment. One action came for trial; Price was represented, on Franklin's instructions, by the Attorney-General, but the jury awarded the plaintiff £50 punitive damages. The action by the other brother was compromised on the Attorney-General's advice.[27] After a protracted exchange of official memoranda, Price was grudgingly reimbursed the amount (about £196) the two proceedings had cost him. He was again the defendant in an action for false imprisonment by one Benjamin Howard, who was apprehended as an absconding convict on an advertisement signed by Price as magistrate. But a mistake had been made in the Convict Department; Howard's time had, in fact, expired and there was no justification for the arrest, and

Howard's claim was legally unanswerable. Price was personally blameless, however, and his claim for reimbursement of about £230, the amount he had to pay, was admitted.[28]

Long after Price was dead Henry Field Gurner, Crown Solicitor of Victoria, told of an instance of his direct and unconventional methods and his laconic humour. Writing to Sir Redmond Barry about a notorious trial in which some Melbourne softgoodsmen were charged with defrauding the customs revenue, Gurner mentioned that the bench was 'packed' in the police court proceedings, and among the justices of the peace who were friends of the accused was one Carter. He wrote: 'This man is commonly known as Piss Pot Carter, from his having left Liverpool packed in a crate of those articles. Some of his Vandemonian friends at the Club were the other day telling a tale about him.' After coming to Van Diemen's Land Carter changed his signature, and when a new arrival from Liverpool presented him with a bill of exchange he had signed in Liverpool, Carter repudiated it. The bearer of the bill consulted Price, 'the same who was murdered here'. Price went to see Carter, and said that the bearer intended to advertise for one Carter who had left Liverpool in a crate of piss pots. 'Carter said, "But people will say that is me." "Very likely", said Price.' Carter met his responsibilities.[29]

However, it was in his dealing with the convicts that Price was in his element. When he gave evidence before the Victorian Legislative Select Committee in 1857, Price divided convicts into three classes: the men who were 'good working men, industrious and honest', who became 'thieves of circumstance'; the 'travelling thief', born to a life of crime, and with no intention of embracing any other; and 'the "Secretary of State's gang" . . . men who had committed some great or sole offence — such as poachers, men convicted of manslaughter, and horse-stealers', to which, on a suggestion from the Chairman of the Committee, he added 'machine breakers'.[30]

It was a crude classification, incoherently presented, and there is little reason to think that Price had ever made any serious study of what Alexander Maconochie called 'penal science'. His concern was not with men who were criminals by circumstance, and such men often suffered at his hands; his great and enduring interest was in the 'travelling thieves' and in the wicked and the vicious. He prided himself upon his knowledge of their habits and their customs, of their cant language and their trickeries. It was his vanity to know the hidden meaning of their slang; to speak it proficiently when talking with them; to see through their cunning stratagems, and to unmask contemptuously their frauds. He was strangely fascinated by their viciousness and depravity, and attracted by the evil in them even as he was repelled by it. It was a psychopathological love-hate relationship. He regarded them as less than human, with no claim to justice in a civilized sense, but his vanity nevertheless demanded they should move in submissive terror of him. At the same time, a peculiar, warped strain in his nature made it necessary for him to have their reluctant regard and grudging respect as a 'fly' or 'wide-awake' man, a man who knew them and their ways better than they did and who, but for the accident of circumstances, might have been a king among them. The Rev. Thomas Rogers had no liking for Price, who suspended him from his chaplaincy and expelled him from Norfolk Island. Rogers published a detailed indictment of Price and his methods when the latter was still Commandant of the island; he asserted that 'the general opinion among the prisoners when I was on [Norfolk Island] was, that Mr. Price, the commandant, had himself been formerly a convict, from his constantly addressing them in their own low burglar dialect.' He wrote, too, that when Price was a police magistrate, he frequently disguised himself as a constable, and, attended by some favourite policeman, went about Hobart Town at night, entering the taverns and public houses in search of disorderly characters; that Price was notorious at Hobart Town for 'his harsh repulsiveness and brusquerie' and 'delighted in acquiring and speaking the vulgar slang of thieves and pick-pockets'. This is not improbable; according to Price himself he used to go into the 'lower class of houses' at Hobart to see how convicts lived when at liberty. He found conditions 'horrible and disgusting beyond imagining'.[31] Fairly enough, Rogers described these as 'peculiar habits and propensities',[32] though it must be remembered that, as the title indicated, a police magistrate was then more closely connected with police measures and activities than are stipendiary magistrates nowadays. James Lester Burke made similar assertions in the autobiography he 'ghosted' for Martin Cash.[33] Of great strength and physically handsome, his manner at times deceptively mild and at others brutally overbearing, his piercing scrutiny made more unendurable by a monocle in his left eye,* Price was a terror to evildoers during his seven and a half years as a magistrate in Hobart Town.[34] Perhaps because of his very lack of judicial qualities, most convicts went in awe of him.[35] Most, but not all; there were on Norfolk Island and in Victoria the 'crawlers' who fawned on him and wormed their way into his good graces, and whom he treated with a rough and capricious favouritism. For the rest, soul-destroying severity was the rule. As early as 1840 he came under public criticism for his partiality for the 'hateful lash'.[36] It was a partiality that was to remain with him, though in his later years he was to put forward the dubious claim that he was averse to flogging; that he thought it a bad form of punishment, and used it because it was the only means of compelling convicts to work.[37]

Price's marriage was fruitful, and his responsibilities as a family man increased rapidly. His widow's death certificate stated there were eight children of the marriage. That certificate, and an affidavit sworn on 10 June 1857 by Mrs Price in support of an application to the Supreme Court of Victoria for Letters of Administration of her husband's estate, establish that six of the children survived to maturity. The eldest child, John Frederick, was born on 3 October 1839, when his parents were living at Lindisfarne, Restdown (or Risdon), and other children followed in quick succession; James Franklin on 20 March 1841, Thomas Caradoc on 21 October 1842, Emily Mary on 5 October 1844, and Anna Clara on 30 January 1846. Price was then living at New Town Road. The sixth of the surviving children, Jane de Winton, was born on Norfolk Island in 1852.

By 1846 Price's health was giving cause for concern. In April of that year he applied for leave of absence 'to recruit his health'. He was then only thirty-seven years old, but whatever ailed him must have been serious. The Colonial Secretary supported his application, and wrote to the Lieutenant-Governor that 'Mr. Bedford, surgeon, has called upon me to state that it is very desirable

---

*G. W. Rusden, who knew him personally, asserted Price was shortsighted (*History of Australia* (London, 1884), vol. 2, p. 591).

that he [Price] should absent himself from business, or else he will be laid up seriously'.[38] Later, towards the end of his period on Norfolk Island, his health again deteriorated, and the next Lieutenant-Governor, Sir William Denison, recognized that 'the nature of the complaint under which he has laboured' was such that he could not continue as Commandant.[39] There is, however, nothing to show whether the illness in 1846 was the same as afflicted him in 1852, or what was the nature of either ailment. Price was subject to sudden fits of cold rage, and it is tempting to speculate that he suffered from some psychoneurotic complaint. Indeed, one writer about Tasmania's past asserts that in 1846, when Price was appointed to the command of Norfolk Island, he was on the verge of a nervous breakdown, and that he begged the Lieutenant-Governor, Sir John Eardley-Wilmot, not to insist that he should take the position.[40]

V Norfolk Island Appointment

Price's application for leave was approved, but before he could enter upon it, events at the penal settlement at Norfolk Island changed his destiny, giving him a permanent notoriety in the grim history of 'the System'. Transportation of convicted persons to Australia, and the repressive disciplinary measures associated with it, were popularly known as 'the Convict System', but more briefly as 'the System', for it had no need of identification. As with most human institutions, its development was gradual. Devised originally to mitigate the harshness of the criminal law, which prescribed death as the penalty for trivial as well as grave offences, and to provide a supply of labour for the colonies that were a source of wealth for England, its beginnings go back to the sixteenth century.[41] When the American colonies were lost to England, it was necessary to find another territory to which convicts could be transported, and on 18 August 1786 Lord Sydney informed the Lords Commissioners of the Treasury that the British government had chosen the land discovered by Captain Cook sixteen years previously. Towards the end of January 1788 Captain Arthur Phillip brought the first fleet into Sydney Cove, and approximately a thousand persons were disembarked, about 736 of whom were transported male and female convicts. Transportation to Australia, regulated by a series of

Hobart Town in the time of John Price

Plough Gang, Port Arthur

Acts of Parliament that were ultimately replaced in 1824 by the Act 5 Geo. 4, c.84, continued for eighty years, from the departure of the First Fleet in May 1787 to the last convict ship that arrived in Western Australia in January 1868, and by its operation over 160,000 convicted persons (approximately 137,000 men and 23,000 women) were brought to New South Wales, Tasmania, and Western Australia.[42] By the 1830s transportation was under vigorous attack, both from repressionists who considered it did not operate sufficiently harshly as a punishment to be a deterrent to crime, and from humanitarians who believed that reformation of character was impossible under a system that operated haphazardly, treating alike the hopelessly corrupt and the potentially reclaimable. As with most controversies, there were exaggerations on both sides, but

whatever advantages may have resulted from it and whatever excuses may be offered for it the convict system was intrinsically and fundamentally evil. It was evil in the naked power it entrusted to human beings over an outcast minority; in the use it permitted to be made of that power; in the terror it had to inspire to maintain control; in the debasing effect it had upon gaolers and gaoled alike; and in the social corruption and in the brutalizing of manners of both bond and free, which inevitably resulted from the indifference to human misery, from the disappearance of compassion and from the denial of human dignity . . . Measures were introduced by the local administrations to limit abuses but the official attitude towards the convicts all too often deprived them of effectiveness, and instances of misuse of power by higher officials, and right down the chain of command, were appallingly frequent.[43]

Section 8 of the 1824 Act vested 'the property in the service of the offender' in the Governor of the Colony, with power to assign the offender to any prison. The majority of convicts were assigned to settler-masters, a form of slavery sometimes ameliorated by the goodheartedness of the masters, and more rarely by effective official supervision. But the opportunities for abuse were too frequent and too tempting, and in its report of 3 August 1838 the Select Committee on Transportation, under the chairmanship of Sir William Molesworth, condemned it root and branch in forceful and explicit language.[44] They recommended the instant discontinuance of the assignment system, and the abolition of transportation. Transportation to New South Wales ceased in 1840,

but convict ships continued to land their cargoes in Van Diemen's Land until the last vessel to carry convicts to eastern Australia, the *St Vincent,* arrived at Hobart Town on 26 May 1853.

In 1842 the 'Probation System' was introduced on the instructions of the English authorities. It was an ingenious and elaborate
product of theorists wedded to harsh punishment as the chief
means of repressing crime. It provided for five stages in the duration of the period of probation. Convicts sentenced to transportation for life, and other heinous offenders, had to serve the first
stage at hard labour on Norfolk Island for not less than two
years. The period of two years could not be abridged, but bad
conduct (or what the Commandant said was bad conduct) could
extend the period indefinitely. The second stage involved hard
labour in gangs in unsettled areas in Van Diemen's Land. In the
third stage, the offender could obtain a 'probation pass' and could
engage in private service for wages, the amount he received for
his own use depending on whether he was in the first, second or
third class. An offender in the fourth stage held a ticket-of-leave,
a 'probationary and revocable pardon, valid in the Colony but
not elsewhere'. To those reaching the fifth stage a pardon, conditional or absolute, was granted as 'an act of pure grace and
favour'.[45] This 'fatal experiment' as Lieutenant-Governor
La Trobe called it[46] was the last and perhaps the most notor-
iously unsuccessful phase of the convict system.

It is common in a dying institution depending for its efficacy
upon harshness that the controllers should intensify repressive
measures. The last years of the convict system exhibited this
feature, and nowhere more brutally than on Norfolk Island. The
island prison from which escape is well-nigh impossible has
always had a morbid fascination for authorities in search of secure
confinement for outcast criminals. In a chronicle of such experi-
ments by various nations, Norfolk Island must be given a dreadful prominence. Discovered and named by Captain Cook in
1774, the island is the only one of any size in a group situated
about 930 miles east-north-east of Sydney, in latitude of 29°3′
south and longitude of 167°57′5″ east. It is about 5 miles long
and 3 miles wide, with a total area of about 8,528 acres, and
because of its climate and its beauty has been called 'the Madeira
of the Pacific'.[47] There is no safe harbour, and it is difficult of

access from the sea except in favourable weather. Lieutenant Philip Gidley King took possession of it in 1788, to forestall the French and found a penal colony; thus, after Sydney, it is the oldest English settlement in the Pacific. No complete history of its use as a penal settlement has been written, and he who undertakes the task will need a strong stomach, for except for a period of disuse between 1813 and 1825, and the years between 1839 and 1844 when Major Thomas Bunbury, Major Ryan, and Captain Alexander Maconochie were successively in command, the story of the island is consistently one of appalling inhumanity.[48]

In February 1840 Captain Alexander Maconochie, who had come to Van Diemen's Land as Sir John Franklin's secretary, took command of the penal settlement. He left the island four years later. His period was notable for a conception of penal discipline entirely different from the traditional approach of maximum severity and debasement. He formulated the conceptions upon which modern penology is based, and he put them into practical operation.[49] It was the official attitude that his policy of leniency was responsible for the trouble with the convicts that occurred later. He was replaced by Major Joseph Childs, R.N., who was chosen because his reputation was that of a strict disciplinarian.[50] Whether Childs was grossly incompetent or badly served by his officials is difficult to determine on the available material (probably it was a combination of both), but there can be no question that by January 1846 control by the authorities was seriously threatened, and that unrest among the convicts had reached flash point. In May 1846 the Van Diemen's Land administration sent a magistrate, Robert Pringle Stewart, to investigate conditions. His comprehensive and well-organized report is an excellent description of the island and the penal settlement, and it provides a startling account of the insubordination of a section of the convicts known as 'the Ring', and of corruption, incompetence, vacillation and retaliatory harshness on the part of the authorities.[51] According to the Anglican chaplain, Rev. Thomas Rogers, the prisoners were defrauded of half their daily rations, and during the sixteen months before Price took command 20,624 lashes had been inflicted on convicts under sentences imposed by the resident magistrate. Rogers wrote:

On several of the flogging mornings the ground on which the men stood at the triangles was saturated with human gore, as if a bucket of blood had been spilled on it, covering a space three feet in diameter, and running out in various directions in little streams of two or three feet long. I have seen this.[52]

Samuel Barrow was the resident magistrate, and the appalling treatment of the convicts may have been of his doing rather than Childs.[53] On 30 June 1846 came the final act of tyranny that sparked off the revolt and the murders of 1 July 1846. The convicts used their own utensils ('billies' and tin kettles) to cook their meagre rations, and it was thought by the authorities that this practice favoured the 'flash' men and facilitated the enjoyment of thefts of government supplies and livestock. Magistrate Barrow ordered that the cooking utensils be impounded, and the constables seized the vessels from the tables of the convicts' mess room. In the morning, a notorious convict and former bushranger, Lawrence Kavenagh, broke into the room where the impounded utensils were stored, and retrieved them. This done, the men ate their meagre breakfast, and the next move seemed to be with the authorities, when a crazed convict, William Westwood, known as 'Jacky-Jacky', asserted leadership, and at the head of a mob of about twenty prisoners rushed into the cookhouse. They snatched up billets of wood and agricultural tools, but, though others were involved, it was Westwood who was the main assailant of the four men—three constables and an overseer—who were murdered, two of them in their beds. Three other officials were wounded. The outbreak was over almost as soon as it had begun; the mob were subdued by the mere appearance of the soldiery, and retreated to the lumber yard. It was a wanton, crazed but inevitable explosion; its cathartic effect was rapid and complete, and the threat to authority promptly exhausted.[54]

The authorities at Hobart Town were gravely perturbed by Pringle Stewart's report, and the tidings of the murders intensified their worst fears. A strong man was required to restore order and exact vengeance, and John Price was the obvious choice. There is no reason to disbelieve the assertion that he was loath to take the appointment. He was ill; he was a married man with a young family, the youngest a baby still at the breast, and the tales of the perils on the island lost nothing in the telling. It is

not unlikely that strong pressure was brought to bear upon him.
However that may be, he accepted, and he was seconded from
the magistracy and his appointment as Commandant of Norfolk
Island was proclaimed.

The announcement brought convincing proofs of the esteem
in which Price was held by the respectable elements of Hobart
Town. At a large public meeting a resolution was adopted urging
him to remain as a magistrate, and promising to make up the
difference between his salary as a magistrate and that of his new
appointment, with a guarantee of free house-rent. However, un-
like some of his predecessors, Price seems never to have been
greatly concerned with financial considerations (when he died
his estate was sworn not to exceed £700) and he adhered to his
decision to accept the appointment. The disappointed citizenry
then presented him with a service of plate valued at £300.[55]
Part of it, a handsome salver, is now preserved at Entally, Launceston, Tasmania. It is engraved with the Price crest, and bears
an inscription:

Presented with a service of plate to John Price, Esquire, as a Token
of the Esteem in which he is held by the Subscribers, being inhabitants of Hobart Town and its vicinity and in testimony of the important services which he has rendered to his Country by the able
and zealous discharge of his duties as Police Magistrate during a
period of nearly eight years in Hobart Town, Van Diemen's Land,
18th July 1846.

Chapter Three

COMMANDANT OF NORFOLK ISLAND, 1846-1853

I *Arrival*

The new Civil Commandant of Norfolk Island arrived there at the beginning of August 1846.[1] His appointment had been notified in the *Hobart Town Gazette* of 21 July 1846, where it was stated that his salary and allowances would commence on the day he assumed his duties, and that if the Secretary of State for the Colonies did not confirm the provisional appointment, he would return to Van Diemen's Land to resume his position of magistrate. His wife and five children accompanied him. The eldest child, John Frederick, was not yet seven years old, and the youngest, Anna Clara, was just six months. Born in Bengal, Mary Price had been educated at Neuchatel, Switzerland, and among her fellow pupils were two sisters of Charles Joseph La Trobe,[2] the first Lieutenant-Governor of Victoria, with whom she remained on friendly terms and corresponded when circumstances permitted.[3] Though she was a soldier's daughter, she must at times have reflected sadly on the harsh fate that sent her, with children of such tender years, to an island remote from civilization, a place of terror and repression, avowedly used to cage men regarded officially as the most debased of English and colonial criminals under conditions of shocking inhumanity. She was to remain there for six and a half tense years, in surroundings whose unexcelled natural beauty were tainted by the viciousness of the gaoled and the gaolers, linked with a husband of marked peculiarities of temperament, who was ill when he began his term of office and whose health was even more precarious when he left. During that time she bore three children, Emma Julia in 1847, Gustavus Lambart in 1849 (or 1850), and Jane de Winton in 1852. Emma Julia died on the island on 28 March 1849, at the age of sixteen months, of cynanche trachealis, a

24

virulent infection of the windpipe that probably resulted in suffocation.[4]

It has been said that Price went to Norfolk Island as 'the Avenger'; that he was a man fitted to deal brutally with brutes.[5] Perhaps he saw himself in that role, but if he did he was exceeding the law, which gave him the custody of prisoners and control of them by reasonable discipline while they were on Norfolk Island under lawful sentences, but conferred on him no authority to torture or torment them. The evidence that he did both is too massive to be ignored. Alexander Maconochie revealed a true understanding both of ethics and its pale reflection, the law, when he wrote:

It may be said that I . . . overlooked, or even sacrificed, the great object—that of punishment—for which the prisoners were sent on the island: but, as I still conceive, not so. I carried into effect the full letter and spirit of the law, and merely did not indulge in excesses beyond it. Every man's sentence was to imprisonment and hard labour; the island was his prison, and each was required to do his full daily government task . . . before bestowing his time on either his garden or education. What I did really spare was, the unnecessary humiliation which it is the fashion to impose on prisoners besides; and which, I believe, does more moral injury than all other incidents put together of ordinary prison life. It crushes the weak, unnecessarily irritates the strong, indisposes all to submission and reform, and is, in truth, neither intended by the law, nor consistent with the professions made by lawgivers when framing it. It is merely one infirmity of human nature, one exhibition of its worst qualities, aggravating others. It is trampling, where we ought to seek to raise, and is thus at once un-Christian and impolitic.[6]

It is doubtful if John Price would have fully comprehended these notions; it is certain that he would not have allowed them to constrain him in the exercise of his despotic authority. According to the common law (though the penal authorities disregarded it when it suited them) a prisoner did not lose all his rights as a human being when he was imprisoned or transported. Where a form of punishment, such as transportation, derives entirely from an act of parliament, 'the manner of carrying it into effect, as well as the legal consequences attending on it, depend upon the specific provision of the legislature'.[7] Unless there is a law specifically authorizing the infliction of a punishment in addition to imprisonment, such as flogging, solitary confinement or fetters, neither the judge nor the gaoler has power to impose it. While a gaoler is bound to keep his prisoners in safe custody, he is also under a duty not to place them in irons or other physical restraint unless there is danger of escape. If the legality of his use of fetters is called into question, the gaoler must be able to justify his action by showing it was reasonably necessary, and if he does not he is criminally liable for his abuse of power. Discretionary control over persons in custody is always liable to abuse; Sir William Blackstone, after observing that a prisoner should 'neither be loaded with needless fetters, or subjected to other hardships than such as are absolutely necessary for the purpose of confinement only', continued, 'though what are so requisite must too often be left to the discretion of the gaolers; who are frequently a merciless race of men, and, by being conversant in scenes of misery, steeled against any tender sensations.'[8]

In Price's day (and for years after), the sentence often directed additional punishments, such as flogging, solitary confinement, and working in irons, and it was the gaoler's duty to carry out these directions. Harsh though these judicial penalties were, and wretched the fate of the prisoner subjected to them, it was not in them but in the virtually unlimited power of oppression possessed by a commandant that the real mischief lay. Commandants of penal settlements were also appointed magistrates, and they had the power to punish for summary offences by flogging and working in irons.[9] There were, too, other and more dreadful punishments; the 'spreadeagle', the violent search of the prisoner's mouth and throat for 'the tobacco track', the tube-gag, inserted in the victim's mouth and throat, and the 'scavenger's daughter', or trussing of the head to the knees. These were not authorized by law, of course, but incontestable evidence establishes they were in use on Norfolk Island.[10]

Major Childs was still on the island when Price arrived; he remained until 19 August, when he left for Sydney by the ship *Mary*. He is a shadowy figure in the island's story; some found him humane,[11] though the evidence that the lash was in constant use, and that there were other and more dreadful punishments, is overwhelming. How far this was Childs' doing, and how far it was the work of Samuel Barrow, the resident magistrate, is (except for an assessment of their characters) largely immaterial. Within the island the authority of the Commandant was supreme, and Childs must carry the responsibility for excesses, though it has been asserted that when Barrow arrived in November 1845, Childs was instructed not to interfere with him.[12] Price ignored Childs and conducted a minute examination of the penal settlement without reference to him.[13] It was clear from the moment of his arrival that he was determined to administer his command according to his own ideas, and that he would brook no opposition. On one pretext or another he got rid of Gilbert Robertson, the able and experienced Superintendent of Agriculture, of Lieutenant Butler, R.N., and of the Anglican chaplain, Rev. Thomas Rogers, as well as lesser officials.[14]

Rogers asserted the outbreak led by 'Jacky-Jacky' Westwood, resulting in the four murders on 1 July 1846, was 'altogether an unpremeditated out-break, originating . . . in a protracted disregard of the men's legal rights in the matter of food.' It was, he said, confined to a perverse small minority of the men at the main prison at Kingston, and there was no tumult, no fear of insult, much less any apprehension of violence from the rest of the convicts.[15] The extracts Rogers quotes from Magistrate Barrow's routine reports concerning the prisoners stationed at the Cascades, on the north of the island, confirm the truth of his assertions.

Price's account of conditions given in January 1857 to the Select Committee of the Legislative Assembly of Victoria, was far different. He claimed that 'nothing but the musket and lash was left to the civil-commandant of Norfolk Island, to coerce the prisoners with.'[16] He told how twenty-five men, charged with murder, were in heavy irons, reeved to a chain cable which passed between their legs. They were guarded day and night by an armed sentry who paced up and down outside the building. He described an unsuccessful attempt to smuggle to Westwood two small saws concealed in a Bible, and the convicts' opposition to his order that the chain gangs should go out to work. It was a lurid account, of more than doubtful reliability.

Barrow committed twenty-six men for trial, but Francis Burgess, the judge sent from Hobart to conduct the trials, became ill, and he was replaced by Fielding Browne. The trial of fourteen of

the prisoners began on 23 September and proceeded (with a break
due to the illness of the judge) until 5 October 1846. The prisoners were not given legal assistance and some of them behaved
indecorously during the trial.[17] They treated the result as foregone and any attempt to defend themselves as futile, and made a
mockery of the proceedings as they derided the convicts who
came forward as witnesses against them. There had been some
doubt whether, since Norfolk Island was detached from the government of New South Wales and annexed to the Van Diemen's
Land administration, criminal trials should proceed under New
South Wales law or that of Van Diemen's Land. Judge Burgess
thought the former, but Judge Fielding Browne held that the trial
was governed by the law of Van Diemen's Land, and that the five
military officers who sat with him were a jury charged with the
responsibility of deciding guilt or innocence.[18] Twelve of the
fourteen prisoners were convicted and sentenced to death. The
sentences were carried out on 13 October, when the condemned
were hanged in two groups of six in the presence of the convicts
paraded to witness the dreadful spectacle and guarded by the
soldiery.[19]

The twelve bodies, in coffins, were hauled in three bullock-
drays to an old saw-pit beyond the burial ground, which, at Price's
orders, was used as a mass grave. The unceremonious haste with
which Catholics and Protestants were interred together prevented
the Anglican chaplain, Rev. Thomas Rogers, from reading the
burial service before the grave was filled in, and Rogers made this
one of his heads of complaint of Price's behaviour.[20] To avoid dis-
tressing scenes, Rogers (who considered himself Catholic, as distinct from Roman Catholic) persuaded his communicants not to
make speeches on the gallows, and three of the men made 'dying
declarations' which they left with him. The declarations were as
follows:

I, William Westwood, wish to die in the communion of Christ's
Holy Church, seeking the mercy of God through Jesus Christ our
Lord, amen. I acknowledge the justice of my sentence; but as a
dying man I wish to say that I believe four men now going to
suffer are innocent of the crime laid to their charge, namely, Lawrence Cavenagh, Henry Whiting, William Pickthorne, and William Scrimshaw. I believe that I never spoke to Cavenagh on the

morning of the riots; and those other three men had no part in the killing of John Morris, as far as I know of. I die in charity with all men, and I ask your prayers for my soul.

William Westwood, aged 26 years.

I, Henry Whiting, profess myself a member of Christ's holy Catholic Church, and in that communion to die, looking for the forgiveness of all my sins through Jesus Christ my only Lord and Saviour. I am now brought out to die, and as a dying man I declare my innocence of the crime for which I suffer. I forgive every man, as I hope God will forgive me.

Henry Whiting, aged 22 years.

I, William Pickthorne, desire to profess myself a penitent member of Christ's holy catholic church, and I hope that I shall find mercy with God, through Jesus Christ, for all my sins. I am now dying, and I declare with my last breath that I am innocent of the crime laid to my charge. I pray God to forgive me and all men, and to receive my departing soul.

William Pickthorne, aged 27 years.[21]

The celerity with which the sentences were carried out prevented any effective examination of the legal correctness of the trial or the sufficiency of the evidence against some of the condemned men, but there is room for uneasiness on both these aspects. In 1847 Bishop Willson told the English Select Committee of the House of Lords of his doubts, and the Rev. Thomas Rogers made no concealment of his.[22]

Five other men were executed during 1846, after Price's arrival. One, Brown, was hanged on 19 October for complicity in the murders on 1 July, and, for other murders, two men were hanged on 3 November, and two on 9 December. Thus within eight weeks seventeen men were hanged. The sentences of death recorded against seven other convicts were commuted by the Lieutenant-Governor of Van Diemen's Land.[23]

It is clear that Price had made up his mind before he took up his duties as Civil Commandant that he would remove from the island any person who might oppose him in his use of despotic power. When he did so he was upheld by his superiors, but an unforeseen consequence was the publication, in 1849, of a scathing denunciation of his administration by the Rev. Thomas Rogers, whose dismissal Price engineered. Rogers' assertion bears the stamp of probability that Price 'commenced his commandant-ship with a headlong exercise of arbitrary power. He conducted himself towards the civil officers as if they were conspirators against the peace of the community.'[24] In his intercourse with his officers, he abandoned his customary suavity; though cruel, he was no longer composed and bland.[25] Domineering in manner, rough in speech, and given to outstaring the object of his displeasure and surveying him from head to foot through his eyeglass in a most offensive manner,[26] Price quickly established mastery over weaker characters among the officials on the island. The men he could not cow he got rid of. When the office of resident magistrate was abolished in 1847, Barrow returned to Van Diemen's Land, and, except for the military garrison, Price was able to concentrate all authority in himself. From the moment he assumed command to the time he relinquished it, Norfolk Island was the reflection of the personality of John Price. The system he administered was one of retribution, and that, too, was to be his fate.

II *Witnesses*

Before a judgment upon Price's character and conduct can be made, the reliability of the material relating to him must be assessed. The contemporary evidence falls broadly into three groups: the first, statements, reports, and communications in the course of their duties by officials (including Price himself); the second, statements by free individuals who knew Price; and the third, statements by convicts who came within his jurisdiction, either as magistrate or as penal administrator. Sometimes it is not easy to determine what credit is to be given to a particular item in any of the three categories. To assess their worth, knowledge of the legal framework of the convict system and familiarity with the way in which it was administered are essential. Something must be known, too, about the individual whose statements are under examination. Thus equipped, an investigator can arrive at a fair estimate by applying the tests which mankind has devised from long experience for ascertaining the worth of human testimony. They are largely the product of common sense. Obviously the credibility of evidence is determined by a variety of considerations, such as the integrity, disinterestedness, and ability of witnesses, the consistency of their testimony, its conformity with experience, and its consonance with collateral circumstances.[27] People differ significantly in their capacity to observe, to recall, and to narrate accurately, and each of these idiosyncracies may be affected by partiality or self-interest. Absolute certainty is not usually to be attained where versions conflict, and while in grave questions proof beyond reasonable doubt is rightly sought, human belief and judgment commonly have as their basis the balance of probabilities, a rather misleading metaphorical phrase that means the balance must be inclined significantly in favour of the truth of the allegation before it can be accepted as proven.[28]

It is to be expected that some convicts who were subject to Price's discipline would tell horrifying stories of harsh and capricious punishments. Thomas Jones, a criminal hanged later in England, was on Norfolk Island in 1848 and in his life story, told while awaiting execution, he asserted that 'although directed by the Lieutenant-Governor to release me, Mr. Price, from sheer spite, and from a desire he always manifested in torturing the minds of prisoners, detained me several months on the island'.[29] In what purports to be an autobiography, but which was certainly written by another hand, Mark Jeffrey described his experiences on the island, and narrated how Price arbitrarily sentenced him to fifty lashes, remarking, 'I will take the flashness out of you, my joker.' After the flogging he was put in irons weighing fifty-six pounds and was manacled, and Price visited him in his cell from time to time to see if his spirit was broken.[30] In James Lester Burke's *Martin Cash,* too, there is an account of Price's tyrannical treatment which certainly does not square with the statement in a recent biography of Cash that 'Martin Cash had no reason to complain of the treatment meted out to him at Norfolk Island by John Price'.[31] There is nothing intrinsically improbable in these stories; indeed, it is quite likely the narrators were telling the truth as they saw it. But where the accounts came from convicts who hated Price, and whose accounts were propagandist and designed by the hacks who 'ghosted' them to attract readers by horrifying details sensationally presented, the temptations to invent or to embroider and exaggerate were so great that, standing alone, they cannot be regarded as trustworthy sources. This is particularly so with stories appearing after Price's death. There is a presumption against wrongdoing, usually called the presumption of

innocence, and this must prevail until it is rebutted by evidence
of sufficient cogency to produce a conclusion of guilt. Witnesses
of repute with less obvious reasons to lie or distort or exaggerate
must be found before it can be fairly concluded that Price mis-
used his powers. If there were such witnesses, and their allegations against Price were made in his lifetime and brought to the
notice of the proper authorities and of Price himself, a basis is
shown for treating the convicts' stories of similar happenings as
worthy of examination, though not necessarily of acceptance. If,
too, a combination of circumstances is established, such as a consistent pattern in the conduct alleged, opportunities and temptations to behave in the manner described without genuine likeli-
hood of adverse consequences, and consistency and constancy in
the allegations by different witnesses of abuses over a period of
years in conditions differing superficially but fundamentally similar, one is justified in undertaking an evaluation of the probabilities of the truth of the allegations by convicts as well as those
made by reputable witnesses. If the actions denounced as misconduct occurred in situations favourable to their happening, so that
it is not inherently unlikely that Price behaved in the fashion
alleged, it is then legitimate to inquire whether in all the circumstances incredulity is justified, or whether the assertions are probably true. If it is established, as well, that grave charges went
publicly unrefuted in circumstances that called for refutation, this
(unless satisfactorily explained) may fairly be regarded as a circumstance that may be given weight. Guided by these considerations, it is possible to arrive at a just estimate of the truth of the
allegations against Price, provided always that the testimony in
Price's favour, both as to his character and his administration, is
also taken into account. Because of their standing and personal
qualities, and also because of the striking similarity of their accounts, the two most important witnesses against Price in respect
of his Norfolk Island administration who speak from actual observation and investigation are the Right Reverend Robert William
Willson, Catholic Bishop of Van Diemen's Land, and the
Reverend Thomas Rogers, an Anglican clergyman.

Rogers, who had gone from Yorkshire to Dublin with his
family in 1842, was appointed in 1844 by the English government a 'Religious Instructor' of convicts at Norfolk Island.[32]

Leaving his family in Dublin, he arrived on the island in 1845 when Major Childs was Commandant. Rogers was a man of courage and ability, with no illusions about his charges, but with a highly developed sense of justice. While he was chaplain on the island, he espoused the cause of William Henry Barber, an English solicitor who was wrongly convicted of uttering a forged will, sentenced to transportation for life, and sent to Norfolk Island. When they were both on the island, Rogers did all he could to ameliorate the appalling treatment to which Barber was subjected under Childs' administration, and he and another Anglican clergyman, Rev. T. Beagley Naylor, whom he replaced, were prominent in the successful efforts to establish Barber's innocence and to obtain for him a free and unconditional pardon and compensation for a grievous miscarriage of justice. He befriended Barber when the latter was discharged by the indifferent authorities at Impression Bay in Van Diemen's Land, penniless and without adequate clothing, and left to make his way unaided to Hobart Town over ninety miles of wild country.[33] According to an unpublished biography by his grandson, when he returned to England Rogers 'piloted Barber's case' through a parliamentary committee. Barber received an absolute pardon and was awarded £5,000 compensation, but Rogers' biographer asserts that he refused to pay the out-of-pocket disbursements Rogers had incurred.[34]

Rogers clashed with Price soon after the arrival of the latter and before they had formally met each other. The Anglican chaplains were also justices of the peace, and when they visited convicts committed for trial at the assizes held on the island from time to time, it was customary for them to examine the depositions of the evidence. The object was to ensure that the accused men (most of whom were illiterate) could present such defences they had. On 6 August, Rogers (who had been notified on 15 July that his commission as a justice of the peace had been terminated) paid a visit to the boatshed, where the men charged with murders during the July outbreak were chained, and handed to the chief constable, one Baldock, depositions he had received from the men before his commission as a magistrate was withdrawn. Though he had the impressive title of chief constable, Baldock was a ticket-of-leave convict, and a highly unpleasant individual. Price, who had just assumed command, happened to be present. He took exception to Rogers having had the depositions, and in 'a loud, haughty, overbearing manner' officiously rebuked the chaplain in the hearing of the officials and convicts.[35] From then onwards he missed no opportunity to humiliate Rogers. He recommended that he should be removed, and a pretext for doing so was found when a private letter which Rogers had sent in October 1846 to the Superintendent of Convict Chaplains, Archdeacon F. A. Marriott, was forwarded to the Administrator, C. J. La Trobe, who was in charge until the arrival of the new Lieutenant-Governor, Sir William Denison. This letter was vigorously and explicitly critical of Price. Rogers asserted that he wrote it to prove to Archdeacon Marriott that it was urgently necessary that, as Superintendent of Convict Chaplains, he should himself visit Norfolk Island, and that he did not foresee it would go beyond the archdeacon. La Trobe sent some pages of the letter to Price for comment, and Price's statements, and those of his officials, are set forth in Rogers' publication, *Correspondence relating to the Dismissal of the Rev. T. Rogers from His Chaplaincy at Norfolk Island*. On 10 December 1846 Archdeacon Marriott was notified that the Administrator considered Mr Rogers should be transferred from Norfolk Island to Van Diemen's Land. The archdeacon wrote immediately to Rogers, informing him of the government's determination to remove him, and continuing, 'I am informed that this decision is made on account of your communications in writing on various subjects, from the whole tone of which the administrator of the government thinks you are not well qualified to meet the peculiar difficulties of your position.' Rogers left Norfolk Island on 1 February 1847, arriving in Hobart Town on 27 February. At once he sought out the archdeacon, who was at Launceston, 120 miles away, and began his pertinacious but unavailing efforts to get the authorities to right the injustice done to him. When the new Lieutenant-Governor, Sir William Denison, read the file, which by then included Price's 'counter statements', he decided, without hearing Rogers, that the charges against Price were unfounded. Indeed, he went further than La Trobe; Rogers was dismissed and informed that because of a 'deficiency in temper and discretion', he would not be employed further in the Convict Department. Both the Bishop of Tasmania (Rt Rev. F. R.

The Penal Settlement, Kingston, about 1848

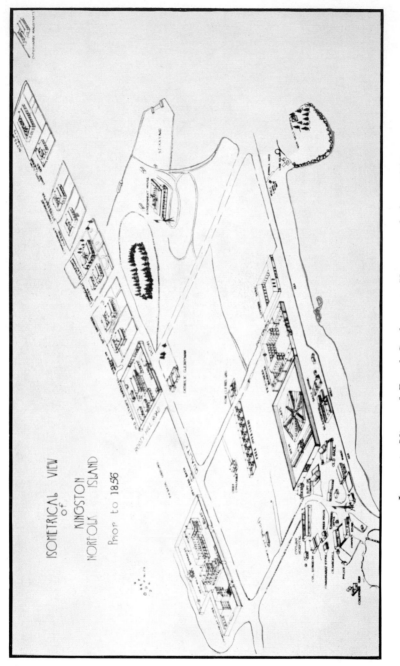

Isometric View of Penal Settlement, Kingston, before 1856

By courtesy of the Administrator of Norfolk Island

Nixon) and Archdeacon Marriott recorded their opinion that Rogers was unjustly dismissed,[36] but despite unceasing efforts by Rogers and others to obtain redress the authorities remained obdurate.

It is because of this official obduracy that there still exists a critical account from a responsible observer of Price's conduct on Norfolk Island in the first year of his command. Failing in his efforts to move the authorities, and in defiance of the warnings of their displeasure, Rogers published the correspondence relating to the affair, and included with it extensive descriptions of conditions that existed on the island under Price. This substantial book of 230 pages was printed in Launceston in 1849, and Rogers added to it *Review of Dr. Hampton's First Report on Norfolk Island,* a vitriolic and detailed condemnation not only of Price, but also of the new Comptroller-General of Convicts, Dr J. S. Hampton. Though debarred from the Convict Department, he was appointed in April 1847 to the colonial chaplaincy of Windermere (involving a loss of £100 a year in salary) and from there he pursued his campaign for vindication. In the course of it he antagonized not only the Lieutenant-Governor and the civil service, but also his bishop. However, testimonials reproduced in the *Correspondence* reveal that he commanded the admiration and respect of citizens of repute and ability. Gilbert Robertson, formerly senior superintendent on Norfolk Island; Robert Pringle Stewart, the commissioner who had exposed conditions on the island under Childs; Fielding Browne, the judge who tried the murderers in 1846; Dr H. Graham, formerly a medical officer on the island; clergymen, including the senior chaplain, Rev. Dr W. H. Browne, the Rev. J. S. Ison, the Rev. F. Brownrigg, and the Rev. Henry Plow Kane (headmaster of Launceston Church Grammar School); and his parishioners at Windermere, all testified in far more than conventional terms to his integrity, his capacity and his worth as a minister, confirming the impression left by his own writings that he was a man of the highest Christian principles, incapable of inventing and promoting baseless charges against Price. Indeed, the church-wardens of Windermere (M. Gaunt, J.P., W. Neilley, J.P., late Captain 63rd Regiment, and W. Browne) presented to Sir William Denison in October 1849 a vigorous expostulation against the wrong done to Rogers. They

reminded the Governor of the archdeacon's declaration, in a letter of 10 March 1847, that Rogers was 'a man enthusiastically
devoted to his calling, zealous, faithful, talented, superior to any
employed in this country in the convict department, with every
qualification that could fit him for winning the respect of the
prisoners, and in acting as their spiritual instructor'. But it was all
to no avail.[37]

Rogers, then in his early forties, was afflicted by personal sor-
rows as well as official injustice. His wife died in Dublin, and his
son, John Foster William Rogers, and two daughters set out to
join him in Van Diemen's Land. By then Rogers had decided to
return to England to press his claims for redress upon the English
authorities, sailing in the *Phillip Oakden* on 27 March 1850, and
while his children were in course of journeying to Australia, he
was on his way back to England. He found many changes. The
Oxford movement and the conversion of John Henry Newman to
Rome had created doubt and turmoil within the Church of
England. Caught up in this fervour, Rogers gave up the Anglican
ministry and became a Roman Catholic. Returning to Australia,
he settled in Melbourne. His grandson claims that he held some
official position that he lost on 'Black Wednesday', 9 January
1878, when the Berry ministry, after the Legislative Council refused to pass an Appropriation Bill, dismissed more than two
hundred public servants, but this lacks confirmation. Later he
worked as a freelance journalist, and as a regular contributor
(under the pseudonym *Peutêtre*) to a Catholic periodical. Tall,
erect of carriage, and impeccably attired in suit of black, white
vest, starched collar, cravat and silk hat, he was a well-known
figure in the 1860s when it was the convention of Melbourne
saunterers in Collins Street to 'do the Block'. Abstemious throughout his life, he lived to his ninety-ninth year, and when he died
at Malvern, a suburb of Melbourne, on 17 January 1903[38] the
press failed to note the passing of the chaplain whom Marcus
Clarke had used (with a good deal of fictional licence) as the
prototype of the Rev. James North in his enduring novel, *For the
Term of His Natural Life*.

Robert William Willson (1794-1866) had many qualities in
common with Rogers, and held similar views about the injustice
of executing some of the men hanged for the July 1846 murders.[39]

He took up his appointment in 1844 as the first Catholic bishop of the newly created see of Hobart. He visited Norfolk Island three times: in May 1846, in October 1849, and in March 1852. On his first visit, when Childs was the Commandant, the commanding military officer was so appalled by what was happening that he said to the bishop, 'For God's sake go home, and let them know the truth.' Returning to England, Bishop Willson told the grim story of his observations to a Select Committee of the House of Lords in June 1847.[40] When he came again to the island in 1849, Price then being Commandant, he found conditions were better, though there were still aspects that troubled him.[41] By March 1852 he had reason to believe that great severity was in use, and the state of the convicts was most unsatisfactory. His worst fears were confirmed when he landed on the island. On his return to Hobart Town, he sent (on 22 May 1852) a very long and detailed description to the Lieutenant-Governor. It is a powerful and horrifying document, exposing the worthlessness of the official versions and the callousness of the official attitude.[42] A biographer records a conversation the bishop had (presumably in 1852) with a person not named, but who must have been Price.

The man who was chiefly responsible for the occurrences met him one night and said, 'Bishop Willson, I am sorry to see you carried away by the stories of these men; you know what a miserable lot they are; do not permit their stories to make any impression upon you.' 'What, sir,' said the good prelate, 'do you not know that I am a Catholic Bishop, and do you dare call me to order for the discharge of my duty? When I was last in England I told the Government to take away one third of the convicts on the island, and now I will recommend the Government to take the whole of the men from the island.' That man, hard as he was, burst into tears, and implored the Bishop not to ruin him.[43]

Bishop Willson cannot be dismissed as a mere sentimentalist, nor can his capacity and integrity be doubted. Indeed, his qualities were officially acknowledged; the Duke of Newcastle, when Secretary of State for the Colonies, wrote on 3 August 1853 to Lieutenant-Governor Denison that

the zeal and abilities which he [Dr. Willson] has displayed under circumstances of a more peculiar kind, when it became his duty to investigate, and combat the great social evils developed under the then prevailing system of convict discipline, deserves more special notice from those concerned in the administration of the civil government.[44]

Five years after Bishop Willson's last visit, confirmation of the charges made by him and Rogers was furnished from an unexpected source. When he was Lieutenant-Governor of Van Diemen's Land Sir William Denison rejected all complaints against Price, but when he was Governor of New South Wales, on hearing of Price's death in 1857, he wrote to his mother that Price 'was a good officer, that is, earnest and zealous in doing his duty, but his system was a bad one, depending very much on corporal punishment, and upon an organised system of espionage.'[45]

The most capable of Tasmanian historians was the Rev. John West, later for nineteen years editor of the *Sydney Morning Herald*.[46] A man of high principle, West was not one to repeat baseless or doubtful charges. In his *History of Tasmania,* published in 1852 when Price was still Commandant, he observed that Price, 'remarkable for his knowledge of prisoner habits, language, and artifices . . . commenced his career with a vigorous, summary, and, it is said, merciless exercise of authority.' Mentioning that a clergyman on the island had exhibited the most serious charges against Price and persons acting under his authority and encouragement, he gave lengthy extracts from Rogers' *Correspondence* and *Review of Dr. Hampton's First Report,* and commented, 'In part these charges have been disputed, but their substantial truth is, at least, rendered probable, by the accumulation of similar facts in the history of such settlements.'[47] West was right. In an isolated penal settlement, removed from public scrutiny, where the commandant knows that the merciless use of degradations and corporal punishments of various kinds will not only be tolerated but approved by his superiors, excesses are inevitable. The excesses on Norfolk Island were Price's, but the responsibility for them was not his alone; it rested also on the authorities in Van Diemen's Land, and on the English politicians and civil servants who administered the Colonial Office and devised the convict system.

However, there were witnesses who spoke highly of Price as a man, and found no fault with his administration. Until the year

1852, when doubts began to creep in, the Lieutenant-Governor had complete confidence in him, though early in that year Denison was troubled by his increased use of corporal punishment, and required an explanation.[48] Major G. de Winton of the 99th Regiment was stationed on the island for three and a half years, from September 1848 to January 1850, and from 1851 to 1853. He and Price, with their families, left on the same vessel in January 1853. de Winton thought highly of the Civil Commandant; writing forty years after Price's death, he asserted that, 'Mr. Price, take him all in all, was the finest character I have met with in a wide experience'. He also wrote:

Mr. Price was by many qualifications eminently suited for his post. He was a man of commanding presence, of great physical strength, and absolutely without fear . . . He was a classical scholar, an athlete, and an oarsman, and he had a practical knowledge of many trades. He was a carpenter, turner, blacksmith, whitesmith, locksmith, baker, cook and confectioner, and was even an expert in sewing. Children were devoted to him; he would devise games for their amusement, and freely join in their diversions. In cases of sickness among them he would send them choice fruit from his garden, and sick comforts from his store, and with his own hands make broth and jellies for the sufferers.[49]

The friendship must have been deep between the Civil Commandant and the military commander, for Price named his youngest daughter, born on the island about 1852, Jane de Winton. The military commander and Price sat together as magistrates, and de Winton must have been aware of the state of affairs Bishop Willson described in 1852, and of the sympathy which the bishop asserted was felt by the military on the island for the convicts because of 'a harsh and merciless system of punishment for trifling offences . . . sometimes awarded without that careful and scrupulous investigation they are accustomed to witness in military law.'[50] He must have known, too, of the excessive use of the lash that caused concern to the authorities in Hobart Town. His description of Price's accomplishments may be taken as having a good deal of truth in it, though coloured by the memory of a valued friendship, but his recollections of the treatment and conditions of the convicts, written forty years later, are far from reliable.

The most significant witness in Price's favour, however, was

William Henry Barber, the English solicitor, already mentioned,
who was a victim of a gross miscarriage of justice. Barber's horrifying account of the way in which he was treated when Childs
was Commandant is adequately confirmed by convincing testimony, but he offered no criticism of Price; indeed, on his return
to England, he wrote of 'the temperate, strict and judicious control of Mr. Price'.[51] He was removed from Norfolk Island in
March 1847, while still a convict, to Van Diemen's Land, where
he was discharged soon after, at first on a conditional pardon.
Price gave Barber a favourable certificate, stating that he had
conducted himself entirely to Price's satisfaction.[52] Barber was on
the island during the same period as the Rev. Thomas Rogers,
who befriended him there and also on his discharge in Van
Diemen's Land. He must have known something at least of the
grave and detailed charges which Rogers made against Price, for
in April 1847, when Barber was a free man, Rogers obtained a
statement from him to support Rogers' claim that it was a usual
practice on the island for a chaplain to obtain the depositions
from convicts committed for trial at the assizes with a view to en-
suring adequate presentation of their defences.[53] It was, of course,
over this practice that Price and Rogers had first come into conflict. Undoubtedly Price's treatment of Barber was very different
from Childs', and Barber's estimate may have been tempered by
gratitude or by favourable comparison with what he had endured
under Childs. Because Barber's assessment of Price's administration lacks particularity, it is not possible to set this against Rogers'
specific and detailed charges, but it is only fair to give some weight
to the pronouncement of a man of character who, though innocent, had suffered grievously under the system and had every
reason to denounce it and its controllers.

As his role was essentially repressive and sterile, Price has received little attention from Australian historians. Henry Gyles
Turner may have known Price, for he came to Melbourne a
couple of years before Price was murdered, and from his *History
of the Colony of Victoria* it is clear that he admired him.[54] G. W.
Rusden certainly knew him; they were both pioneering members of the civil service of the newly created State of Victoria,
and Rusden's tributes to Price—'capable, determined, fearless
and strong in mind and body'—were an expression of his own

regard.[55] That partiality, and his authoritarian approach, impaired the factual accuracy of the brief passages in which Price is mentioned in his vigorous but idiosyncratic *History of Australia*.[56] It was natural, of course, that conservatives should esteem Price; to them he was the personification of just retribution, a trusted protector standing between them and the debased and disorderly elements that genuinely threatened the stability of an infant community. Fear and compassion are incompatibles, and so long as Price kept criminals in subjection, whether in Van Diemen's Land, on Norfolk Island, or in Victoria, the propertied and the timorous sections were not disposed to trouble greatly about his methods. In that lay the tragic and ever-recurring dilemma; the end, the protection of society, was necessary and praiseworthy; the means, which denied compassion and human dignity, were corrosive of the essential basis of social living.

III   *The Harsh Régime*

The circumstances under which John Price took command at Norfolk Island were favourable to tyrannical behaviour. There were, broadly, three periods in the official English attitude to the convict system, and these were mirrored in the approach of the local authorities. In the first, from 1787 to about 1820, the emphasis was upon getting the outcasts to the new penal colonies and keeping them there; while harshness and brutality were concomitants, they were often incidental and inevitable, and the official mind was not obsessively concerned with the reclamation and reformation of the convicts. In the middle and the final periods, moral regeneration of criminals became a dominant objective, to be achieved through pain and degradation. That was not quite the way Lord Stanley put it in his famous 'Probation System' despatch,[57] which embodied the results of the twenty years' cogitation by the British government. Discreetly avoiding the crudities of clarity, His Lordship expressed it in ornate language:

to keep alive an invigorating hope and a salutary dread at every stage of the progress of the Prisoner from the commencement to the close of his punishment appears to us to be an indispensable part of the discipline to which he should be subjected . . . I should leave unnoticed the most important of all the general principles to which the Ministers of the Crown look . . . if I omitted to add that we anticipate from a systematic course of Moral and Religious

Instruction, which the congregation of the Convicts in masses will afford the best means of applying, such salutary influences as may best qualify them for entering on the temptations of an independent course of life, and may induce them to betake themselves to industrious and useful pursuits.

By 1846 religious, moral, economic and personal considerations combined to support the opposition to transportation, and the attitude of the free Australian population was one of hatred and fear of convictism and all it implied.[58] It was forgotten or disregarded that convicts ranged from the irreclaimably wicked and depraved to the merely unfortunate, and though a substantial section had followed criminal pursuits as a livelihood in England, that this was largely a consequence of appalling social conditions. Even in Norfolk Island's worst days, the proportion, albeit significant, of hardened and vicious criminals among the doubly convicted men, or 'old hands' as they were known, was much less than popularly supposed, and among the prisoners were men sent to the settlement, not for great crimes or wickedness or depravity, but because it suited the authorities. From Maconochie's time (1840-4) the island held two classes of convicts, the 'old hands', and the probation prisoners sent direct from England. When the Governor, Sir George Gipps, visited the island in March 1843, there were 876 old hands and 593 probation prisoners. Under Stanley's 'Probation System', prisoners sentenced in England to transportation for life went direct to Norfolk Island, and prisoners similarly sentenced in the colonies could also be sent there. Price himself told a Select Committee of the Legislative Assembly of Victoria that among the 2,000 men on the island when he arrived, boys of 14 to 16 years were herded together with men 'grown grey in crime'.[59] The Rev. Thomas Rogers stated that 'nearly all the turbulence was confined to the "old hands"', and that even of these the really perverse were a very small minority.[60] Anyone familiar with the management of penal institutions will recognize that it is highly likely his statement was true. But this was not the popular, nor perhaps the official, view; it was thought, in G. W. Rusden's words, that 'like pitch the miserable felons begrimed all with whom they came in contact. Their island lair was [as] awful as one of Dante's circles—an abyss of unutterable horror.'[61] Doubtless it was, but the responsibility for that state of affairs lay largely with authorities corrupted by the immoral doctrine of maximum penal severity.

No useful purpose would now be served by an examination of Rogers' allegations that Price treated him discourteously or used his authority high-handedly in their relations as Commandant and chaplain. There is not much point, either, in discussing whether Price needed to use disciplinary measures of great severity, or could have maintained order by milder methods. After all, Price was a prison governor, sent for the purpose of exercising harsh control, and it is idle to censure him for doing what his superiors required of him, or for mere errors of judgment in carrying out his allotted task. Rogers criticized the use of convicts as overseers and constables. So did Bishop Willson, and there can be no doubt the criticisms were justified. Solomon listed first among the things that disquiet the earth and which it cannot bear 'a servant when he reigneth';[62] even worse is the prisoner put in authority over his fellow prisoners. But Price did not introduce that practice; he found it in full vigour when he assumed command. He cannot fairly be criticized for continuing its use, though he may be held blameworthy if he encouraged grave abuses of authority by overseers or constables, or even if he failed to check them. To justify an indictment of Price for using his despotic powers in disregard of the dictates of humanity, specific instances of inexcusable abuse must be established. It is at this point that the testimony of Rogers and Bishop Willson is impressive in its cogency and it is the more so because it was never convincingly refuted. Rogers himself stressed the failure by Price and Hampton, the Comptroller-General of Convicts, to meet his charges:

it is worthy of remark that Dr. Hampton or Mr. Price never ventured to publish in the colony any refutation of the charge of brutal severity. If the charges were altogether deliberate falsehoods, they were nevertheless highly libellous attacks on the government and official character of Mr. Price. They excited general execration against the convict department throughout the whole colony. Yet no authorised contradiction of them ever appeared: no newspaper was prosecuted for publishing such atrocious calumnies . . . What means this shrinking from denial in the colony? Is it the loftiness of proud contempt for public opinion, or is it the serener consciousness of injured innocence? No such things. Dr. Hampton knew by his visit to Norfolk Island, that indisputable proof of Mr. Price's barbarity existed.[63]

About three weeks after he took control, Price directed that eighteen ounces of flour should be served out to each prisoner daily. Rogers considered that once this was done, the most potent factor disposing the half-starved prisoners to insubordination was removed. His allegations were explicit and unequivocal, as the following passage shows:

His arrogant and insufferable exercise of authority neither removed nor mitigated any one moral evil. With the exception of the flour issue, no improvement took place. Miscreants were not expelled from the police. Perfidy was not discountenanced. The gaols and cells were crowded more than ever. Men who slept in garden huts and stables were ordered into barracks at the very time when, from official representation made by Mr. Burgess to Mr. Latrobe, it was known that the wards were already over-filled. Officers were brow-beaten. Second and third-convicted felons were as formerly appointed to be policemen, and often countenanced in their insolent demeanor to free officers. It was made a part of these convict policemen's duty to search any fellow-prisoner anywhere, or at any time they met him. This 'searching' was often conducted in the most obscene and disgusting manner; and if the least resistance was offered, the man resisting might be knocked down by a blow from the searcher's bludgeon, and run the risk of having his limbs broken. Every man was exhorted to play the spy upon his fellow, and treachery was rewarded as a virtue. *'Anything and everything might be made a charge.'* Perjury on the part of the constables was rife. Innocent men were inveigled into crime by those set over them to prevent crime. An inquisitorial vigilance and undiscriminating harshness presided everywhere, until the lives of hundreds of prisoners were reduced to a continued agony of terror. Every agency for their *reformation*, except physical force, was derided.

That no moral benefit could accrue to prisoners from such a discipline as this, is evident. Rather they were deteriorated by it, and rendered unfit for returning to free society. It made them unbelievers in all the social charities. It caused religion itself, and all religious exercises, to be regarded by them as an hypocrisy. It hardened their hearts, and eradicated from their minds all sense of probity and fidelity. It made the service odious and degrading to officers. It accomplished nothing noble in penal science. It was debasing and inhuman.[64]

As he revealed in a letter in June 1848 to the Quaker missionary, George Washington Walker, Price was fully aware of the criticisms of his methods that came from others as well as Rogers. In a passage expressed in the phraseology peculiar to the Friends, the devoutness of which is strangely out of character with his usual language, he wrote,

Be assured that whatever man says of me provided the inward monitor tells me I am right avails but little. I have attained to that point of philosophy and trust that He who has strengthened me in that respect will ever befriend me and teach me to fear self reproach when in error.[65]

The claim itself discloses a remarkable self-sufficiency.

In the *Correspondence*, Rogers supplied specific instances of brutal and capricious punishments ordered by Price, and some of them he set out compactly in the *Review of Dr. Hampton's First Report*.* There can be no doubt that Price read both the *Correspondence* and the *Review*, and as both are very rare (indeed, the only accessible copy of the *Review* is in the Mitchell Library, Sydney) it is desirable, instead of paraphrasing them, to reproduce the passages in the language in which they were originally expressed.[66]

H— was servant to Mr.—. He was one day bringing home his master's monthly ration of flour from the store. Near his master's house he was met by a fellow-prisoner acting as constable. The constable stopped H— and demanded to know what he was carrying; he replied, 'I'm carrying home my master's flour.' The constable ordered him to put the bag down until the flour was searched. The servant replied, 'my master sent me for his flour—I am obeying his order—you have nothing to do with the flour—you have no right to detain me.' The constable insisted on searching the flour. The servant would not let him put his stick into the bag. H— was then taken into custody, charged with obstructing a constable; and the servant, for what he believed to be the faithful discharge of his duty to his master, *received thirty-six lashes!* The same high state of discipline forbids and renders penal all such interchanges of goodwill and sympathy as the following between one convict and another. A man whose age prevented his employment at any heavier occupation than that of gate-keeper was one day eating his dinner: he had a mouthful or two of salt beef and maize bread left: a fellow prisoner happened at the moment to pass by, and was asked if he would have the morsel of bread and meat; it was instantly accepted. While he was eating it, a constable who had

*The report, dated 10 March 1848, of the Comptroller-General of Convicts, Dr J. S. Hampton, made after he visited Norfolk Island in January 1848, is set out in Further Correspondence on Convict Discipline and Transportation, presented Feb. 1849, P.P. (H.L.) 1849, MS. pagination 202-9. It exonerated Price completely, and Rogers pronounced it 'a deceptive document'.

been watching the giving and eating of the bread, rushed up and took the two men into custody. Mr. Price sentenced them, the one for giving, the other for eating the morsel of food, to *a month's detention* on the island; which detention might prolong their sentence for several months.

Feelings of pity or compassion were also repressed. It was customary in my time on the island to return any men of the gaol-gang to their cell for the remainder of the day on which they were flogged. The man who happened to be flogged was washed by his companions with cold water, the mangled skin pressed down, and a wet cloth applied to the wounded parts. Subsequently the cooling leaf of the banana was applied. One Sunday I was told that an officer's servant was in gaol. On making enquiry I found that he was sent to gaol for having given a few banana leaves out of his master's garden for the use of the gaol-gang in dressing each other's backs. A constable saw him and took him to gaol. I forget the man's name, and what punishment he received for giving a few banana leaves to lay over the lacerated shoulders of men who had been flogged. But I submit that to deal with such an act as an offence against discipline, or sternly treat it as a crime, was a process of extirpation against the minor virtues. The giving of banana leaves was never before regarded as irregular or wrong.

That the gentler feelings could find little place in Mr. Price's high state of discipline may be inferred from the following. The surgeon superintendent of the *John Calvin*, probation ship, on his landing at Norfolk Island, recommended a man named S— as an inoffensive man with very fine feelings. 'Oh,' said Mr. Price, 'I'll soon take *them* out of him!' 'Whenever a fellow is recommended to me by the religious instructor or the surgeon superintendent,' said Mr. Price on another occasion, 'I always set that fellow down as the greatest hypocrite in the whole lot!' This man S— was made prisoner clerk by the commissariat officer. One evening after the duties of the day were over he went out, as he was accustomed, for a walk. Mr. Price met him, and roughly demanded where he had been. S— terrified and confused, said he was out on duty. This was a falsehood. Mr. Price ordered him to the police office, charged him with telling a lie, and sentenced him to receive thirty-six lashes. S— a man of nervous temperament, shrieked dreadfully under the flogging. Yet I know of a case where a sub-overseer was falsely accused by an impudent constable who, before Mr. Price, swore to a charge that was fully disproved by the testimony of another constable; yet the man who swore to a false charge escaped without even a reprimand. In selecting men for the police one day, Mr. Price asked a man what he had been at home, the man replied he had been a farm servant; 'well then,' was the remark, 'you are not thief enough for me.' Another who professed to have been 'a honest traveller' in England, *i.e.* a thief by profession, was made a police man, and an agent in maintaining a high state of discipline. Another instance:— One day the Black Rock gang, of sixty men and upwards, left off work at the usual hour for dinner. When the messes came to the field, it was found that there was no vegetable or bread, and scarcely meat for half the men. The gang accordingly refused work until they got a proper ration. The officer in charge proceeded to the settlement, and reported the occurrence to Mr. Price. Of course Mr. Price directed the deficiency in the dinners to be rectified? No such thing. He took a party of five or six constables with him, and riding out to Black Rock, marched the whole gang into the barrack yard. Here he held a court, and ordering the triangles to be erected, he sentenced four of the men to receive fifty lashes each, all the rest to three months extension of their original sentence on the island; and so to bring about a high state of discipline, the convicts were first cheated of their food, and then flogged for remonstrating against the fraud.

Another instance:— When the probation prisoners from England by the *John Calvin*, were landed at Cascade, every man was stripped stark naked on the beach to be examined. If any had a garter, shoe, hat, vest, or drawers not having the government mark, the article of clothing was taken from them. Several men who had worn flannels all their lives, or for many years, had their vests and drawers taken away by order of Mr. Price, under whose personal observation the examination was made. Several of these men were then marched across the island, four miles, to Longridge, some without shoes, some without waistcoats, some shivering without their flannels: for several days after I saw many of these men thus mustered at day light for prayers on the Longridge parade ground, which was quite wet after a showery night. The medical officer of the station, finding many of them on the sick list from sore throats, catarrh, and rheumatism, wrote a memorandum recommending their flannels to be restored. Mr. Price referred the memorandum to Dr. Everett, the senior medical officer, who declared that the flannels were *not* necessary for the men's health. Two days after, there were no less than thirty-five men by the *John Calvin* on the sick list, from exposure on landing, and loss of their clothing. Such was the mode, and such the means in raising up the discipline at Norfolk Island to the high state in which Dr. Hampton reports he found it; a state of discipline that discouraged all the benevolent sentiments; that treated honorable feelings as a crime; that punished fidelity in servants as a breach of discipline; that patronised the bold crafty ruffian; that crushed the weak and inoffensive; that built itself up by fomenting ill will, malice, hatred, envy, revenge, suspicion, and perfidy, among the members of the community whom it purported to reform; a state of discipline whose reformatory products are admitted to be *a sham* by its own advocate, who yet coolly tells the home government and

British parliament that the sham is *a 'step in advance'* in the convict
polity of Norfolk Island.

*   *   *

Take the case of Waters. This man was sentenced to the gaol gang
for eighteen months. He had sore eyes. He was charged with wilfully
preventing them from getting well. He was placed in a strait-
waistcoat by order of Mr. Price, and tied down by the arms and
ancles to the iron bedstead on which he lay. This torturing process
is called *'strapping down'*. Waters was strapped down for a fortnight
or three weeks until the lacing cord of the strait-waistcoat excoriated
his back, causing him excessive pain. Mr. Price saw him in this
condition, but would not release him, although he positively denied
the charge of hurting his eyes. The weight of his body pressing on
the cords of the strait-waistcoat rendered his posture so intolerable
that he asked to see Major Harold, the officer in command of the
troops, and visiting justice of the gaol and island. The turnkey told
Mr. Price that Waters wanted to see Major Harold: Mr. Price
charged him with 'insolence' for so doing, and sentenced him to
receive thirty-six lashes. The man was taken off the bed and flogged
upon his already bruised and lacerated back. After being flogged
for the *insolence* of asking to see Major Harold, Waters was again
strapped down. In a day or two his back stank so much that the
turnkey interceded for him with Mr. Price, and a slight relaxation of
his torture took place: he was allowed to sit up on the bed, but his
hands were still tied to the foot of the bed frame. Dr. Hampton in
his report declares that having held a *private* enquiry he was convinced that Mr. Price had not tyrannically abused his power; and
this report was laid before parliament as a refutation of the charges!
At Norfolk Island Dr. Hampton declared that the case of Waters was
one of established cruelty against Mr. Price.

Kelly, a convict, was charged with having tobacco improperly in
his possession. In the police office he stated that he had not more than
a quarter of an inch of tobacco, and before he got it he read a notice
on the barrack gates, *signed by the commandant,* giving the men
leave to use tobacco if they got it honestly. The tobacco he had was
given him by one of the chaplains. Notwithstanding the fact of the
written notice on the barrack gate, and his having got the tobacco
honestly, Mr. Price sentenced Kelly to receive thirty-six lashes. Was
this no tyrannical abuse of power?

A man employed as gardener at Orange Vale, was met by a constable on one of the walks with a twig in his hand. The constable
asked him what he was doing. The gardener thought the constable
was joking, and jocularly replied, 'why, I might be after a parrot.'
The constable took him into custody on the instant, and lodged him
[in] gaol. He was brought before Mr. Price. He was charged with

'*intending to catch a parrot!*' and for intending to catch a parrot he received thirty-six lashes. Both the English chaplains then on the island considered this case to be one of reckless oppression. But probably Dr. Hampton does not think it any tyrannical abuse of power!

Graham, a cart driver, at Longridge, found a young bird in the bush. He brought it home to the stable and tamed it. He was brought before Mr. Price, charged 'with having a tame bird.' He got thirty-six lashes for having a tame bird!

Higson, a stock man, was passing along his run. Mr. Ison's gardener said 'give this tree a push, I want to roll it down the hill to mend the garden fence where your bullocks come in.' Higson put his foot to the tree: one push sent it to the bottom of the hill. A constable saw him and charged him with 'pushing a tree with his foot.' For this *crime* he got thirty-six lashes. For an equally trivial offence he also received thirty-six lashes on his back, and thirty-six on his breech. Six days afterwards he was flogged for having tobacco. Four or five days after this last flogging, he was reported for not having the bullocks in by bell ring. He hid in the bush—was taken—and received one hundred lashes!

Clayton was flogged four times within a month, for trifling breaches of discipline.

Launder was charged with having government paper improperly in his possession. He had once been a very respectable man at home, and felt the charge keenly. The government paper was three or four small slips which the commissariat officer had torn and thrown on the floor to be swept out. Launder wished to explain this to Mr. Price at the police office. Mr. Price bid him hold his tongue. He begged a second time to be heard in his defence. Mr. Price then cried out 'give him the gag!' The constable seized, and dragged him to the gaol; he was in a very feeble state of health, and nearly blind with ophthalmia; yet the gaoler forced the gag into his mouth with so much violence as to dash out two of the man's teeth—cut his gums—and caused such distension of the jaw, that it was supposed for a time to be dislocated. Next day, on another false or frivolous charge Launder was brought before Mr. Price again, and sentenced to four months extension.

Peart, an officer's servant, standing at his master's door, said 'good morning' to a waterman who was passing: not another word was spoken: for saying 'good morrow,' Mr. Price put Peart seven days in chains.

Lloyd, a young man 27 years of age, was transported when a boy. He was again transported in the colony, and sent to Norfolk Island. In October, 1845, he joined in robbing an officer's house. I was one of the sitting magistrates who committed him for the robbery. He remained in gaol nearly ten months before he was tried. He was sentenced at the assizes in 1846 to three years' further imprisonment, with three months in each year in solitary. After he had gone through a year of his sentence he was charged with indecency in the gaol yard, and sentenced by Mr. Price to nine months extension in gaol. He became so despondent that he hung himself in his cell: the turnkey discovered him before life was extinct. Mr. Price was informed of what had taken place. He went down to the gaol and sentenced him to receive fifty lashes for attempting to hang himself. The medical officer, however, would not answer for the man's life, and the lashes were not inflicted. But what does Mr. Price gain on the score of humanity from the surgeon's intervention? Instead, however, of being flogged, he was 'strapped down,' and kept in that exhausting posture on his back for six weeks. The chaplain who visited him, told me that he looked more like a pale distended corpse than a living being, and his voice so weak that it could scarcely be heard. One day the chaplain seeing his lips moving, leaned down to his ear to the man's mouth, and at length distinguished the words— 'Loose me—oh, loose me.' The chaplain replied, 'no, Lloyd, I dare not do that.' A deep sigh followed the refusal, and the tears trickled down the culprit's emaciated face. But a list of instances were almost endless. They were of daily occurrence. I have not picked out a few rare cases. I have given a fair specimen of what was frequent and usual, neither have I set down one that I believe to be doubtful— much less deliberately false. My authority is either personal knowledge, or information from credible parties who had personal knowledge. Finally, no contradiction of the charges against Mr. Price has even been openly and fearlessly put forth in the colony.

A comparison of the texts and the footnotes in Book Five of the original version of *For the Term of His Natural Life* establishes that Marcus Clarke drew extensively upon Rogers' *Correspondence*. He used, almost verbatim, a shocking instance of brutality that appears among several incidents which Rogers said were 'taken from written communications made to me by several respectable officers with whom I am acquainted'.[67]

In one of the turnkeys' rooms in the new gaol is to be seen an article of harness that at first sight creates surprise in the mind of the beholder when considering what animal of the brute creation exists of so diminutive a size as to admit of its use; but on enquiry it will be found to be a bridle, perfect in head band, throat lash, etc., for a fellow creature. There is attached to it a round piece of ironwood of almost 4 inches in length, and 1½ in diameter; this again is secured in a broad strap of leather to cross the mouth. In the wood there is a small hole, and, when used, the wood is inserted in the mouth, the small hole being the only breathing space; and when the whole is secured with the various straps and buckles, a more complete bridle in resemblance could not well be witnessed. This is one of Mr.—'s instruments for torturing the unhappy and fallen men, and on one occasion I was compelled to witness its application on a poor blind wretch, named Edward Mooney. My duty required my attendance at the gaol occasionally. I came in one evening after eight o'clock. I was conversing with one of the turnkeys; the notorious —, who robbed Mr. Waterhouse of £700, was present; he also at that time being a turnkey, holding a third class pass, and in receipt of 2s. per diem. Everything was quite still. I could not help remarking how quiet the gaol was, when the said — exclaimed 'there's some one speaking; I know what b— it is;' and forthwith took from its pegs one of the bridles just described and a pair of handcuffs. I followed him to one of the cells which he opened, and therein was a man lying on his straw mat undressed, and to all appearance asleep. — desired him to get up, calling him by his name, and to dress himself. He did so, and came out into the yard where — inserted the iron-wood gag in his mouth, and the sound produced by his breathing through it (which appeared to be done with great difficulty) resembled a low indistinct whistle. He then led him to the lamp post in the yard, placing him with his back to it, and his arms being taken round were secured by the handcuffs round the post. As the night was very chilly, I buttoned his jacket up to the throat, speaking at the same time a few words to cheer him that brought tears from his sightless eyes to think that some one yet felt for his miserable and forlorn condition; and this convinced me still further that even the most hardened villain can be melted by kindness, however trifling. Having enquired how long he was to remain in the condition described, I was told THREE HOURS!

It is only fair to Price to stress that this incident seems to have occurred before he came to the island, though the harness and the 'spreadeagle' remained accessible at the cells during at least part of his tenure. The spreadeagle consisted of two ring-bolts, about six feet asunder, and five and a half feet from the floor, securely fastened to the wall, and a third bolt in the floor, the three placed to form the letter V. The victim was placed against the wall; his arms were outstretched and one attached to each of the wall bolts, and his legs made fast to the floor bolt. Often the bridle and ironwood bit were used as well. The turn-keys could resort to this punishment without consulting the head gaoler.[68] The passage quoted exposes the brutality of the gaolers who were certainly no more restrained when Price was Commandant, as the following incidents establish.

August 6.—Visited the general hospital; found a man named Lemon dreadfully beaten, and having his arm broken. It appears that constable Baldock was taking a man to gaol, charged with either having or using a towel irregularly. He threw his shirt to Lemon, and asked him to get it washed. Baldock would not allow him (Lemon) to have it. Upon this the man Lemon gave Baldock either a blow or, as he says, a push, when a number of constables fell upon him and beat him with their clubs. It was just as divine service was commencing yesterday evening. All the officers and constables left the church, except Mr. Duncan, and the 'old hands' made a general rush towards the windows to see what was going on. Mr. Bott told me he interfered to cause the constables to desist after the man was down, but Baldock said 'lay it into him—lay it into him.' While down he was handcuffed with his hands behind him; after this he was taken to gaol and gagged two hours, with his hands chained behind him to the lamp post, *having all this time his arm broken!* He was then taken to the new gaol, and Stephens sent for the doctor who received him into hospital.

*   *   *

In one of the yards in the new gaol, exposed to a nearly tropical sun, was another appliance of gaol discipline: this was a large hand-mill for grinding maize corn. At this mill I one day saw a man working, whose agonised features I shall not soon forget. The turnkey told me that he had frequently seen the men vomiting while grinding at this mill.

A convict named Jackson, for stabbing an overseer, was sentenced to death and confined in the new gaol until such sentence should be approved of by the executive council. Whilst awaiting this decision, although fully impressed with the awfulness of his situation, he frequently gave way to violent temper. On one occasion he found some fault with the food sent him, and threw the tin plate out of the cell door as the acting turnkey left it. This turnkey, a fellow convict, in a few moments returned with his bludgeon, and beat the unhappy man in a most brutal and unmerciful manner about the head *whilst chained in his cell,* although the confirmation of his sentence was hourly expected; and he was scarcely healed of his wounds when he went to the gallows. The man who had beaten Jackson boasted of what he had done. The name of this man is —, and he may (if not already a policeman) soon be added to the police of the colony. [Note.—*This man told me that the first time he saw men flogged at Norfolk Island, he trembled, and turned quite sick: but that after he had been constable awhile he could stand by and see a dozen men flogged of a morning, and watch the infliction with the utmost unconcern.* —T. R.]

*   *   *

Perkins had another drubbing some time since coming out of church. ——, a prisoner constable, was the first to fall on him, and after him a host who soon covered him with blood and wounds, for not walking in a proper manner out of church. And the commandant allowed this drubbing to stand as a sort of instalment of punishment when the man was brought up for trial. On account of the beating he received a lighter magisterial sentence. Mr.— told me one day that the commandant censured the conduct of the constable who complained of some man not opening his mouth to have the inside of it searched for tobacco. It seems they were deemed blameworthy for having in this instance neglected to use violence. 'Why didn't you knock him down like a bullock?' was the interrogatory at Norfolk Island!

During the early years of Price's command there were two murders. A sub-overseer named Clarke, who was murdered on 27 August 1846, had been a witness against two prisoners who were hanged for the murder of a convict policeman. Fifteen sub-overseers wrote to Price that they feared for their lives if they had to drive men to work on hungry bellies, and would have to give up their billets as sub-overseers. Presumably this protest influenced Price in directing an increase in rations.[69] Price himself is said to have always gone with loaded pistols in his belt.[70] The second murder occurred on 20 March 1848, when Michael Sullivan killed a man named Payne. He was convicted but sentence of death was recorded, which meant that it would not be exacted unless confirmed by the Lieutenant-Governor. On 9 July 1848 Sir William Denison directed the execution be carried out and Sullivan was hanged on the island.[71]

Severe punishments for trifling offences were high among Price's methods of enforcing discipline. Until its use was permitted in 1848, offences in connection with tobacco were punished with savage penalties. Convict constables were encouraged to bring men in on charges relating to tobacco; they were allowed to seize a prisoner by the throat and forcibly examine his mouth for the 'tobacco track', or sign of tobacco, or to force him to strip and submit to an indecent examination of his private parts for contraband. Four to fourteen days' solitary confinement were imposed for a minute's lateness at mustering; for not walking fast enough; for not performing tasks that were physically impossible; for having a pipe; for talking; for possession of a

needle or of articles of no significance; for laughing when going in
to prayers; for not touching the hat by way of deference. Solitary
confinement, however, meant no solitude; men were herded together in fetid, cramped and airless cells, where the heat and
the stench of unwashed bodies and of the night buckets brought
them close to suffocation, and the opportunities for gross homosexual practices were seized upon, if need be with violence. The
sentence meant rations of maize-corn bread and water, and the
harshness of the punishment lay in near starvation and in the
degrading physical discomforts. Floggings were ordered for trifling reasons; one man received thirty-six lashes for losing his
shoe-laces. Rogers lists the trivial offences and the names of over
one hundred men confined in the old gaol in February 1847,[72]
when the need for harshly repressive measures no longer existed.
There was, he asserted, but 'one law, if law it can be called,
the law of arbitrary caprice'.[73] The records of court proceedings
were defective, and the proceedings summary in the completest
sense of the word:

The business . . . was thus indeed disposed of in a morning with
amazing celerity; the only misfortune . . . was, that the administration of justice in the police office at Norfolk Island, was turned into
an iniquitous and demoralizing farce; and the magisterial records . . .
were rendered as deceptive as a registry of crime, as they were defective in the number of criminals tried.[74]

For years the English authorities vacillated in their attitude
to the retention of Norfolk Island as a penal settlement, and,
though the decision turned out not to be final, Earl Grey decided to abandon it. By about the middle of 1847 practically all
the probation prisoners had been transferred to Van Diemen's
Land, leaving Price with about 450 'old hands', or colonial prisoners, and 50 or 60 probation prisoners. However, the numbers
of the staff and the military were the same as when there were
almost 2,000 prisoners on the island, though the garrison was
reduced later.[75] When the Comptroller-General of Convicts in
Van Diemen's Land, Dr J. S. Hampton, visited the island in
January 1848 it was to ascertain if it could receive convicts
from Sydney, enabling the Van Diemen's Land authorities to
find a temporary solution for a thorny problem. The inhabitants
of Van Diemen's Land, embittered still because the probation

prisoners were dumped on them, were vigorously hostile to taking the Sydney convicts. Rogers asserted Hampton's report was a 'deceptive document' that defended barbarity and palliated injustice.[76] Hampton, formerly a surgeon in the Royal Navy, succeeded as Comptroller-General Colonel William Thomas Napier Champ, a man of excellent quality and capacity. Hampton was as unscrupulous as Champ was upright, and his career in Van Diemen's Land revealed his worst features. Later by some inexcusable freakishness on the part of the English authorities he was appointed Governor of Western Australia, where, as in Tasmania, he earned and richly deserved public detestation. He was a cold-hearted and devious opportunist, and a fitting target for Rogers' strictures.[77]

In October 1849 Bishop Willson made his second visit to Norfolk Island. He found 'a marvellous change' had taken place; the 'frightful evils' he had seen on his visit in 1846 had been corrected; unnatural crime had been eliminated, and violent crime was rare. He attributed the improvements and the 'perfect unanimity which existed among the whole staff of officers on the island, whether civil or military, lay or clerical . . . to the judicious control of Mr. Price the Commandant.' He declared Price possessed 'a master mind for carrying out the work entrusted to him—[he is] one who possesses such a combination of qualifications for the discharge of duties so important as rarely to be found in one man.' Yet three things still troubled him: the evil system of employing convicts as constables and overseers; the practice of extending sentences for petty breaches of discipline, usually on the word of a convict constable or overseer; and the distance of 1,400 miles that separated the island from Hobart Town. So long as Price had charge of the penal settlement he thought there was little reason to fear that abuses to any extent could exist, 'yet, from its immense distance from the seat of government, and comparatively infrequent and irregular visitation, it is not difficult to imagine circumstances occurring from which evils of a fearful description might arise and exist for a considerable time before a remedy could be applied'.[78]

Bishop Willson's satisfaction was short-lived; when he came again to the island he was to find that his confidence in Price was misplaced, and that the evils he feared were flourishing, with no sign of remedy. Reports that great severity was in use, and the plight of the convicts deplorable, induced him in March 1852 to make his third and final visit to the island. Dr Hampton travelled on the same vessel. On his return to Hobart Town the bishop sent a very long letter, dated 22 May 1852, to the Lieutenant-Governor, Sir William Denison.[79] His description of conditions as he found them is an even more powerful indictment of Price than the account given by Rogers; whatever justification Price may have had to use brutally repressive measures when he took command after the rising in 1846, this could not be claimed in 1852. According to Bishop Willson:

Gloom, sullen despondency, despair of leaving the Island, seemed to be the general condition of the men's minds, except those who were employed as servants or engaged in billets . . . My observation was particularly directed to the number of men in chains; and it was stated that about a fortnight before my visit, on one morning, for some cause they were ignorant of, the Commandant ordered every man wearing chains to have both legs secured, or, as it is technically termed, 'chains crossed', which adds, I am told, greatly to the punishment, especially to those in heavy irons (14 lbs. for instance), and who have to walk much with water and wood carts, bullock wains, etc. I could not learn that there had been any general cause for this measure . . . The exact number of men in chains I am not able to state, but on Sunday, 14th March, out of 270 convicts who attended the church when I officiated, only 52 were without them . . . Complaints, regarding the frequency of the lash, were great indeed. It was stated . . . that on the Monday previous to our arrival . . . thirty-nine men belonging to the settlement had been flogged, and fourteen from Longridge Station next day . . . The description, or rather remarks—I could not avoid hearing both—from free and bond, respecting the time consumed in the infliction of that day's punishment—the state of the yard, from the blood running down men's backs, mingled with the water used in washing them, when taken down from the triangle—the degrading scene of a large number of men standing in the outer yard waiting their turn to be tortured, and the more humiliating spectacle presented by those who had undergone the scourging, especially towards the end of this melancholy business, were painful to listen to, and now raises a blush, when I reflect that by a rational system of discipline, and judicious management of the whole of the convicts in Van Diemen's Land, not one lash has been inflicted for many, perhaps not for twelve months. Sir, either the system pursued in Van Diemen's Land is very unsound, or that on Norfolk Island.

In his letter of 10 December 1849 Bishop Willson had expressed concern over the power of the Commandant to pass a sentence for a petty breach of discipline (generally on the word of a convict overseer or convict) that had the effect of extending the original sentence of transportation. Price strongly opposed the suggestion that this magisterial power should be abolished, and disingenuously asserted that in every case in which the evidence of a free officer or free constable could be had, 'and there are very few cases in which it is otherwise', that evidence was required.[80] Officially it was claimed that unless the magistrate's sentence was added to the period the prisoner had to serve on the island, the penalty would be meaningless. This ignored, of course, the trifling offences, the perjured evidence, and the prejudiced bench, but it concealed, too, the practice of adding to the sentence as well a period of probation equivalent to the magistrate's sentence. Bishop Willson raised the matter again in 1852 with Dr Hampton when they were both on the island, and Hampton agreed that the practice of adding a period of probation was wrong, and directed that existing extensions be cancelled.

The bishop found that every one of the 130 cells had an occupant, many in heavy irons which were placed on them not to prevent escape but, contrary to law, for the purpose of increasing punishment. Some of these prisoners from long and close confinement and spare diet presented 'a very attenuated and blanched appearance'. Many men out of the cells had 36 lbs. of iron on their legs and some were in manacles with their hands separated by bars; 'in fact, with their bodies placed in a frame of iron work'. He was shocked by the pallid countenances and shrunken appearance of men who, he was told, had been discharged from gaol the previous day. 'The image of one of these living skeletons (he too had been lately flogged) is so strongly impressed on my mind that no day passes without having it many times vividly before me.' This man died not long afterwards, and Father Lucas, a chaplain on the island, considered that the 'air of his cell was intolerable' and confinement there had hastened his death. Hampton explained officially that he had been left in his cell because the greater degree of ventilation in the hospital would have been 'prejudicial to his case'.[81]

As was inevitable in such an environment, callousness was not confined to the penal staff; it corrupted also the medical officer.

Bishop Willson put his finger squarely on the basic factor that enabled these horrors to take place. It was 'the system which invests one man at this remote place with absolute, I might say irresponsible power of dealing with so large a mass of human beings . . . and which also leaves the medical superintendence of so many to one unaided officer.' He continued:

It is proper also to make every allowance, in reason and justice, for gentlemen so completely cut off from all social intercourse with others, except the very limited circle of society on the island, all of whom who compose it breathe the very air of convictism. This fact most probably tends to work strongly on minds, and add to the difficulties of no ordinary nature, and perhaps also to create fears and apprehensions which may cause a system of coercion and severity to be pursued which under other circumstances dare not be thought of.

Hampton's official comments followed the customary pattern. Though no one had thought to mention it to the bishop, Hampton claimed there had been a conspiracy to break out of the barracks, and the chains were crossed as a 'necessary precaution'. He said, in any event, 'crossed chains' had formerly been the general rule and 'split chains' were a relaxation, and there had only been a return to the previous practice. His Lordship's figures about the floggings were wrong; the number was not thirty-nine at Kingston, and fourteen at Longridge, but twenty-nine and six respectively, and only eight of the floggings were for offences connected with tobacco! He observed that the medical officer disagreed with the description of the flogging yard; he had never seen any blood, and after floggings the men were not washed in the yard but in the cells. Only twenty-six were in gaol for tobacco offences. No one was convicted without the evidence of a free constable or officer or confirmation 'by concomitant circumstances'.[82] It was as evasive and unconvincing as most official explanations.

In due course, the Duke of Newcastle expressed his gratitude to Bishop Willson, but as it had been decided to break up the settlement, he thought it was needless to discuss future management, and as for the past, the explanations given by Hampton and Price satisfied him that there was no cause for censure.

Somewhat inconsistently, though, he added, 'I shall be very glad,
however, if milder measures should be found to be sufficient for
the management of the convicts on their transfer to the mainland.'[83]

Despite official palliations and equivocations, there is no reasonable doubt that the Rev. Rogers and Bishop Willson described truly the conditions under Price's administration. Long
ago Herodotus pointed out that evils must result where a man is
allowed to do whatever he pleases without having to answer for
his actions:

Even the best of men, were he granted such power, would alter the
train of his thoughts. Insolence will be engendered in him by the
advantages of his position: and envy he has already, implanted in
him, as in all men, from his birth. With these two in his soul he is
filled with every wickedness; for insolence will cause him to break
out in many acts of wantonness, and envy into many more . . . He
very readily listens to calumny and is the most inconsistent of all
men.[84]

Remote from supervision, confident his superiors would always
support him, contemptuous of his charges and relishing their
misery as proof of his mastery, Price was the more readily corrupted by his despotic powers because of his temperamental
defects.

Abandonment of the penal settlement was constantly under
consideration, however, and the position of Commandant carried no prospects and many drawbacks. In a communication of
12 December 1850 he had asked to be 'removed from this Lazar
House of crime' and given employment 'elsewhere than in the
Australian Colonies'. His expressed reasons were

the necessity of educating my family and removing them from the
influence of a penal settlement . . . unable as I am to obtain tuition
for my children, female servants for my family, with ultra penal
convicts as my domestic servants, I should be wanting to my family
were I not to bring my case under your Lordship's notice.[85]

Yet there were compensations if the function of the settlement
and the misery of the convicts were ignored. Price's salary was
£600 a year when he was appointed, and it was increased to
£800 in 1849, with much else provided. Looking back through
rose-coloured memories forty years afterwards, Major de Winton

saw it as 'a terrestial paradise'. Officials had free quarters, free rations and free gardens, poultry in abundance and vegetables in profusion. The lemon, guava, and cape gooseberry grew wild all over the island. The services of tailors, shoemakers, and other artisans were available for sixpence a day. 'We were', he wrote, 'a happy and united family, a sort of social commonwealth.'[86]

Price was suffering from some unspecified and mysterious malady when he accepted the appointment as Commandant, and by 1851 his health was again causing concern. He had received only a non-committal answer to his application for a transfer to a position outside Australia,[87] and in December 1851 he asked for two years' leave of absence, to enable him to go to Europe. Denison forwarded the application to England, recommending it for favourable consideration, and adding, 'It is necessary I should add that reports which have been received respecting the state of Mr. Price's health, render it not improbable that it will be necessary for me to anticipate your Lordship's decision by granting to Mr. Price the leave of absence required.'[88] He did not need to do so, however, for approval for leave of absence was given by the Secretary of State for the Colonies, and Price left the island in January 1853.

Before this there had been a significant exchange between the Hobart Town authorities and Price. Though Lieutenant-Governor Denison officially supported Price in the traditional manner against all complaints, privately he thought Price's system was bad because it depended very much on corporal punishment and on organized spying.[89] In March 1852 Price was asked to explain the increased use of flogging revealed by the yearly returns of corporal punishments inflicted. Price regarded this as a censure, and in fairness his vigorous defence should be given in his own words.[90] He wrote:

I have the honor to acknowledge the receipt of a letter from the Assistant Comptroller of the 2nd February ultimo, in which I am informed that the attention of His Excellency the Lieutenant Governor has been drawn to the increasing amount of corporal punishment which returns from this Island show to have been inflicted, that His Excellency regrets very much that I should have considered such punishment necessary to so great an extent; and lastly, that His Excellency trusts that I may find it in my power to adopt for the future effective means of enforcing proper discipline without recourse to such frequent infliction of this mode of punishment. Implying, as this communication does, a censure on the course I have pursued for some months past, I feel it due to myself to point out, for His Excellency's consideration, the causes of my deviating from my former course in the allotting of punishments for offences by convicts on this settlement.

Before adverting to these causes, however, I may point your attention to past communications to yourself, and more especially to my observations on the report of the Roman Catholic Bishop after his last visit to this Island to show my utter aversion to corporal punishment, and I assure you that it has been only the absolute necessity arising from the causes which I shall presently detail which has compelled me to have resort to the lash more frequently than for some years past.

Since the introduction of the task-work system which has had effect here from the 1st of January 1850 the better behaved portion of the convicts have taken advantage of it, and by operation of the credit they have obtained have been removed from the Island. In their place I have received the cullings of the Convict Department in Van Diemen's Land—men who in Van Diemen's Land had rejected the inducements—utterly neglected all the advantages which are held out to the convict by that system. English incorrigibles also, the worst that could be selected from Gibraltar and Bermuda, from Millbank, the Hulks, Pentonville, Portland, and Parkhurst, and convicts from India represented as most dangerous characters have been landed here, most of these too young men of vicious characters who are readily influenced by the desperadoes remaining on the Island under sentences from all the adjacent Colonies including some of the worst from New South Wales, or rather I should say, from Cockatoo Island.

On looking at the magisterial sentences passed in Van Diemen's Land, you will find that numerous protracted periods of hard-labor in chains are there awarded, and I have on the Island a considerable number of men under long sentences to irons; I have others here with allotted probations extending over various periods to the maximum of fifteen years, while some few have been ordered to be detained here for life.

These convicts for the greater part are reckless of future consequences, and regardless of any sentences to chains which may be passed upon them, founding some indefinite hope on a prospective change of officers on the Island, and a chance of a change in the system hitherto pursued in respect to convicts, before their periods of detention can expire. The consequence is that those who are unwilling to exert any self control, or to pay such obedience to orders as must be exacted from convicts, are constantly appearing at the Police Office charged with breaches of the Social Regulations. Strin-

gent these regulations are—and stringent they must be—but they are
not more so than those imposed on soldiers, or indeed on boys at
public schools in England. They are however disregarded by the
great mass of the convicts until they are driven to obedience. Persuasion is useless—advice is thrown away—they will not listen to me,
who have turned a deaf ear to the appeals of a parent, a wife, a
brother, or a friend. Ere they reached Norfolk Island they had
chosen their paths in life and they doggedly pursue them until
driven from them.

I might mention very many instances of the good effect of such
men being so driven to obedience. I might refer you to the cases of
George Strong, of *T. H. Larchens*, of *McBurns*, of *George Smith*,
now on the Island, of *B. Smith*, of *Daniel Fagan*, of *I. McManus*,
of *T. Brown*, and many others who have left the Island and are now
holding indulgences, who were handed over to me as incorrigible
ruffians, but who having been compelled to have regard to regulations, and thereby to acquire a power of self control, have become
comparatively good men and have been or soon will be returned to
society.

To return however:— the same men week after week appeared
at the Police Office, charged court after court with similar offences.
They laugh at sentences in irons, and I have no sufficient means of
carrying out sentences of solitary confinement. I have not cells
enough. What then remains but to have recourse to the Scourge?

I had for a long period abstained from the infliction of corporal
punishment, but the men (I mean the incorrigible and reckless)
finding that a certain breach of the regulations brought with it a
certain sentence to irons, learnt as they termed it, 'the price' of such
offence, and disregarding it they pursued the bent of their own inclinations. Indeed it was no uncommon occurrence to hear them, to
myself and other officers, enumerate the various 'prices' they expected
when they have committed themselves. I was at length driven to
corporal punishment. That it has had a beneficial effect, I have no
hesitation in asserting. The magisterial returns will show a very
material reduction in the number of offences brought under the
notice of the Police Court, and more especially at Longridge.

The number of cases there ranged weekly from one hundred to
one hundred and fifty until scourging commenced, but it is now reduced to an average of forty.

The convicts cannot plead ignorance of the regulations. They
are the same throughout the Island and they are read to every prisoner on his arrival, and on every Sunday that he remains here. The
greater number of offences are breaches of the tobacco regulations,
and for His Excellency's information I insert a copy of them. Extract
from Prisoners' Regulations. The use of Tobacco:—

'Tobacco is not permitted to be smoked or chewed in the Mess-room at any time, or in the privy of the Lumber yard during labor hours, or in any public thoroughfare—at any Muster, or in presence of any officer (except the Officer in charge of the Lumber yard). When a prisoner is addressed by an Officer, the pipe is to be withdrawn from the mouth. Tobacco or pipes are not permitted to be brought out of the Lumber yard.'

Every prisoner arriving on Norfolk Island is now allowed tobacco (formerly it was not allowed, only to men out of chains) and the ration is continued to them until they more than once or twice infringe the regulations above quoted. They will not regard these regulations and they lose their tobacco—and thence are led to the commission of offences so repeated and sometimes so serious that, in the course of last year, I was induced to recommend the discontinuance of the tobacco ration altogether—a recommendation to which I have not been favoured with any definite reply.

I assert fearlessly that offences against these tobacco regulations, as well as against other regulations, are committed wilfully by the convicts who 'chance' their being detected, and at the same time 'chance' the awarded punishment being carried into effect when the sentence is one to irons.

Were I asked what punishment I consider most effective, I would reply—that of isolated cells—Were there a sufficiency of these, the most refractory might be tamed, and corporal punishment abolished by law, and I may here observe that in no case has it been found necessary here to sentence a prisoner to corporal punishment while imprisoned in the isolated cells.

In conclusion I beg you to assure His Excellency that had I followed my inclinations I should not have adopted the mode of punishment that I have deemed necessary, and which I deem will still be necessary, where such a body of incorrigibles is collected without sufficient means of punishment by separation.

Denison was not convinced by Price's explanation.* He wrote to the Secretary of State for the Colonies that he thought the increased use of the lash was caused by Price's failing health. At last he reached the same conclusion as Bishop Willson; the distance of Norfolk Island from Hobart Town involved that 'more power must inevitably be entrusted to a single subordinate officer than he is entitled to exercise'. He outlined a scheme for relinquishing Norfolk Island and establishing instead a penal

*Price's letter, and the comments of the Lieutenant-Governor, Sir William Denison, and the Comptroller-General of Convicts, Dr J. S. Hampton, are set out in Further Correspondence on the Subject of Convict Discipline and Transportation, presented 18 July 1853, P.P. (H.L.), 1852-3, MS. pagination 251-9.

settlement at Port Arthur on Tasman's Peninsula.[91] Bishop Willson, too, had mentioned in his letter of 22 May 1852 that Price was anxious to be relieved on account of the state of his health. Price was in his forty-third year, of powerful physique, and Denison's belief that there was a connection between the increased use of the lash and his health, and his statement that the 'nature of the complaint under which he has laboured' would prevent him from resuming duties as Commandant,[92] suggest that the illness was of some psychopathological kind. His capricious harshness, his preoccupation with the enforcement of the tobacco regulations, his sudden rages, his morbid determination not to be outwitted by any convict, and his abnormal suspiciousness, taken in combination, point to a paranoid condition. But information about peculiarities of behaviour with his family and in private intercourse is wanting, and no description of the symptoms of his ill-health has been discovered. Lacking these, it is difficult to be certain that Price suffered from some psychiatric abnormality, though there is ample reason to suspect it. He had been on the island for six and a half years, and there were many good reasons for him to give up his command. He told the Select Committee of the Legislative Assembly of Victoria that he did so because he was not prepared to accept a system under which free officers leaving the island to join the gold rush were to be replaced by convicts of good character.[93] That may have been a factor, though alone it is unlikely to have been a dominant consideration; so long as they were subservient to him and did his bidding promptly, Price was not likely to trouble much about the character of his subordinates. It is more probable that his decision resulted from a combination of factors; the needs of his family, the bleakness of his prospects, his malady (whatever it was), and a realization that his methods were no longer viewed with favour by his superiors.

On 17 January 1853 Price and his family left Norfolk Island. He was still Commandant, and retained the position (and salary) for another twelve months. He may have had some notion of visiting England, but, according to his friend de Winton, he planned to take up farming again in the Huon River district. He had kept his farm there and in May 1854 had fifteen convicts in his employ.[94] One thing is certain; he had no intention of returning to Norfolk Island. On the voyage to Hobart Town the *Lady Franklin*, the vessel in which the Price and de Winton families were travelling, ran into a gale near Bass Strait and began to take in water. Convicts were set in shifts to work the pumps incessantly until the vessel made Hobart Town, where it was found that a large piece of coral had pierced the bottom, but was so tightly wedged that the ship remained watertight until caught by the gale.[95]

Although Denison recommended Price strongly, the English authorities showed no enthusiasm to find Price a position in England or in some colony outside Australia. Denison was told merely that if he could find Price some post in Van Diemen's Land, he should do so.[96] Price went to live at first at Devonshire House, Murray Street, Hobart, and later at Vallis Vale in Holbrook Place, now Upper Davey Street.[97] With him were his wife and seven children,[98] the youngest, Jane de Winton, a baby in arms. Sorrow lay ahead of them; Gustavus Lambart, aged three, died from scarlet fever on 31 July 1853. The other three boys, John Frederick, James Franklin and Thomas Caradoc, were aged thirteen, eleven and ten, respectively, and they were admitted to the Hutchins School, Hobart Town, in February 1853. The eldest, John Frederick, had not reached his seventh year when the family went to Norfolk Island, and he and his brothers and three sisters had known as their world only the natural beauties and man-made horrors of Norfolk Island. But normal home life in Hobart Town was brief; in January 1854 John Price was provisionally appointed Inspector-General of Penal Establishments for the State of Victoria. He took up his duties in that month, and his family's new home was again within a prison, the Pentridge stockade at Melbourne.

Chapter Four

INSPECTOR-GENERAL OF PENAL ESTABLISHMENTS, VICTORIA, 1854-1857

I *Assignment in Victoria*

When Price and his family arrived in Melbourne in 1854, it was to take part in the exciting task of moulding a frontier community into an organized and civilized society. Proclaimed as part of New South Wales in 1835, Port Phillip began its official history with the arrival of the resident magistrate, Captain William Lonsdale, on 1 October 1836. He brought with him two or three surveyors, some soldiers, and a couple of constables. The order in which the rudimentary institutions of social organization developed is not without significance. A few months before Lonsdale's arrival, and at a time when the future city of Melbourne was known variously as Bearbrass, Bareburp, Glenelg, Yarrow Yarrow, Batmania, the Settlement, and the Township, the residents, less than two hundred in number, met and appointed an arbitrator, James Simpson, and bound themselves to accept his decisions in all disputed matters, and in cases of aggression by or upon the aborigines.[1] In December 1836 the prison at Port Phillip was proclaimed a common gaol. Thus, as Professor Edward Jenks commented, the first institution was an arbitrator, the second a police magistrate, the third a constable, and the fourth a gaol. The Governor of New South Wales, Sir Richard Bourke, visited the settlement in March 1837, and by proclamation of 10 April 1837 the sites of two towns were named. In compliment to King William IV, Williamstown was the name given to the site on the western shore of Hobson's Bay (as the waters of Port Phillip at the mouth of the Yarra were called), and the other, on the right bank of the Yarra, was designated Melbourne, after the Prime Minister, Lord Melbourne.

The new settlement prospered in a manageable fashion until

1 July 1851, when the colony of Victoria came into being. In the same month specimens of gold found at Clunes and at War-randyte were exhibited on the one day, and in September came the first inkling of the fabulous riches of Ballarat. The character of the colony changed almost overnight, and the story of the next ten years, never adequately told until the publication, in 1963, of Geoffrey Serle's *The Golden Age*,[2] shows man's constructive genius at its best. At the opening of 1851 the estimated population of Melbourne was 20,000 people, and of the whole colony 77,000. In the next three years, an average of 90,000 persons a year arrived by sea, which spread over the period, meant close on 250 immigrants a day. Between 1855 and 1858 the arrivals exceeded the departures by 30,000 a year. Censuses showed that in 1854 the colony's population was 237,000; by April 1861 it exceeded half a million. During that period the number of people in Melbourne and its suburbs grew from 80,000 to 140,000.[3] Incredibly, the social organization not only adapted itself to this extraordinary impact, but in a spirit of creativeness never since matched its leaders brought into existence the apparatus of a vigorous and basically democratic society. During a decade, in Jenks' words,

In spite of the almost overwhelming difficulties of the situation, the leaders of the period had laid in Victoria the solid foundations of enlightened future prosperity. They had organized the administration of justice and police; established a system of universal education; reformed the financial administration; and started great institutions such as the Public Library, the Museums, and the University. They had provided a system of local government, and organized a provision for the maintenance and extension of the means of communication. They had placed the granting of state aid to religious denominations upon a systematic footing. And they had done this in the face of a social, political, and economic revolution which shook the community to its very centre, and which would have overthrown the civilization of many a state which had an established tradition of fifteen hundred instead of fifteen years to rely upon. That there were some in high places who preferred their own interest to that of the community few who are familiar with the history of the period can doubt. All the more credit is therefore due to those who, in spite of traitors in the camp, presented an unflinching front to the threats of anarchy and the temptation of private gain.[4]

Crude in its lusty adolescence, Melbourne was a city of contrasts, where a surfeit of extravagant personal luxuries did nothing, even for those who could afford them, to lessen the daily asperities of a primitive, insanitary and grossly overcrowded settlement. Arriving to endure the rains and gales of April and May 1854, Céleste Mogador found it a place of mud and potholes, but already the city was organizing the rudiments of municipal services; thoroughfares were being macadamized, reticulated water was becoming available, gas lighting a reality, and the transformation from wood and daub to stone and brick had begun.[5] But the conditions of the newly arrived migrants in the closing months of 1851, and during 1852 and 1853, defy description. The congeries of human folly and wretchedness at Emerald Hill and in Canvas Town, on the Government Domain, received little attention and less assistance from the authorities. Philanthropists were stirred to action, and efforts were made to allay the increased misery and destitution brought by the harsh winter of 1853 and the inclemencies of 1854. Although the situation never got completely out of hand and private vengeance never replaced the orderly processes of the criminal law, the flimsy barriers against lawlessness were strained not far short of collapse. Everything favoured the relaxing of social constraints, and inevitably crimes ranging from heartless frauds to brutal violence increased perturbingly. Between 1844 and 1849, before the gold rush began, more than 1700 'Pentonvillains', as hostile residents called them, had been received at Port Phillip. They were English convicts who, after a period of reformatory imprisonment, or 'secluded punishment', at Millbank or Pentonville or Parkhurst, were shipped to the colony on condition they did not return to England. They were officially dubbed 'exiles', and were free so long as they remained out of the United Kingdom. The citizens of Melbourne were determined Victoria should not be a convict settlement, however, and in 1849 the intensity of popular opposition forced the authorities to turn away the *Randolph* without disembarking its exiles.[6] A like number of freed convicts had arrived from Van Diemen's Land between 1846 and 1849.[7] After the discovery of gold, criminals flocked to Melbourne and the goldfields. Greed and its misshapen bodyguard, aggression, stalked the land, and though for one reason or another the majority resisted the temptations

to criminal behaviour, the proportion of the vicious and the ir-
retrievably corrupted was dangerously high. Crimes increased,
and with the increase fear and insecurity became general.

In 1852 two particularly brazen exploits infuriated the people
of Melbourne. Five criminals took possession of St Kilda Road,
almost within sight of the city, and for some hours held up and
robbed every passer-by. One citizen on horseback was shot in
the leg as he dashed for safety past the ambush, and when the
desperadoes made off with their booty, they left twenty victims
tied to trees. None of the robbers was apprehended. On 2 April
1852 the boldest of the gold robberies was staged. With black-
ened faces, twenty-two armed men put off in two whale-boats
from Sandridge, as Port Melbourne was then known. They
boarded the barque *Nelson,* which was at anchor at Williamstown, surrounded by other ships. The ship was about to sail for
London with 8,000 oz. of gold, valued at £30,000. A skeleton
crew of seven was on duty, and these were overpowered, one
being wounded by a bullet. The robbers stripped the vessel of its
guns and ammunition and threw them into the sea. Boxes containing the gold were then taken from the lazarette and the
bound crew members thrust into the vacant space; the robbers
then departed unmolested with their booty. A seaman had
managed to hide himself and remain unobserved, and he released the crew. The alarm was given but although there were
customs officers and water police in the neighborhood, and forty
ships at anchor, it was ineffectual, as were offers of rewards for
the apprehension of the criminals. Later four men were arrested
and convicted, and heavy sentences imposed, but none of the
gold was recovered.[8]

When the robbery became known, the demand for vigorous
action was universal and irresistible. It was popularly believed
that the criminals were 'Vandemonians', as ex-convicts and con-
ditionally pardoned men from Van Diemen's Land were
known, and a public meeting insisted that they be excluded
from the colony. An Act 'to facilitate the apprehension and prevent the introduction into the Colony of Victoria of Offenders
illegally at large' commonly known as the Convicts Prevention
Act (16 Victoria No. 13) was passed by a Legislative Council
eagerly responsive to the general perturbation. It recited that

great evils had arisen within the colony of Victoria from the continual influx of runaway convicts from Van Diemen's Land, and enacted a code that disregarded fundamental legal principles relating to the Royal Prerogative and the liberty of the subject. It embraced past and future, and caught within its definition of 'offenders illegally at large' any person transported thereafter as well as those who had already been sentenced. It included any person convicted of any transportable or capital offence in any British colony (other than Victoria or New South Wales) who had not served the full term of transportation, or the full period of his sentence, or received a free pardon from Her Majesty. The master of a ship who brought to Victoria an offender illegally at large was liable to a fine of £100, or six months' imprisonment, or both, at the discretion of the justices of the peace to whom jurisdiction under the Act was entrusted. A person suspected of being illegally at large could be arrested without warrant, and if he did not prove he was *not* an offender illegally at large, a justice could order him (or her) to be held in custody. Two justices were empowered to send an offender back to his place of departure, or to impose three years' hard labour in irons on public works on a male, or two years' imprisonment at hard labour on a female. Oral proof, as distinct from formal proof by production of records, was good prima facie evidence, as was a statement that the offender was commonly deemed or reputed to be a transported felon or a convict under sentence. The offender's property was forfeited, and half of any pecuniary penalty went to the colony and half to any informer.

Lieutenant-Governor C. J. La Trobe, a civilized, sensitive and balanced man in a community gripped by frontier passions, recognized that the measure jettisoned important constitutional safeguards for what might be illusory benefits, but he realized that if he did not bend to the storm he and the precarious institutional stability he represented were in danger of being uprooted. He saw clearly that a person at large under the Queen's conditional pardon was not an 'offender illegally at large',[9] and that the measure was obnoxious in reversing the onus of proof, exposing the innocent but unwary to harsh punishment, and reviving the worst mischiefs inherent in the use of informers and

irresponsible delation. But he knew, too, the vigour of local feeling, and, yielding to it, he assented to the measure.[10]

The Act was expressed to operate for two years, and came
into force on 23 September 1852, but the Queen later directed
it be disallowed. The disallowance was to operate from the passing of an amended version. As La Trobe foresaw, the English
authorities, remote from the turbulence, were shocked by its dra-
conic illogicalities and the Duke of Newcastle, in explanation of
Her Majesty's disallowance of the Act, pointed out how it disregarded legal theory and constitutional safeguards, and suggested legislation to replace it. But the Legislative Council would
have none of His Lordship's proposal; in October 1853 it passed
a revised version of the Act that was even more drastic in its
terms. La Trobe reserved it for the Royal assent, but, interpret-
ing his instructions liberally, he abstained for the time being
from disallowing the earlier Act, which thus continued in
operation. He left Victoria before the conflict was resolved. Sir
Charles Hotham, who succeeded La Trobe, found the temper
of the colony made it impossible to carry out the wishes of the
English authorities that the drastic legislation should be watered
down. On 16 November 1854 he perforce assented to an 'Act
to prevent the Influx of Criminals into Victoria' (18 Victoria
No. 3). This Act Her Majesty did not disallow, and it was continued by Act 19 Victoria No. 3, and made perpetual by Act 22
Victoria No. 68.[11] It survives to this day in the Crimes Act 1958
(Victoria), sections 336-50. Some innocent persons suffered under the legislation, but popular passion is rarely abated by individual injustice. Between 23 September 1852 and 18 October
1854, according to a return printed by order of the Legislative
Council on 30 January 1855, one hundred and thirty-one males
and nine females were convicted under the Acts. Twenty-nine
males and one female were then under sentence, eighty-three
males and eight females had been returned to Van Diemen's
Land or elsewhere, and the rest had been discharged, either upon
subsequent proof they were free persons or on completion of
sentence.

In some ways the story of the Convicts Prevention Acts is not
a pretty one, for it showed that the fragile protections of indivi-

dual liberty will be ignored when fear and prejudice take over. But it disclosed, too, a healthy determination not to be subservient to dictatorship by the English authorities, who were believed by Victorians, with good cause, still to entertain a hope that they could use the far-off Australian colonies as a dumping place for at least some of their criminals, despite assurances that the colonists' detestation of the transportation system would be respected.

It was to this explosive community, harassed by the seemingly intractable problems of crime, of Chinese immigration, of a repressive goldmining licensing system, and of inequitable land laws, that John Price came with his family in January 1854. Lieutenant-Governor La Trobe had appealed to Lieutenant-Governor Denison for a man to control the penal system. Denison could conscientiously recommend Price, and was happy to do so. On 25 January 1854 John Price was appointed Inspector-General of Penal Establishments in the colony of Victoria at the substantial salary of £1,000 a year.[12] It was an assignment that would have daunted most men. The number of prisoners convicted in the Supreme Court had increased from 29 on 31 December 1851 to 279 on 31 December 1852, and to 560 (excluding 92 deserting seamen) on 30 June 1853. When Price took office, there were 1,056 offenders, including 205 'refractory' (or deserting) seamen, confined in the colony's inadequate penal institutions.[13]

Price's predecessor was Samuel Barrow, the resident magistrate on Norfolk Island at the time of the 1846 rising, who remained there for only a brief period after Price became Commandant. A barrister of the Middle Temple, he came to Hobart in 1842 to take up an appointment, made by the English authorities, as assistant police magistrate at Waterloo Point. Sir John Franklin had already filled the position, however, and Barrow had to be content with a junior magistracy at Bothwell. In August 1845 he was sent to Norfolk Island as resident magistrate. He was a bumptious and brutal fellow, whose arbitrary assertions of authority there caused great resentment among the free officials, and Rogers and others ascribed much of the discontent among the convicts to his harsh punishments and the brutal methods of his convict police.[14] When the Norfolk Island post was abolished in 1847, Barrow became visiting magistrate to the Central convict gangs in Van Diemen's Land, but in July 1848 that office was also abolished. He held temporary positions until December 1848, and when no other employment was found for him, he went insolvent. In 1850 his luck changed, but only temporarily. He was appointed Superintendent of Penal Establishments in Victoria on 28 October 1850, and also visiting justice at the Pentridge stockade, which was proclaimed on the same date. On 1 July 1853 he was given the title of Inspector-General of Penal Establishments. He gave up that position to become Immigration Agent, but not long afterwards, on 5 May 1854, he was drowned when a boat in which he and others were farewelling Lieutenant-Governor La Trobe capsized in Hobson's Bay. He was then thirty-eight years old.[15]

Barrow thought the great increase in convicted persons was traceable to the influx from Sydney and Van Diemen's Land of ex-convicts and convicts on conditional pardons, who 'drawn hither by the attraction of our gold-fields commenced anew their career of crime with an atrocity without parallel'.[16] Convicting them of crime or of being offenders illegally at large was one thing; keeping them in confinement another. When the gold rush began, the sheriff's gaols and the places of penal confinement were the ramshackle Eastern and Western city gaols, the rudimentary main depot and stockade at Pentridge, and the Richmond stockade. None of these provided security against escape. To build a maximum security penitentiary sufficiently capacious to contain the enormously increased number of prisoners and to provide against foreseeable future needs required time and money (Barrow estimated a prison to house 1,000 men would cost £200,000) and in 1851 the colony had a sufficiency of neither. In desperation the authorities drew upon English experience,[17] and hulks moored in Hobson's Bay were used as prisons. The usage was inhuman and the consequences horrible, as they were bound to be, but, given the inescapable assumption that malefactors had to be confined, it is difficult to see what else could have been done to meet the serious emergency. Between 1852 and 1855 five hulks were acquired for use for penal confinement. The *President* was opened for the reception of prisoners on 15 December 1852, the *Success* on 23 June 1853, and the *Sacramento* in the latter part of 1853. Seamen, guilty by desertion of an offence against the Merchant Shipping Act, were a serious problem, but they were properly regarded as not being ordinary criminals and were confined in the hulk *Deborah*. This derelict was vacated on 19 March 1855; it was retained to provide accommodation, if needed, but thereafter it disappears from official reports. The *Lysander* was fitted out for the reception of convicts in 1855.* Henry Augustus White, a penal officer who wrote about the beginnings of Victoria's penal system, stated that the *Success, President, Sacramento* and *Lysander* were vessels abandoned by their crews, which the government of Victoria bought and had fitted out as penal hulks under the directions of the government engineer.[18] The hulks were painted yellow, and the neighbourhood where they were moored was marked by buoys as a prohibited area. The regulations of 1853, prescribing the treatment of prisoners on the hulks and the duties of officials, are set out as an appendix to this work. To read them is to gain some idea of the horrors of the hulks, but they were only the bureaucratic framework within which the callous brutality of officials, corrupted by power and habituated

---

*After Price's murder the hulks were moved from Hobson's Bay to waters opposite Sandridge, now Port Melbourne (H. A. White, *Crime and Criminals, or Reminiscences of the Penal Department in Victoria* (Ballarat, 1890), p. 129). From the annual reports of various Inspectors-General, dated 10 November 1855 (Price), 26 October 1859 (Champ), and 18 June 1878 (Duncan), it appears that *Deborah* was abandoned for confinement of adult males in 1855, *Lysander* in 1857, *Sacramento* in 1857 (but used for some purposes until March 1878), *President* in 1858, and *Success* in 1859. The most notorious, because later exhibited the world over as a 'convict ship', was *Success*, which was used for some years after 1859 for the confinement of females and juveniles (Inspector-General's annual report, 26 October 1859; H. A. White, op. cit., p. 168). It was sold to one Alex. Phillips in 1890. Phillips fitted the vessel out with wax figures for exhibition as a chamber of horrors. There are various editions of *The History of the British Convict Ship 'Success'*, and all are sensational and untrustworthy. Built in 1839-40 as an East India merchantman, it was never a convict ship, but was bought in 1853 by the government of Victoria for use as a prison hulk. See *The Story of the East India Merchantman 'Success'*, by 'Cygnet', Swan River Booklet no. 11 (Perth, n.d.). For a vigorous criticism of Joseph C. Harvie's *History of the Convict Hulk 'Success'* . . . (London, 1897), see H. A. White, 'The True History of the Hulk "Success",' *Austral Light*, vol. 7 (1898), pp. 150-60, 205-12. See also W. A. Hall, 'The Convict Hulk "Success",' *Victorian Historical Magazine*, vol. 14 (1931), no. 2, p. 73.

to cruelty, could manifest itself as capricious inclination suggested. In his report of 1 May 1853, Superintendent Barrow minced no words about the purposes of the hulk *President*. He wrote:

This hulk is intended for the coercion of prisoners of the longest sentences and most desperate character, and is fitted with separate cells capable of containing eighty-four prisoners, who are as it were, during the periods of their servitude on board, entirely shut out from the world, being permitted to hold no communication whatever with each other or any of their friends or associates, either by letter, message or otherwise . . . I am of opinion that it will be found fully to answer the purposes for which it was designed, viz., to act not only as a severe punishment to the convict himself, but as a wholesome check upon the commission of crime, by shewing indisputably that a commensurate punishment awaits the criminal, and that too without a hope of escape.[19]

The largest cell on the *President* was 8 feet 4 inches high, by 4 feet 1 inch wide, its length varying from 7 feet 8 inches at deck, or floor, level to 8 feet at ceiling level. The 'box', a closed receptacle used for punishment, was 2 feet 6 inches at deck and ceiling levels, 2 feet 2 inches wide, and 6 feet 6 inches high. It was ventilated by a pipe $2\frac{1}{2}$ inches in diameter, passing through the vessel's side. The dimensions of the solitary cell, also used for punishment, were, at deck level, from 3 feet 1 inch to 5 feet 6 inches, and at ceiling level, from 4 feet 11 inches to 6 feet 6 inches, width being 4 feet $2\frac{1}{2}$ inches and height 6 feet 10 inches.[20] Some cells on the lower deck were 5 feet long and 4 feet 4 inches wide, and on the main deck a little over 7 feet long by less than 4 feet wide.

The eighty prisoners on the *President* were never allowed ashore, and were confined in cells below water level. They were given no work; enforced idleness was part of the punishment. Each prisoner, whether his sentence directed it or not, was placed in irons, as soon as he was brought on board, the lightest 14 pounds, and some weighing 28 and 36 pounds. Price acknowledged that the irons were for punishment and to break the spirit of the convicts. Thus fettered, prisoners remained on the *President* for periods varying from twelve months to three years.

depending on their sentences and behaviour.[21] Even when a convict was in the punishment box or in the solitary cell, his irons were not removed. Price asserted that the men had to be kept in irons to prevent escape, but if he really believed that claim it was contrary to the opinion of Angus McPherson, the superintendent of the hulk. McPherson thought that when in the cells men would be secure without fetters, though irons might be necessary when they came out of their cells for exercise.[22] They were allowed on deck for that purpose once a day in groups of ten, wearing irons, and handcuffed in couples.

For dietary purposes, prisoners were divided into seven categories, each with a prescribed scale of rations. They were set out in an appendix in the 1857 Report of the Select Committee of the Legislative Council. The daily ration of a prisoner in solitary confinement was 16 ounces of bread and a half-ounce of soap. Prisoners in separate confinement on the hulks received daily 16 ounces of bread, 8 ounces of fresh meat, 8 ounces of vegetables, 8 ounces of maize meal, one ounce of sugar, a quarter-ounce of soap and a quarter-ounce of salt. Prisoners from the hulks or stockades at hard labour were given a double allowance of meat and vegetables. Barely if at all sufficient to sustain the prisoners, the diet was likely to result in nutritional deficiency ailments and acute or chronic diarrhoea.[23]

The men on the *President* were reputed to be the wickedest and most dangerous of the convicts. Price knew many of them from his Norfolk Island days; 'I have men down there', he said, 'whom I have known sentenced three times to be hanged, and who are, at this minute, absconders from Van Diemen's Land.'[24] There was no gaol hospital, and the *Lysander* was used for the reception of sick and infirm convicts. Able-bodied convicts from the hulks, except from the *President,* were required to labour on public works. Hours of labour varied with the seasons: from November to February they were 5.45 a.m. to 5.30 p.m., in March and October, 6.15 a.m. to 5 p.m., in April and September, 6.30 a.m. to 5 p.m., in May and August, 7.30 a.m. to 4.15 p.m., and in June and July, 7.45 a.m. to 4 p.m. Working hours in the stockades were half an hour longer.[25] When Price became Inspector-General, free labour was scarce and finding work for convicts did not present great problems, but diggers returning empty-handed from the goldfields eased the labour shortage, with a consequent fall in prices and wages, and Price's hopes of a satisfactory revenue from convict labour were disappointed.

The institutions available to Price in 1854 consisted of the main depot and new stockade at Pentridge, holding 290 prisoners; the Collingwood, Richmond and Marine stockades, capable of holding 117, 46, and 127 prisoners, respectively; and the hulks, on which about 400 were confined. With refractory seamen, the total prison population was 1,117 on 30 September 1854. Price's sensible object was to construct a maximum security prison at Pentridge, where a rudimentary prison had been established in November 1850.[26] He designed and brought into being a movable stockade, derisively known as the 'Crystal Palace'. It was 'a most unsightly and repulsive building'.[27] The walls, painted black externally, were of hardwood planks, 1½ inches thick, and 12 feet high, and enclosed a quadrangle of about two acres. Within the quadrangle were eight huts, of primitive workmanship, 14 feet long, 12 feet wide, and equipped with wheels to enable them to be moved from one spot to another. Each hut was supposed to accommodate 84 men. For sleeping, hammocks were slung in rows, one above the other, and spy-holes were provided to enable inspection by the guards. When the convicts were in the labour yards they were watched by armed sentries stationed on four platforms that gave an entire view of the interior of the gaol. The 'Crystal Palace' continued in use, though on a different site within the gaol limits, until 1863.[28] Henry Augustus White, who served as a penal officer on the hulks and at the Collingwood stockade and at Pentridge, finishing his service as second officer at the Ballarat gaol, and whose reminiscences provide a useful account of the early penal system, asserted that within the 'Crystal Palace' were the most dangerous criminals in the British dominions. He wrote:

here . . . could be formed the 'Devil's regiment of the line', as many bore on their bodies the terrible effects of floggings; others had contracted deformities from the constant practice of wearing heavy irons on their legs . . . it must be admitted that there was, in some instances, unnecessary severity shown towards them, which crushed out the last spark of humanity, and endowed them with the ferocity and remorselessness of tigers.[29]

Female prisoners were housed in the completely unsuitable Western gaol. It must have been common for their children to accompany them, for No. 6 of the Dietary Scale for prisoners was headed, 'Children of female prisoners confined in gaol', and entitled the innocent victims to wheaten bread, 8 ounces; beef (fresh), 4 ounces; milk, 1 pint; soap, quarter-ounce. When the Western gaol was abandoned the women were transferred to hulks, at first the *Sacramento,* and later the *Success.* A Select Committee of the Legislative Assembly recommended in 1857 that female offenders should be transferred to Pentridge, but it was not until May 1894 that a prison for females was opened at Pentridge. The strange dilatoriness about taking the decision to establish it was reflected in the five years it took to build the prison.[30]

The system of control over the places for the confinement of persons sentenced to imprisonment was bewildering in its complexity. In his evidence to the Select Committee of the Legislative Assembly, the sheriff, Claud Farie, said only the Melbourne gaols were under his immediate control. He named them as the main gaol, the Melbourne gaol (in Russell Street) which was 'an excellent gaol, very healthy and commodious . . . but altogether too small for the demand made upon it'; the female gaol at the western end of Collins Street, and the Eastern Hill gaol which was used almost exclusively for the reception of lunatics. He mentioned Geelong, Sandhurst (now Bendigo), Ballarat and Beechworth as the country gaols, of which the Geelong gaol was 'very good' but also inadequate to cope with the demand. The other country gaols were 'logged huts' containing three or four cells, though in 1857 new gaols were in course of erection at Castlemaine and Ballarat, and financial provision had been made for new gaols at Sandhurst and Beechworth. The country gaols were under the control of deputy sheriffs, and the sheriff did not supervise them, but acted only as the medium of communication between the deputy sheriffs and the government. Lock-ups, too, were outside his control. Farie said that the Melbourne gaol held persons imprisoned for debt as well as those sentenced for crimes, and that the penal establishments, consisting of the stockades and the hulks, were entirely the concern of Price as Inspector-General. In his evidence to the Select

Committee of the Legislative Council Price said that the establishments in his charge in December 1856 were

Pentridge, with accommodation for 450; Collingwood in which I can accommodate 364 prisoners; the penal hulk *Success* with accommodation for 130; the *Sacramento* capable of containing 128; the penal hulk *President,* 80; and the *Lysander,* which is not looked upon as a penal hulk, which is capable of containing 300. When I receive notification from the gaoler in Melbourne, or when in my visits to the gaol I see that it is overcrowded, or that it is desirable to remove prisoners, I attend personally, and, together with the gaoler, select from the prisoners in the gaol prisoners to supply such vacancies as may exist in the various establishments. Long-sentence men, over ten years, . . . are invariably removed to the hulk *President,* as are such men as have been refractory since their punishment . . . On arriving at the stations the prisoners are searched, and have their hair cut, and are washed and clothed, and then told off to their gangs by the superintendent.

Price had had many difficulties to surmount, and he was exposed to constant frustration by governments that wanted protection from criminals for the community but would or could not supply him with adequate means to provide it. In November and December of the year in which he took office, he was involved in the turmoil of the Eureka stockade which, in his annual report, dated 10 November 1855, he mentioned merely as 'the disturbances on the Gold Fields'. The Governor, Sir Charles Hotham, required him to furnish daily a hundred of his staff in aid of the police. He was instructed to prepare for the reception of three hundred prisoners, and the *Sacramento* was brought up from its moorings off Geelong in readiness to take them.[31] His own administrative problems were exacting enough to occupy his energies fully, but he was called on as well for guidance on other aspects of preserving law and order. In 1855 he was a member of a commission of four members to enquire into the state of the police and was a signatory of the Commission's sensible and constructive report.[32]

When a body of prisoners banded together to effect an escape, it was called a 'rush'. 'Rushes' were Price's constant concern, and tales by informers hoping to get remission in return kept him and his staff in constant tension. In March 1854 a notorious convict, Isaac Thompson, led a 'rush' of eight men, but when one prisoner was shot in the leg it was quickly abandoned. In May of the same year a convict named Rider achieved the impossible and unforgivable by outwitting Price. Employed as a servant in Price's house at Pentridge, he got hold of some of Mrs Price's clothing and, disguised as a woman and carrying his mistress's handbag and parasol and wearing a veil, he made his way past all the sentries who saluted him as the Inspector-General's wife. He was not missed until the evening muster.[33] There were other unsuccessful attempts during the troubles on the goldfields,[34] and occasionally a prisoner got away, but most were soon recaptured. The year 1856 was noteworthy for 'rushes'. Four prisoners cut through the deck of the *Lysander* but were recaptured; and an absconder from Pentridge was soon retaken. In March a 'rush' failed when its leader, Gisborne, was shot through the body. Uneasiness over these happenings, and criticism of Price's methods, led to the formation of a committee of citizens to enquire into the penal system.[35] It was the murder of Owen Owens and the trial of the notorious 'Captain' Melville for the crime, however, that precipitated contemporaneous inquiries into the penal system by two Select Committees, one appointed by the Legislative Council, and one by the Legislative Assembly.

Melville (whose real name was Francis McNeish McNeil McCallum) was a man of some capacity, whose criminal activities were thought by some to have a Robin Hood quality. After the trial, Richard Hengist (Orion) Horne wrote a letter to the *Argus* supporting a proposal for an account of Melville's exploits, and narrating an incident that showed him in a favourable light.[36] Melville, who was under sentences totalling thirty-two years' imprisonment, was not a tractable prisoner. When confined on the *President* he attempted to bite off an officer's nose.* He was severely beaten with 'neddies', as the warders' clubs were known, and chained in his cell in such a way that for a couple of days he was not able to lie down. Later the chain was lengthened, but he served twenty days in solitary confinement in acute physical discomfort.[37] When Price became Inspector-General his conduct improved, and Price transferred him to the

*Biting off the nose or ear of an opponent was a not uncommon practice among the worst class of convicts. See Price's evidence, Report of Legislative Assembly, p. 17.

Success, where he was allowed ashore to work in a gang on alternate days.

On 22 October 1856 at the end of the day's labour, a gang of ten convicts was returning to the *Success* in a launch towed by a boat. Suddenly they hauled in the towrope and attempted to seize the boat. The warder, Owen Owens, was beaten to death with a hammer, and a seaman named Turner was thrown overboard and drowned. One of the convicts disappeared overboard; possibly he was shot by guards on the *Success*, but as his body was not recovered it was not known with certainty whether he died from drowning or a bullet. Another felon, Richard Hill, was seriously wounded but survived to be tried for Owens' murder, and later to be hanged in New Zealand as one of the Maungatapu murderers. The convicts were apprehended almost immediately, and were brought to trial for the murder of Owens. Melville was tried first, on 19 November 1856; he was convicted, and on 21 November Mr Justice Molesworth sentenced him to death. On 24 November two other prisoners were convicted and also sentenced to death. The remaining six were arraigned on 25 November and, surprisingly, were acquitted.[38] Melville conducted his own defence (though volunteer counsel were in court to assist him) and told a shocking story of brutal and degrading treatment on the hulks. Mr Justice Molesworth, an able judge, was sufficiently impressed by legal points taken by counsel intervening on Melville's behalf to state a case for the opinion of the Full Court. In his defence Melville claimed the dead convict, Stevens, had killed Owens, and the jury had announced with its verdict that it was not unanimous that Melville had inflicted the fatal blows. The prosecution's evidence that Melville was the killer having failed to convince every member of the jury, to support the verdict the Crown had to contend that it was the law that when several persons were acting in concert to carry out a common illegal purpose a homicide committed in the prosecution, or with a view to the attainment, of the illegal purpose was a murder for which each was responsible, no matter which of them did the actual killing. Even at that time the proposition, stated in that way, was dubious; the true rule is that the other participants as well as the actual killer may be found guilty of murder only if the prosecution proves to the satisfaction of the jury, as a fair inference from the evidence, that it was understood expressly or impliedly by all participants that if anybody sought to prevent them from carrying their unlawful purpose into effect, violent measures of a kind likely to cause death or grave physical injury would be used to deal with him.[39] The trial judge had directed the jury that it was the law that a common design to escape from lawful custody was enough to make all the prisoners engaged in the enterprise liable for all the consequences that ensued, including Owens' death. As the statute 17 Victoria No. 26 made an attempt to escape a felony, this direction was probably correct as the law stood in 1856, but on this view it was necessary for the Crown to establish that the custody from which Melville had sought to escape was a lawful custody. The Crown proved his original sentence, which was to imprisonment at hard labour on the roads, and it proved also that he was transferred by valid warrant to the hulk *President*. However, no warrant was produced for his transfer from the *President* to the *Success,* and the Full Court held that a link in the chain was missing; there was no proof that in escaping from the *Success* he was escaping from lawful custody. It was the kind of point that delights a lawyer's heart, and perhaps it was a quiddity; the true question was surely whether he had escaped, not from a place, but from a state, of confinement. However, exactly a century later a Full Court of the Supreme Court of Victoria considered *Melville's Case* still good law on this point.[40] Judgment of death was reversed, and Melville resumed serving his heavy sentence of imprisonment. But not for long; on 12 August 1857 he was found lying in his bunk in his cell strangled by his scarf. The verdict at the inquest was suicide, but it was whispered by knowing persons that it was impossible for Melville to have killed himself in such a fashion and that his death was the work of prison guards.[41]

Price had an office at 137 Lonsdale Street West, between William and King Streets, and every prisoner completing his sentence had to come there to be discharged.[42] He lived with his family at Pentridge, however, and everything in the stockade was under his sharp and critical scrutiny. Woe betide any prisoner or officer who incurred his displeasure. On his own version, he found a very unsatisfactory class of subordinate officers when he first took charge. A warder's wage was ten shillings a day. There was a good deal of drinking by the staff, who paid little regard to the regulations, either as they applied to themselves or their prisoners. During his first six months as Inspector-General, Price summarily got rid of subordinates he regarded as unsatisfactory.[43] He appointed or advanced men who were with him on Norfolk Island, and the names of Henry William Blachford, James Holles, James Hendry and Thomas Hyland (to mention some only), crop up in accounts of the early Victorian penal system, and are found also in the Norfolk Island story. The unpleasant reputations they had earned there came with them (for example, Blachford was deputy sheriff and in charge of the hanging of the twelve men on 13 October 1846), and old hostilities were intensified.

The legal framework of Price's authority was 'An Act to make provision for the better control and disposal of Offenders', which became law on 22 January 1853 and replaced, for the colony of Victoria, the Act 4 Victoria No. 20 of New South Wales that regulated mainland gaols in eastern Australia. Later, on 11 April 1854, the Victorian Act was amended significantly by Act 17 Victoria No. 26, which empowered the Lieutenant-Governor *or any officer specially authorized by him* to cause a convict to be employed at such labor or in such place as directed. Attempt to escape was made a felony. Regulations were made under the Act, and it was from them that Price obtained his greatest power. But in practice regulations did not mean a great deal; within wide limits Price interpreted them to suit himself, and there was little chance of his being called to account for any particular abuse. His powers were not as great as on Norfolk Island, because he did not combine the roles of Inspector-General and magistrate, and though on some pretext he could delay release on ticket-of-leave, he could not sentence prisoners to additional imprisonment. Jurisdiction to do so resided in the visiting justice for lesser offences, such as insolence or idleness, and for graver offences, such as absconding, assaults or rioting, in two justices of the peace, one of whom had to be the visiting justice. A sentence so imposed was added then to the original sentence, as, indeed, it still is.[44] Price had limited powers of punishment enabling him to impose solitary confinement and reduced rations

for no more than three days. He asserted there was no corporal
punishment under his rule,[45] but this was an equivocation. It is
true that floggings were not inflicted for prison offences, but the
use of irons on the hulks was undoubtedly corporal punishment,
as was confinement in the 'box'. Warders were equipped with
'neddies', a life-preserver made of whalebone with lead at each
end, which could be carried in the pocket,[46] and there can be no
doubt they were used, but at a warder's caprice and not by way
of official punishment. A prison governor does not need much
ingenuity to devise effective punishments that are not authorized
by law, but are unlikely to arouse much criticism. 'John Price's
stone' was an instance. This stone was still at Pentridge as late
as 1882. It weighed about a ton, and was flat on one side, with a
bolt about 18 inches long in the centre. It was placed close to a
wheel of one of the wooden huts, and a recalcitrant prisoner
was chained to the wheel, sat upon the stone, and fastened from
behind to the bolts. The physical discomfort was great because
he was left there on no or meagre rations, exposed to the elements
all day, but the avowed purpose was to humiliate him and
break his spirit. He continued to sit on the stone until Price was
satisfied he was no longer insubordinate. As many as fourteen
prisoners were chained up at the one time in this fashion.[47] But
grave though the physical hardships were that Price could inflict,
it was his arbitrary discretion to order a man to the hulks that
was his most powerful weapon. He had in reserve, with many
prisoners, the Convicts Prevention Act. Reputed to be omniscient with respect to Van Diemen's Land ex-convicts, his statement that a prisoner discharged after serving a sentence was an
offender illegally at large was sufficient to bring the man within
the drastic provisions of the Act and back to prison. To every
prisoner confinement on the hulks was an ever-present possibility if he incurred the displeasure of the Inspector-General,
and of the horrors of the hulks, shipping water in all but the
calmest weather, with their primitive sanitation and harsh discipline, there could be no doubt. William P. Burne, formerly
Superintendent of Hyde Park Barracks, Sydney, and later chief
warder on the hulk *Deborah,* thought that discipline and punishment aboard the hulks was a worse punishment than death; 'I
would rather die', he said, 'than undergo a year of it. I think it is

almost impossible that anything can be worse.'[48] Price himself recognized this was true. 'If I had the option of going out to be hanged tomorrow morning', he said, 'or enduring a year's confinement on the hulk *President,* I would choose hanging.'[49]

When death came violently to him in March 1857, Price had been Inspector-General for a little more than three years. During that time, if the hulks are left out of consideration, he proved himself a capable administrator. His annual reports reveal an effective use of convict labour upon public works; a bridge of blue stone, quarried locally, over 'the Merri Merri Creek, on the road from Pentridge to the Plenty' still stands.[50] Excluding the expense of constructing buildings, the yearly cost to the government of maintaining a man in prison fell from £123.17s.7d. in 1853, when Barrow was Inspector-General, to £109.16s.9½d. in 1854, £70.10s.3½d. in 1855, £63.6s.10½d. in 1856, and Price estimated it would be £61.9s. in 1857.[51] He pressed on with the erection of a maximum security prison at Pentridge, where he gave the construction of a gaol hospital priority in the scheme.

He protested strongly against the practice whereby a prisoner's money was forfeited on conviction, even if there was no doubt that it was not the proceeds of crime. He told the Legislative Assembly Select Committee, 'Criminals of any description who are convicted of felony have every penny taken from them when coming to me, and very few come to me with a shilling. There are some cases I think are very hard.' He said he had known cases where as much as £300 or £400, £500, or even £600, had been unjustly confiscated.[52]

The despotic exercise of power that would have gone without effective challenge on Norfolk Island could not escape criticism, however, in the restive Melbourne of the 1850s. Perturbation grew during 1856 over the stories of the hulks, and of Price's arbitrary behaviour. When the Citizens' Committee of Enquiry into the Penal System came into existence, men of repute were among its members, and the *Age* newspaper threw open its columns to Price's critics. Both in the Legislative Council and in the first Legislative Assembly, whose members were sworn on 21 November 1856, there were prompt moves to investigate the penal system. John Price had now to face the ordeal of explaining and justifying his penal methods and philosophy.

II   *The Demand for Penal Reform*

In many ways 1856 was an eventful year. The political energies of the colony of Victoria were occupied largely in creating and operating the machinery for responsible government. The results of the elections, the first to use the secret ballot, were published in the *Government Gazette* of 6 November 1856. Responsible government became a constitutional reality on 21 November when successful candidates were sworn in, and the parliamentary session was formally opened on 25 November. The tasks ahead of Parliament were many and formidable. It is more than a little remarkable, therefore, that a demand for an investigation into the abuses said to exist in the penal administration, and for the adoption of more constructive penal methods, should have gained the immediate attention of both Houses. On the first business day, 26 November 1856, Mr John Hood moved successfully in the Legislative Council for the appointment of a Select Committee to inquire into the working of the penal establishments of the colony.[53] On the same day in the Legislative Assembly Mr Wills gave notice he would move a resolution framed in four paragraphs, the first of which averred:

That the system of discipline pursued in the penal establishments of Victoria is directly opposed to the reformation of criminals, and alike repugnant to common feeling and common sense.[54]

The motion, amended to remove its contentious aspects, was debated by the Legislative Assembly on 12 December, when it was resolved that a Select Committee should 'take evidence and report upon the most advisable scheme of penal discipline'.[55] Members in both Houses appeared to take for granted the need for an inquiry. The Premier, W. C. Haines, agreed that 'the system pursued in the penal establishments was not so sound as he would wish', and even John Pascoe Fawkner, strangely hostile to convicts for one who had himself known imprisonment and endured the lash,[56] thought an investigation necessary. This unanimity reflected the community's growing disquiet. In retrospect, it is surprising that the community's conscience should have been troubled; only a few years previously the colony had manifested its hostility and dread of convicts by insisting that the Convicts Prevention Act be passed in defiance of the English authorities, and these fears and resentments certainly had not died away. But the stories usually circulating of appalling conditions on the hulks were given vigorous currency by Melville's speech at his trial. Moreover, Price's public image was that of an aggressive and imperious personality who brooked no opposition and arrogantly resented any questioning or criticism of his methods. Enough citizens of repute to influence public opinion believed his measures were harsh beyond what was really necessary, and an increasing section of the public sensed that some of his actions toward individual convicts were undertaken to satisfy his vanity and his craving for mastery. When both Houses separately resolved that the penal system should be investigated, the extent of public feeling was promptly demonstrated. There was a significant body of opinion opposed to Melville's execution, and on 1 December 1856, before the Full Court had quashed the conviction, a public meeting, convened by the Mayor of Melbourne, Peter Davis, was held in the Mechanics' Institute.[57] The meeting was addressed by a prominent journalist, David Blair, M.L.A.,[58] and by Dr John Singleton, M.D., and Lieutenant Amsinck, R.N. Price was vigorously denounced and several speakers gave their versions of his misdeeds. The meeting resolved to set up a Citizens' Committee of Enquiry into the Penal System, 'for the purposes of receiving reliable information, preparing statistics and evidence and assisting the Legislative Committee'. Although H. A. White labelled them 'humanity-mongers'[59] the committee was in no way a collection of radicals and sentimentalists; the members included Sir George Stephen, Dr Singleton, Dr George Mackay, LL.D. (Singleton's brother-in-law) and G. E. Barton, the barristers who volunteered to be Melville's counsel, William Little, Adam Adamson, Henry Jennings, N. Kentish, J. Goulson Bent, Lieutenant Amsinck, R.N., the Rev. Dr Adam Cairns, and three other clergymen, Messrs Ramsay, Townend and Bathurst.[60] The committee held meetings at Dr Singleton's house at 125 Collins Street, where statements were obtained from potential witnesses.[61] On 29 December another public meeting was held, this time in Astley's Amphitheatre. The Mayor again presided. One W. Schultz, a German from Heidelberg, was honorary secretary, and he presented a very long report, purporting to expose the evils of the system, to an audience numbering five hundred when the meeting began but exceeding a thousand before it ended.[62]

The morning newspapers took opposite sides in the controversy. In a vigorous editorial the *Argus* castigated those who sought to make a hero out of the felon Melville,[63] while the *Age* threw open its columns to the indefatigable Mr Schultz, and anyone else who cared to write a letter to the editor supporting penal reform. During December it published a series of articles vehemently assailing Price and Dr Richard Youl, a medical practitioner who combined the duties of coroner and visiting justice to Pentridge. Among other things, Price was accused of hampering the clergy in the performance of their duties, but in letters to the *Age* two Pentridge chaplains, the Rev. C. P. Barden and the Rev. Father O'Hea, refuted this charge. However, Price was under heavy fire, and when he was called as the first witness before the Select Committee of the Legislative Council, he was in no doubt of the strength of the feeling against him.

Six vitriolic articles in the *Age* contributed substantially to public unease about Price's administration.[64] The first article was introduced by a letter from W. Schultz, as secretary of the Citizens' Committee, but the author's name was not given. Vigorously satirical, and highly defamatory if they were not true, they appear to have been the work of an experienced journalist, possibly David Blair. The first, entitled 'Case of Daniel Gisborne', accused Price of deliberately using a 'rush' from the stockade (in which Gisborne was shot through the lungs) as means of terrorizing prisoners, and asserted 'the plain truth is Mr. Price is fond of blood. He rejoices in the opportunity of striking terror into the prisoners, that feeling, which by itself alone, is the warp and woof of his whole system.' Price was said to have had forewarning of the attempted escape from one of his 'dogs' (as informers were known in gaol slang), and to have let it develop for his own purposes. Later Price gave his account of the affair to the Legislative Assembly Select Committee;[65] he agreed an informer had told him of the plot, but he denied the damning features of the *Age* version. The next article dealt trenchantly with the 'Case of Charles Stewart'. Stewart was a first offender under a sentence of three years' imprisonment, which meant he could be released on a ticket-of-leave after serving sixteen months. Dressed in his own clothes, he was about to leave the stockade when Price saw him. The savage pen-picture of Price and the powerful impact of the article are best conveyed by extracts.

Among Mr. Price's numerous pleasant little devices, is a favourite one for impressing on the prisoners a belief in his omniscience. Obtaining information through his 'dogs', he pretends to have discovered it by means only of his own surprising astuteness. Now the hour at which the prisoners for discharge usually quit Pentridge, is one, at which John wanders, like Satan, to and fro the Stockade, in his shirt collar, his glass stuck in his eye, and his hands in the pockets of his shooting-coat, seeking whom he can pick a quarrel with. On the morning in question his mood was not propitious, as indeed, it very seldom is, unless he has got a good batch of fresh prisoners, or has been solaced in some similar satisfactory way.

Misled by an informer, Price said he recognized Stewart and accused him of having been in Van Diemen's Land. Stewart truthfully denied that he was ever there, and despite Price's endeavours, by threats and cajolery, to wring an admission from him, persisted in his denial.

The Inspector-General grew tired and violent. In a twinkling off went Charles Stewart's free clothes, and on again went the badged and tattered rags. Away went, under the remorseless hands of the Stockade barber, the hair, to its very roots, which prisoners, on the roll for discharge, are allowed to grow for two months before they go. For days and days that man was in a solitary cell, on half prison rations. The Visiting Justice never saw, heard of, or interfered with him. And how did he emerge? In hand-cuffs! to be taken to the Upper Stockade at Pentridge, which is distinct from the Main Stockade, and under the control of an old convict, now Mr. Price's crack overseer, named Kilmartin, where the very hardest labor in the penal department which experience and cruelty can devise is inflicted on the prisoners. For twelve long months . . . did Charles Stewart, a man of feeblest frame, toil and suffer . . . Why did Mr. Price keep him so long as twelve months? I verily believe he did not at first mean to do so. In a moment of ungovernable passion, which he so often displays, brooking no obstacles, and believing himself wholly irresponsible, as, indeed, the Government have suffered him so long to be, where a prisoner is concerned, he did a most wicked and illegal act.

The remaining articles dealt with other instances of injustice to prisoners and scathingly criticized Dr Youl as well as Price.

They purported to expose malpractices in the prisons, whereby penal functionaries had used the services of skilled prisoners for private purposes, and they hinted at peculations of government stores. It is impossible now to determine the soundness of the charges, though the account of Price's maltreatment of Stewart rings true. But of the polemical effectiveness of the articles there can be no doubt, and a growing number regarded the charges as true, or at least as inherently probable.

The *Age* continued its campaign even after the parliamentary committees had begun their inquiries; on 21 February 1857 an editorial contained these passages:

The abuses in the Penal Department continue to obtrude themselves on public notice, in a manner which forcibly arrests attention. And now that our Estimates are under the consideration of the Assembly, it is to be hoped hon. members before voting to Mr. John Price his very remunerative salary of £ 1000 a-year, as Inspector-General, with its comfortable concomitants of a house and grounds rent-free, forage, and other allowances, will endeavour to obtain some explanations, if not a pledge of reform, upon those matters of complaint with which the columns of the Daily Press have lately been, and still are, occupied.

All those abuses, though of the most varied kind, are presented to our notice as being directly traceable to the tyrannical and illegal treatment of the prisoners by the Inspector-General himself, and those officers immediately under his personal orders . . .

No one will deny that the Head of the Department of Penal Discipline who can not only suffer, but encourage such cruel out-rages on our common humanity being inflicted upon the unhappy criminals submitted to his custody, is utterly unfit for a position which requires in the man who would fill it properly, not only firm-ness of character and self-control, but also a humane disposition ani-mated by an earnest desire to effect the reformation of criminals. It may not be a very easy matter to meet with such a man for the office in question; but it certainly is not necessary that it should be filled by one whose leading characteristics appear to be cunning and cruelty.

His imperious temperament and hectoring manner made Price many enemies. Among them was Dr John Singleton, a gentle but determined man. Like the Rev. Thomas Rogers, Dr Single-ton was not content to endure Price's treatment meekly or in silence, but devoted himself pertinaciously to exposing the evils of the penal system. Born in Dublin in 1808, John Singleton

arrived in Melbourne with his family in 1851, where he practised medicine for forty years until his death in 1891, in his
eighty-fourth year. He was a zealous Christian and a genuine
philanthropist, whose dynamic compassion stimulated the
founding of the Children's Hospital, and the free medical dis-
pensary and the homes for women that still bear his name, and
whose labours to relieve wretchedness and raise the moral standards of his community deserve remembrance.[66] Singleton combined missionary zeal with dedication to his profession, and Price
grudgingly gave him permission to carry on his work for the
moral and spiritual welfare of prisoners as a voluntary visitor to
Pentridge, though he told Singleton he thought that conversions
and reformations of prisoners were all a sham. The Inspector-
General must have repented of his decision, for Dr Singleton
often encountered hindrances, and he believed Price had a great
aversion to his presence in the prison. Finally, in September
1856, Price seized upon a pretext to exclude him. Singleton was
asked by a prisoner to visit his wife, who was a prisoner in the
gaol at Collins Street West. From concealment, Price watched
Singleton make a note of the request, and then accused him of
breaking a regulation prohibiting a visitor from carrying out a
message from a prisoner. Words were exchanged; Price's de-
meanour was angry and over-bearing, and he told Singleton he
would not allow him to come to the prison any more.[67] Singleton's
previous dealings with the Inspector-General had not brought
him any reason for satisfaction. In March 1855 he inspected
the *President* and appealed to Price without avail to mitigate the
severities of the conditions on the hulk. He spoke to Price about
a runaway seaman, the son of the Coroner of Wiltshire, who was
serving a sentence for horse-stealing, but the unhappy result of
his intercession was that the prisoner's ticket-of-leave was post-
poned six months.[68] Before the Select Committee of the Legislative Council, however, Singleton was asked directly, 'Have you
ever yourself seen any instance of unnecessary cruelty exercised
towards the prisoners in the stockade?', and he answered, 'No,
unless you look upon chaining men to a stone in all weathers as
unnecessary cruelty'.[69]

Singleton was a practising Christian of generous and forgiving
nature who would not have consciously maligned Price, but his

strong hostility survived the Inspector-General's death and remained with him to the end of his days. In his memoirs, published in the year he died, Singleton recorded several incidents to Price's discredit. Price was such a stern disciplinarian, he wrote, that he was known to have placed his own son in one of the solitary cells for some slight misdemeanour. He told, too, of an incident at Pentridge concerning a horse that had kicked Singleton as it galloped past him. Price heard of the happening, and when he met Singleton he told him he had put the horse 'in irons'.[70] Singleton regarded this as an instance of Price's addiction to harsh measures, even when the offender was a dumb animal, but plainly it can be viewed differently; it may have been a sensible precaution to put a fractious horse in hobbles, and Price's remark may have been in jest. He asserted that it was 'painfully patent' that 'old hands' were generally on good terms with the Inspector-General, and were less rigorously treated than young first offenders. To illustrate this, he narrated an incident that must have come to him as hearsay. It concerned a young prisoner named Bacon. Price ordered him to take a set of irons to the blacksmith and have them riveted on his legs. When the prisoner refused to do so, because irons were not a part of his sentence,

The Inspector seized him, placed the irons round his neck, and when the ends had been rivetted on his legs, locked his wrists in strong handcuffs, and then thrust him in a solitary cell. Because the unfortunate lad cried out in his distress, Mr. Price had him gagged and suspended by the hands from a staple in the wall, and with his toes barely touching the ground. He was kept in this terrible situation for some time, the inspector saying 'Your name is Bacon, but I'll take the fat off you before you leave me.'[71]

Even the circumstances of Price's death did not lessen his dislike. Mentioning 'the monstrously savage character of the discipline practised by Price in the prisons', Singleton permitted himself the comment, 'The only expression of surprise that Price's death caused was that it did not occur long before.'

The Select Committee of the Legislative Council received its first check on 1 December 1856, when the sheriff informed the members that, under the law, prisoners of the Crown could not be brought to the Council Chamber for examination, but would be available at the Melbourne gaol if the committee wished. Apparently this led to an abandonment of the notion that convicts should be called as witnesses, and when the Council's committee met on 5 December 1856 to take evidence the first witness was John Price. The orientation of the Legislative Council's inquiry was different from the Legislative Assembly's. The Council's committee was to inquire into the working of the penal establishments of the colony, while the Assembly's committee was charged with reporting on the most advisable scheme of penal discipline. This may account for the different courses taken by the two committees. The Legislative Council's committee concerned itself with conditions in the penal establishments as well as with proposals for reform, and the range of the witnesses was far wider. The Legislative Assembly's committee began its sittings for the taking of evidence on 21 January 1857, almost seven weeks after the Council's committee began its hearings, and, except for Edward Wilson, the editor of the *Argus,* the witnesses before it consisted of officials. They were the sheriff, Claud Farie; Price; the man who succeeded him as Inspector-General, William Thomas Napier Champ; the Superintendent of Pentridge, George O. Duncan; a former Commandant of the Norfolk Island and Moreton Bay penal settlements, Captain Foster Fyans; and the visiting justice and coroner, Dr Richard Youl, M.D.

The atmosphere of the two committees differed, too. Price was on the defensive before the Council's committee, but when he came before the Assembly's committee he was very sure of himself and during six full sessions held on 28 January, and 4, 5, 11, 12 and 19 February 1857 he described his experiences with criminals on Norfolk Island and in Victoria, the working of his department, and the difficulties he encountered when he assumed control in both places. He defended his use of the hulks, and gave his exculpatory version of some (but not all) of the incidents charged against him by his critics. It was an impressive performance, enlivened by descriptions of convicts' exploits and wickednesses that were narrated with relish and something not far short of admiration. He agreed that hulks were an unsatisfactory substitute for the maximum security prison at Pentridge, which he was in course of constructing. He preferred working prisoners in association (or gangs) to the system of solitary cellular labour, and desired to separate first offenders and youths from hardened criminals. In his evidence, and also in his annual reports, he revealed a disposition to believe what suited him. In his first annual report he asserted that unnatural crime, or homosexual intercourse, did not exist in Victorian prisons, a claim his successor, Colonel Champ, stated he was not able to confirm.[72] Whether he had finished his *apologia pro vita sua* when he left the witness chair on 19 February will never be known, for the committee did not effectively meet again until 3 June, and by then Price was dead.

The grave allegations against Price are to be found in the evidence before the Council's committee. He furnished his critics with ammunition when, in answer to the question, 'Do you think there would be more chance of reforming the prisoners if they were in a penitentiary?', he answered incautiously, 'I must say that my hopes of reforming men are gone. I started once with the expectation of reforming men and I have now many men who will not thieve again, and will not come back as criminals, but they are not morally reformed.'[73] A later answer, 'I believe that in about another thirty years there will be a very different class of prisoners to what we have at present, but the class of prisoners we have now must be kept down by a strong hand', probably indicates what he meant, though there is every reason to believe that Price was cynically incredulous about reforming criminals, and even more so about professed conversions.

A dismissed warder named Duffy told the Council's committee he had seen Price strike a prisoner who would not surrender some tobacco he had in his mouth. He said prisoners were stripped and searched for tobacco in Price's presence.[74] Another dismissed warder, John Berkeley, described how a prisoner named Warren, the editor of one of the papers at the Ovens goldfield, serving (he believed) a sentence for libel or perjury, was constantly searched, the wardens examining even his private parts, and he asserted this was a general practice on the *Lysander*.[75] Indecent and humiliating searches were a feature on Norfolk Island, and it is more than likely they were carried out on the hulks and in the stockades by warders who had served under Price on the island. Berkeley described, too, the horrifying treatment on the *Lysander* of a prisoner suffering from syphilis *in ano,* who was pushed into a bath, scrubbed with flannel and sand, and subjected to the torture of having a piece of flannel saturated with caustic soda thrust into his rectum. Charles Tye had been a member of Price's staff for eleven months, serving at Pentridge, Collingwood and on the hulks. He was summarily dismissed for drunkenness by the Inspector-General, who nevertheless gave him a good character reference. He told the committee he had been in the penal service in England, and in Bermuda and Gibraltar, and he had never seen there the cruelty exercised in Victoria. He described a remarkably primitive instance of shock therapy in which the prison medical officer, Dr George Webster, was involved. Webster believed a convict named Maguire was feigning madness, and ordered him to be 'blistered'. The hapless convict was held face down, and his shaven head, his spine, his cheeks and his calves were painted with a feather dipped in vitriol. A fortnight later, when the skin had barely healed, the blistering was repeated.[76] Dr Webster agreed that he had ordered the treatment, and claimed that it cured the man of malingering.[77] Reading the evidence of the medical witnesses, Drs McCrea, Youl and Webster, one is left with the impression that, at least by modern standards, they were remarkably callous.[78]

A number of witnesses spoke of Price in highly favourable terms. The medical officers, Drs Webster and McCrea, and the visiting justice, Dr Richard Youl, saw no fault in him. A penal officer, Ronald C. F. Smith, who had been on Norfolk Island under Price and also with him in Victoria, said that in his opinion Price was a strict and able officer who insisted on strict obedience from both staff and convicts, and who acted habitually from rule and not from caprice.[79] A warder and messenger, William Walsh, told how Price with his own hands made gruel for prisoners when they were sick.[80] Penal officers denied there was unnecessary brutality, but the Rev. Sam Corrie thought the whole system of the hulks radically wrong and calculated to make men worse,[81] and the Rev. W. C. Currie told of seeing a prisoner on the *President* who had been badly beaten. Currie complained of restrictions upon him in the discharge of his priestly duties, and said Price had told him, 'I have been twenty

years in the Penal Department, and I never knew a man reformed or converted, as you call it, yet.'[82]

The evidence followed a pattern made distressingly familiar
by investigations during the eighteenth and nineteenth centuries
into brutalities in institutions such as gaols and asylums.[83] When
the Council's committee reached the stage of reporting, Price
was dead, and with his death partisanships subsided, though the
chairman, John Hood, made it plain that he thought the report
too pusillanimous.[84] Only one witness, Dr Youl, was heard after
Price's death, and the committee's report was presented and
ordered to be printed on 30 July 1857. It stated that 'the condition of the Penal Establishment is . . . (to say the least of it)
unsatisfactory'; that this had arisen chiefly from want of adequate
accommodation for the carrying out of a proper system of penal
discipline, and from the consequent impracticability of enforcing the necessary classification of criminals. The report added,

the Committee are also impressed with the opinion that the reformation of criminals, or indeed their capability of being reformed, has
not been allowed to exert that practical influence upon the management of the institution which its importance demands,

and concluded,

As the bulk of the reliable evidence goes to show the utter hopeless-
ness of accomplishing anything efficiently of a reformatory character
with the present establishments, your Committee are of opinion that
a properly designed building, commensurate with the wants of the
department, ought to be immediately commenced, and completed as
soon as possible.

The Assembly's committee, which consisted of sixteen members (including David Blair), encountered difficulties through
lack of a quorum on some meeting days, and failure of witnesses to attend on others, but it had the advantage of hearing
Price's successor, Colonel W. T. N. Champ. On 11 September
1857 the committee presented a report consisting of eighteen
sections, some of which were divided into numbered paragraphs.
It was a well-organized and intelligent document, and one sus-
pects it may have owed a good deal, both in substance and in
language, to Colonel Champ. It began by stating that, having
made a retrospective inquiry into the state of the Penal Department under the late Inspector-General, the committee had

been led to the conclusion that the administration of that lamented officer was marked, on the whole, by great personal ability and efficiency, but so numerous were the difficulties with which he had always to contend from want of adequate and proper buildings in which to concentrate and classify criminals under sentence, that it was impossible for him to establish anything like an efficient system of organization throughout the department.

The report noted that 'grave and serious charges had been brought against the late Mr. Price of frequent cruelty to the prisoners placed under his control, but your Committee have not found these charges in any one instance substantiated.' This, of course, was misleading; the committee had not heard any witnesses against Price, and in truth had not investigated the charges in any real sense. The draft report had used the phrase 'fully substantiated', but a motion by Mr Haines to delete 'fully' was carried when the committee debated the report. The absence of witnesses against Price, and the circumstances of his violent death, should be borne in mind in assessing the value of the qualified exoneration in the next paragraphs of the report. They were:

3. From his large and intimate experience of criminal life and character, and his acquaintance with convict discipline in the penal colonies of Australia, Mr. Price appears to have been led to the conviction that a system of strict and uniform severity was essentially necessary to secure the maintenance of subordination amongst prisoners; and to the mere casual observer it may have appeared that in particular instances he carried this principle to an extreme length, but it has not appeared in evidence that he was guilty of those deliberate acts of atrocious cruelty which have been alleged against him. Those charges, your Committee find, have been principally brought by criminals whose evidence is not always of a trustworthy character; and it must be borne in mind that there was one circumstance of peculiar significance in the relations of Mr. Price to the criminal population of this country, which made that gentleman a special object of both the fear and hatred of that class. This was his singularly extensive and minute knowledge of them individually. He had a special faculty for detecting and identifying old convicts, whom he had known many years before in Van Diemen's Land and Norfolk Island; and it is of that class that the criminal population of this country is mainly composed. This circumstance was certainly the proximate cause of the murder of Mr. Price; but it was combined with two more immediate causes of a strongly operative kind, namely: his reputation amongst the criminal population as a severe discipli-

narian; and, especially, the evils arising from the maintenance of the
hulk system, for which Mr. Price was not, however, personally responsible.

4. Your Committee find that Mr. Price had been, for several years
before his death, urging upon the Government the introduction into
the penal departments of those very reforms which your Committee
are now convinced, after investigation, are imperatively required.

5. The peculiar circumstances of the country may have prevented
those reforms being carried out; but had the case been otherwise, it
is not probable that the recent frightful occurrences would ever have
happened.

6. With the means at his disposal, however, Mr. Price accomplished a very great deal towards a radical reform of the entire department. He laid the foundation for an improved system, and very
few men, in his situation, could have achieved more.

7. Your Committee cannot refrain, while referring to the late Inspector-General, from expressing their deep regret at the loss to this
country of an officer whose practical ability and immense experience
would have qualified him, beyond almost any other person in existence, for the control of a thoroughly organised system of criminal
management in this colony.

Having disposed of the charges against Price, the committee
addressed themselves constructively to the main task. Unani-
mously they recommended that the hulks should be abolished,
with the 'slight reservation' that one hulk should be retained as
a place of detention for 'refractory seamen', who should, in any
case, be kept wholly separate from criminals under sentence.
The central contention of the Citizens' Committee triumphed;
the report stated flatly,

the system of hulks has been an entire failure. It has entailed a very
large expenditure on the colony, without securing a single compen-
satory advantage, except that of providing safe custody for a number
of criminals; it has been destructive rather than preservative of discipline in the department, and it has been one of the chief causes of
those dreadful outbreaks which resulted in the murder of the late
Inspector-General.

The committee earnestly urged the absolute and immediate necessity of breaking up the hulks' establishment. They did en-
visage the retention of one or two hulks in certain circumstances
to house, not the *worst*, but the *best* prisoners if convicts were
employed on public works around the shores of ports. The com-

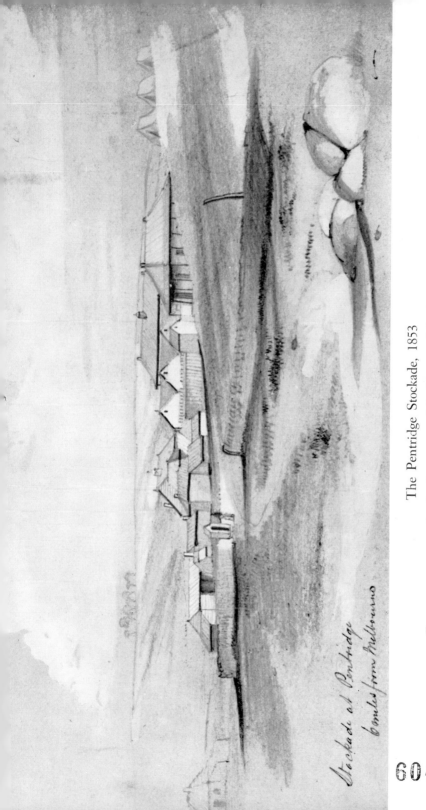

The Pentridge Stockade, 1853

From a contemporary drawing, by courtesy of the Trustees of the State Library of Victoria

Colonel W. T. N. Champ

From a portrait in the possession of his granddaughter,
Miss K. R. Green

mittee suggested this could be done if the recommendation were adopted that prisoners in their last year of probation for tickets-of-leave, on the Inspector-General's recommendation, should be employed away from the prison on public works. These prisoners should be 'indulged by the addition to their ordinary ration of tea and tobacco in moderate quantities'. The system they recommended was, they said, based on four principles: (a) centralization; (b) classification of prisoners; (c) employment of prisoners; (d) uniformity of discipline. Regular and full employment of prisoners was essential in any effective system of prison discipline. The practice of permitting lunatics to be mixed up in a narrow yard with other prisoners was mischievous and objectionable. 'Confirmed lunatics' not charged with serious crimes should be sent to the Yarra Bend Asylum, and youthful lunatics, or idiots, should in every case be sent there. They roundly condemned the Western gaol of Melbourne, used for females, and recommended that females should be housed in a new building at Pentridge, and be employed in 'washing' (that is, laundering) and in sewing for prison domestic purposes. Destitute orphans, taken into custody under the Vagrant Act, should not be confined in gaol; and children of female prisoners should be kept apart from their mothers during the day, with adequate playing space and simple amusements, and returned to their mothers at night. The Eastern gaol was badly ventilated and had a sickening atmosphere; it was hopelessly inadequate; and should be 'removed' forthwith. A building should be erected at Pentridge to house juvenile offenders under fourteen; they should be kept separate from other prisoners and given proper instruction by regular teachers for three hours a day, and employed at some trade or in the garden or farm. Boys should not be sentenced to lengthy imprisonment; instead, they should undergo a short imprisonment with corporal punishment not to exceed two dozen lashes, inflicted always under the observation of the visiting justice. Schools should be established in penal institutions, and instructive and amusing books should be available during the week, and on Sundays books of a religious and moral tendency, sanctioned by the chaplains. No official from the visiting justice down to the lowest class of warder, should address a prisoner in 'sarcastic, contemptuous, harsh, or familiar language, but always with the strictest gravity and reserve'. No prisoner should be led to expect any indulgences except those officially authorized. A fund of £200 a year should be entrusted to the Inspector-General for distribution at his discretion to prisoners on release, and no prisoner should be discharged in prison clothing. The sentencing powers of the visiting justice should be curtailed, and an Act consolidating the laws relating to penal management should be introduced. The committee were satisfied that escaped and manumitted convicts were entering Victoria, and urged the Convicts Prevention Act should be strictly enforced. Two chaplains, one Protestant and the other Roman Catholic, should be appointed by the government, and they should have no other duties in their respective churches. By way of rebuke to Dr Singleton, presumably, the committee added that no other person, male or female, should be allowed to visit the prison as a religious instructor unless sanctioned by the Chief Secretary, and chaplains should never convey messages from a prisoner to friends outside without the permission of the Inspector-General. To secure the establishment, once for all, of the system recommended, the committee were 'decidedly of opinion that almost any expenditure, in reason, might be justifiably incurred'.

It may be doubted if the committee's pious belief was well founded that John Price would have been either happy or successful in controlling such a system of criminal management. His successor, William Thomas Napier Champ, devoted his great energies and experience to creating a system that embodied the best features of the report, and he achieved a great deal. He introduced most of the ameliorations Price asserted were impossible, but even Champ could get so far and no further in the face of governmental indifference. Champ's official career was at times linked with Price's in Van Diemen's Land; Price succeeded him as Muster Master, and Champ was Comptroller-General of Convicts in 1846. Born in Essex on 15 April 1808, he was educated at Sandhurst and joined the army at eighteen. He was sent with his regiment to Sydney in 1828, and in the following year to Hobart. Later he resigned his commission and was appointed an Assistant Police Magistrate and Muster Master. He succeeded Captain O'Hara Booth as a firm but humane commandant of the Port Arthur penal settlement. He retired from this position, and for a time was Comptroller-General of Convicts. In 1852 he became Colonial Secretary, and when Van Diemen's Land became Tasmania in 1856 and achieved representative government he was Tasmania's first Premier in the colony's first ministry, though he held office only briefly, from 1 November 1856 to 26 February 1857. After Price's death Champ accepted appointment as Inspector-General for Victoria, a position he occupied until 31 December 1868. Three years later he was elected to the Legislative Assembly, but he found Victorian politics not to his liking and went into a retirement that ended with his death on 25 August 1892, in his eighty-fifth year. He was a man of impressive integrity, whose innate fairness and exceptional ability as commander of men assured him of success in any undertaking. In May 1852 Bishop Willson had urged that Champ should replace Price on Norfolk Island, stressing that his 'universally acknowledged talents, his zeal, energy and unflinching integrity, his character for justice, even among the worst description of the convict class, render him . . . in a remarkable degree qualified for such a task.'[85] A firm disciplinarian, Champ's administration in Van Diemen's Land and in Victoria was never disfigured by the excesses ascribed to Price, and his fervent admirer, Henry Augustus White, who served under him during his eleven years as Inspector-General, claimed that during his period of office 'no board of inquiry was ever appointed to investigate charges against any of the officials; the management of the department was never questioned, nor did any comment appear in the public press unless in praise of his public career.'[86]

Champ took up his duties in June 1857, and proceeded energetically to organize the penal department. There were 1,221 prisoners, of whom 29 were refractory seamen. Three hundred and sixty-one prisoners were at Pentridge, two hundred and ninety-three at the Collingwood stockade, seventy-three closely confined on the *President,* one hundred and nineteen on the *Success,* of whom sixty-seven were confined similarly to the men on the *President,* one hundred and twenty-three on the *Sacramento,* of whom twenty-three were in close confinement, and one hundred and ninety-three on the *Lysander.*

The convicts on the hulks who were not in close confinement

were landed daily and were employed on public works at Williamstown. In his first report Champ stressed that existing facilities and arrangements were completely unsatisfactory, though he stated explicitly that he attributed no blame to Price for this state of affairs. He set out briefly his own ideas of penal management. 'I am', he wrote, 'no advocate for corporal punishment where any other can be effectually substituted, considering its tendency to be brutalizing and its effects uncertain.' He took for granted that 'it is the duty of a humane government to endeavour, if possible, to combine reformation with effective punishment', to be achieved by classification of the various grades of offenders, and a complete separation of the evil from the better disposed; the appointment of religious instructors, whose duty it should be not only to address the men collectively, but to administer consolation to the sick in hospital, and to visit the cells, advising and reasoning with each occupant individually; and the establishment of schools, to afford at least to those who were disposed to learn, the opportunity of doing so.[87] Adopting Jeremy Bentham's scheme,[88] he envisaged a panopticon at Pentridge, where a prisoner should pass through progressive stages, as he earned them, from confinement in his cell in absolute silence at the beginning of his sentence to relaxed discipline and labour in association before its expiration. He shared this strange attachment to the inhuman Separate System (under which a prisoner worked in silence confined to his cell) with a good many well-intentioned penal reformers.[89]

Under Champ, Pentridge took on much of the aspect it still wears; the high stone wall was completed and the grim prison buildings constructed in accordance with the standards of prison architecture then favoured, but now outmoded. A few years after he retired, penal discipline again occupied the attention of a Royal Commission. With no hostile intent against the government, and primarily because of his interest in penal reform, David Blair raised the question in the Legislative Assembly in 1870, seeking the appointment of a select committee.[90] Instead, the government appointed a Royal Commission, consisting of Sir William Stawell (Chief Justice), Archibald Michie (Attorney-General), Messrs S. H. Bindon, W. H. Fancourt Mitchell (who had been Chief Commissioner of Police under Lieutenant-

Governor La Trobe), Charles MacMahon, M.P. (who had also been Chief Commissioner of Police), David Blair, M.P., Richard Youl, M.D., William Templeton, P.M., and Charles Edward Strutt, P.M. Blair acted as the commission's secretary. Champ was called out of retirement to give evidence. Between 1870 and 1872, the commission returned three extensive reports, which, with the appended evidence, still make interesting reading for social historians and penal reformers.[91] Champ's immediate successors lacked his capacity for command and control, however, and in 1884 events at Pentridge gave rise to public scandal, another investigation was ordered and senior officials were replaced.[92] But all this lay in the future when, on 26 March 1857, Melbourne was shocked and fear-stricken by the tidings from Williamstown that the invulnerable John Price lay unconscious and mortally injured, the victim of a murderous attack by a gang of convicts ashore from the hulk *Success*.

Chapter Five

THE MURDER OF JOHN PRICE AND THE TRIALS OF THE MURDERERS

I *The Murder of John Price*

In the afternoon of 26 March 1857, at Williamstown, John Price kept his appointment with destiny. Confident he could do so by sheer force of personality, he went there to quell the dangerous unrest among the convicts from the hulks labouring on an ambitious scheme of public works.

In the annual report[1] which he was writing but did not live to complete, the Inspector-General described the works:

The gangs from the different hulks have been chiefly occupied in reclaiming a portion of land from Hobson's Bay at Gellibrand Point and erecting a Battery thereon. The area reclaimed is about three quarters of an acre which has had to be filled up in some parts to a depth of seven or eight feet, with rubble quarried some distance off and removed by prison labor. The interior of the Battery is built of stone dressed in a superior manner, all quarried, worked, and built by the prisoners. A powder magazine is also constructed (bombproof), the only free labor employed in the whole work being in lining this magazine with asphalt, and building (also in asphalt) the walls of the mouths of the Embrasures, concurrent with the Battery. The jetty has been rapidly progressing, being now faced with dressed stone to the length of 267 feet by a width of 50 feet and reaching (in rough rubble work) a total length of 407 feet to a depth of fifteen feet of water at high tides. A tide gauge house has also been erected of dressed stone and fitted entirely by prison labor.

It is proposed to lay down an iron tramway and employ horses to draw the materials from the quarries to the jetty. When this arrangement is perfected and I am enabled, by the completion of the Battery, to withdraw all the men from thence and employ them on the jetty, rapid progress will be made, but the magnitude of the work is such that years must elapse before any hope can be entertained of its completion . . .

The men on the hulks had become increasingly restive since Owen Owens' murder. In the hulks and the stockades the 'grapevine', the surreptitious but highly efficient system of communication that exists in every prison, brought to inmates information, often distorted, about the attacks on Price and his department by the Citizens' Committee. Despite the most rigorous measures to prevent it, pages of the *Age* containing the Committee's report were passed from convict to convict. Price was perturbed by the ominous behaviour of the convicts, and recognized its explosive potentialities. In his unfinished report he wrote:

Since Melville's trial and the subsequent proceedings taken by the (so-called) Citizens' Committee, I regret to say that a spirit of insubordination has pervaded the prisoners, which not only calls for the strictest vigilance combined with great forbearance on the part of the officers to keep within present control, but which will I fear lead to some serious consequences before it is thoroughly eradicated.[2]

On the morning of Thursday, 26 March, eighty-two convicts from the *Success* were brought by boat from the hulk to the works at Gellibrand Point.[3] The morning held promise of a warm day, later fulfilled, for the temperature reached 82 degrees, and a light northerly wind was blowing from the inland. By evening it had changed to a light south-westerly. As the boat was pulling off, a prisoner complained to James Holles, the hulk superintendent, that portion of his bread had been taken from him by the chief warder, and Holles ordered him aboard again. The other men were taken ashore, but they refused to work. A gang overseer reported to Holles that the convicts demanded to see the Inspector-General. He promised that the Inspector-General would hear their complaints that day, and they began their labours. Holles went to the Inspector-General's office in Lonsdale Street, Melbourne, and reported what had happened. Supremely confident of his ability to handle the situation, Price said he would come to the works during the afternoon, and shortly before three o'clock (according to evidence at the inquest) he went by train to Williamstown. Holles met him and they were joined by Captain Blachford, the superintendent of the *Lysander*. They walked along the works tramway, which was raised above ground level, and Price listened to the grievances of several prisoners.

The working gang from the *Lysander* was quiet, and the omi-

nous discontent seemed to be confined to the men from the
Success. Price summarily rejected most of the complaints. When
a prisoner, William Jones, complained of his treatment, Price
drew one of his own eyes open with his fingers and asked, 'Do
you see anything green in my eye?'[4] The chief warder of the
Success, Thomas Hyland, was hated by the prisoners, who believed that not only did he treat them with unnecessary harshness but he also cheated them of their proper rations. One convict said his bread ration had been taken from him, others that
the bread ration was mouldy and the soap ration was short. The
prisoners claimed, with truth, that soap intended for the use of
prisoners to wash their working clothes was in fact used to scrub
the hulks.[5] Price spoke fairly to some prisoners; two of them,
Simon Russell and Henry Fee, he told he was doing what he
could to have their sentences mitigated. But generally his attitude was in character, autocratic and unreceptive, and his lack
of responsiveness infuriated the convicts. However, the strong
personality of the Inspector-General might have left him master
of the situation had it not been for a prisoner, James Kelly,
whose sentence was about to expire. He asked Price if a sentence
he had received of three days' 'solitary' on bread and water would
mean that he would have to serve a further six months before
being eligible for a ticket-of-leave. Price told him, 'You will have
to do so.' Kelly lost his temper, and shook his fist at Price, saying,
'You bloody tyrant, your race will soon be run.' The Inspector-
General shouldered Kelly to one side, and ordered he should be
taken aboard, but Kelly retreated among the cart-gang convicts
who had come up and grouped themselves about the officials in
a half-circle. Men from the quarry gang joined them. Price was
told by the overseer that they had gathered against orders, and
he commanded that they be sent aboard, where he would see
them individually. The men were in a mind to obey, when a
prisoner called out that they wanted their officers replaced, and
another shook his fist threateningly at Chief Warder Hyland,
shouting, 'That's the bloody tyrant.' At that moment a couple of
clods of earth were thrown from the rear rank of the grouped
prisoners. The convicts snatched up pieces of quarried rock of
various sizes that lay about, and hurled them, some at the
Inspector-General, some at officials near him. A senior overseer

from the *Success*, Samuel Wilson, was injured and Captain Blachford and Warder Gleeson were also hit by stones. The Inspector-General raised a hand to protect his head, and instinctively turned away. When the convicts saw his back turned, the spell of his personality was broken, and a group surged forward. Several convicts seized him. Calling out 'Don't, don't men', and 'Fall back, men, fall back', he defended himself vigorously, but the numbers were too great. He broke loose, and turned to run. A heavy stone struck him in the back, and he fell against the tramway embankment. He got up, and attempted to make his escape, but he stumbled in a gutter and fell again. Dazed, he was getting to his feet when a convict struck him with a shovel. A mob of howling convicts surged about the prostrate Inspector-General, dragging him along as they struck him with stones and fists and, according to some versions, shovels. When it was evident even to his frenzied assailants that he was badly injured and unconscious, a convict called out, 'Come on, he's cooked, he wants no more', and the mob rushed up the embankment. Not all of the convicts were in irons, but some of those who were attempted to remove them. However, there was no organized attempt to escape; irresolute, the mob was at a loss what next to do, and the armed guards rounded them up and, with the bulk of the convicts (who had taken no part in the outbreak), sent them back to the hulks. At muster two prisoners, King and Farrell, were missing, and were later found in a cunningly concealed excavation not far from the scene of the 'rush'. Despite later suggestions that their attempt to escape was connected with a plot to murder Price, it is clear that it had nothing to do with the spontaneous assault on Price and the officials, for the two men had gone into hiding before Price arrived.[6]

Chief Warder Hyland took to his heels when the mob turned on him, and none of the officers and the guards, except Wilson, showed much resolution or initiative. None sought to succour the Inspector-General as he lay in the mud, mortally wounded; this act of mercy was left to a convict, Simon Russell. He made his way to Price, who was lying face downwards in a cavity in the sand. The wounded man was bleeding profusely, and 'groaned fearfully' when Russell lifted his face from the wet sand to enable him to breathe. Russell called to George Ross, another convict, to assist him, and he was joined by Henry Fee and other convicts, one of whom, Alfred Berry, brought a pannikin of water and washed Price's mouth. They lifted the unconscious Inspector-General onto a barrow, and wheeled him to the foot of the lighthouse. Dr John Wilkins lived nearby; he was medical officer to the hulks, and Price's friend. At about a quarter to four he was called to the scene and made a cursory examination of the unconscious and shockingly battered Inspector-General, who was then carried to an upstairs room in the doctor's home. Except for a few seconds, he continued insensible and died shortly after 4 p.m. on the next day. His injuries were so extensive that the medical men called into consultation confirmed Dr Wilkins' opinion that an operation to relieve the brain haemorrhage or to amputate his injured arm was out of the question. On the Saturday morning a post-mortem examination was made by Dr Wilkins in the presence of several other medical practitioners. It was confined to an examination of brain and external injuries, and though the skull cap was removed, the body was not otherwise opened. The bones of the left cheek were grossly shattered; there were five or six large wounds, from 2 to 2½ inches long, on the sides and back of the head; the left shoulder was severely bruised and there was a puncture wound on the left elbow-joint. The middle finger on the right hand was crushed. The base of the skull was completely fractured and the brain lacerated. Dr Wilkins had no doubt that the fracture of the base of the skull was the cause of death. In his opinion it was probably caused by a blow from a stone.[7]

The counter-measures which the authorities undertook without delay showed the terrifying impact of the outbreak on the community of Melbourne. A troop of the 40th Regiment and a large body of mounted police were rushed by the steamer *Comet* from Melbourne to the Williamstown Pier. The Volunteer Corps was marched to Williamstown and 'disposed in a line so as to preclude any chance of the convicts gaining the town'.[8] Victoria's first ship of war, the steam sloop *Victoria*,[9] trained her guns on the prisoners, and some of her crew were landed to reinforce the troops. There was little difficulty in herding the convicts aboard the hulks but, gripped by fear, the people of Williamstown and Melbourne had lost all sense of proportion, and fantastic rumours were rife, whipped up next day by sensational accounts in the *Argus* newspaper.

The inquest opened at the Royal Hotel, Williamstown, on Saturday, 28 March. Because of his friendship with the dead man, the coroner, Dr Youl, did not preside and Dr Wilmot replaced him. Late at night it was adjourned until Monday, and was concluded on Thursday, 2 April. During this period the climate of fear was intensified by the uproar from the caged prisoners on the *President*, who cheered at the news of Price's death. Extraordinary precautions against attempts by convicts to escape and seize Williamstown were maintained; the *Victoria* lay alongside the *President* with guns shotted and trained on the hulk, and soldiers patrolled the town.

On Monday, 30 March, in this atmosphere of dread, the funeral of John Price was held. It was movingly impressive. Over the week-end the body lay at the Williamstown stockade, enclosed in a lead chest covered with the Union Jack. On the Monday the chest was placed in a black coffin, bearing a solid brass breast-plate, inscribed simply 'John Price. Ob. March 27th, 1857, AEtat.48'. The body, thus enclosed, was taken in one of the *Victoria's* boats to Sandridge, and placed upon a hearse. The funeral procession then moved slowly off to the New Cemetery, now the Melbourne General Cemetery. The *Argus* recorded the order of the procession as

The Undertaker
Three Mounted Troopers
Mourning carriage containing the Rev. Mr. Barden,
      Dr. Youl and Dr. Martin
Mutes
THE BODY
Mourning coach, containing three sons of the deceased
Detachments of Warders
Members of the Volunteer Artillery Corps
Citizens and others on foot
Persons on horseback
Private carriages.

As it passed the university (where Price's eldest son, John Frederick, was then a student) undergraduates joined the cortege. Public dignitaries attended and acted as pall-bearers; the streets were cordoned by police, and 'the greatest order, decorum and even silence characterised the crowd during the procession; all the principal shops were temporarily closed, and the peculiar solemnity of the occasion appeared to be universally felt.'

On the following Thursday the coroner's jury found a verdict of wilful murder against fifteen convicts, and reserved two others for the opinion of the Attorney-General. The jury added a rider directed at the Citizens' Committee, condemning the 'misplaced sympathy exhibited by a portion of the public', and expressing approbation of the officers and warders of the hulks, and of the military and naval forces for the alacrity of their assistance. However, two jurors did not subscribe to the rider, considering it 'uncalled for'. The brutal circumstances of the murder shocked and terrified the populace, evoking widespread sympathy for his widow and children, and bitter hostility against the Citizens' Committee. But the *Age* stood its ground. In a leading article it said:

John Price is dead. He has gone to give an account of himself before another tribunal than that of the Citizens' Committee. It is a solemn event, whether viewed as an individual calamity, or in connexion with the circumstances in which his name has recently appeared before the public. Different people will view it with different feelings. By some it will be viewed as a deed of retribution; by others as a martyrdom. Many people look on John Price as a monster of cruelty, who had no right to die other than as he did; while not a few may look upon him as an innocent and ill-used man, whose death is to be attributed to the advantage taken of a merciful disposition, and to the persecution he endured at the hands of a community that did not know his worth . . . But, if the truth be told, there can be no doubt whatever that Mr. Price was guilty of the cruelty attributed to him, and that his untimely and unfortunate end is the melancholy result of that vindictive feeling which his own conduct and policy has fostered in the minds of the convicts under his charge. The whole affair lies in a nutshell. He was a cruel man, and his cruelty came back to him.[10]

Few were found to utter such sentiments publicly, however, and expressions of sympathy and horror were general. In April the staff of the penal department, some of whom had served under Price on Norfolk Island, presented the widow with a vellum-bound address, in which they said 'he proved himself the most disinterested, just, able and zealous Public Officer it has

ever been our lot to serve under or be associated with.' They
continued:

> Of his private worth to you who have been so many years the partner
> of his life, it would be superfluous for us to speak, but we may be
> allowed to say that we amongst those who have enjoyed his friend-
> ship bear equal testimony to his private as to his public virtues and
> we can assure you madam that the memory of his many acts of kind-
> ness will ever be engraven on our hearts.[11]

They subscribed a sum of £270 to erect a granite memorial to
Price, which stands above his grave in the Melbourne General
Cemetery. The tombstone is inscribed:

> In memory of John Price Esqr., Fourth son of the late Sir Rose
> Price, Bart., of Trengwainton, Cornwall, England, who died on
> 27th March 1857 from the effects of injuries inflicted on him by a
> gang of convicts at Williamstown on the 26th March 1857 while
> in the execution of his duty as Inspector-General of Penal Establish-
> ments. Aged 48 years.

and on the west face,

> This monument was erected by the officers and warders of Penal
> Establishments in Victoria as a tribute to the memory of one who
> neither swerved from the path of public duty nor failed to respond
> to the call of friendship.

Mrs Price was known for her kindnesses to sick prisoners, and
this may have prompted what was the most unusual of the expressions of sympathy. One hundred and four prisoners at Pentridge sent a letter of condolence to her. They expressed their
indignation at the rumour that they had 'cognizance of the intended attack upon the late Inspector-General', and stated that
they had not 'the most remote knowledge of the dreadful event'.
They added that had they been present, they would have made
every exertion to save his life.[12]

II   *The Trials and Executions*

Representative and responsible government, newly established
in Victoria, was suffering from teething troubles in 1857, but
the inexorable processes of criminal justice went forward ex-
peditiously and remorselessly. Under a special commission, a
session of the Supreme Court in its criminal jurisdiction opened

on Monday, 13 April, to try fifteen convicts for the murder of John Price. The small courtroom in the unimpressive building in Latrobe Street, in which the Supreme Court had been housed since July 1843, was crowded. Fifteen men stood in the shadow of the gallows. The tension inseparable from a trial which has death as its possible ending gripped the onlookers outside, unable to gain admittance, and the jurors, witnesses and favoured few within the courtroom, when the trial judge, Mr Justice Redmond Barry, took his seat sharp at 10 a.m. It mounted throughout the days that followed.

The first four resident judges in Melbourne—successively, John Walpole Willis, William Jeffcott, Roger Therry, and William à Beckett—were judges of the Supreme Court of New South Wales. In January 1852 the Act creating the Supreme Court of Victoria was passed, and à Beckett became the first chief justice and Redmond Barry the first puisne judge. In 1857 Barry was in his forty-third year, a bachelor, and a competent though not an outstanding lawyer. His interests were wide; by no means indifferent to carnal pleasures, he was zealous, too, in promoting education and culture, and is deservedly remembered on that account. A severe criminal judge, he entertained no doubts of the efficacy of harsh penalties. To him a convicted felon was a hateful threat; in his view, the use of the criminal law, as the regulated brute force of the community, was legitimate to incapacitate or abolish the threat.* He was vain and often pompous, and at times too readily seduced by the awful power his office gave him over the life and liberty of wrongdoers. Human misery personified by convicts moved him little, if at all. It was soon clear he would give the accused men their bare legal rights, but no more.

Difficulties were encountered at the outset of the trial; so freely did the prisoners exercise their right to twenty peremptory challenges each that twelve jurors could not be obtained. The Attorney-General, Henry Samuel Chapman, elected to 'sever the panel', that is, to defeat the obstructive tactics of the accused by removing some of them for trial later, so that those left were

---

*In fairness it should be mentioned that he subscribed to and held office in the Discharged Prisoners' Aid Society, presiding over at least one annual meeting.

not able, by using their challenges, to prevent the empanelling of the requisite jury of twelve men.[13] At first eight prisoners were removed, but still a jury could not be obtained. Two more prisoners were removed, without avail. The removal of another three left Thomas Williams, Henry Smith (No. 1794, used to distinguish him from another Henry Smith, also on trial) and Thomas Moloney, and finally a jury was empanelled. Mr Justice Barry revealed his attitude when Smith asked for counsel to defend them. The Attorney-General was sympathetic to the request, and with a little encouragement from the Bench, counsel would have been available, but none came from Mr Justice Barry. The absence of legal representation placed the prisoners under a grave handicap. Although one copy of the depositions of the evidence taken at the inquest had been provided for the use of all the fifteen prisoners on the Saturday before the trial began,[14] this meagre concession to fairness was of little advantage, because none of the three accused could read or write. The selection of these three prisoners to be tried first seems to have been haphazard, for James Kelly, whose outburst triggered off the outbreak and who was alleged by a convict witness to have taken up a stone in his two arms and thrown it upon Price's head, saying, 'There you bloody tyrant (or wretch), take that', was among the prisoners removed. The Attorney-General was fair enough in his opening address, and this outward semblance of fairness was maintained through the long sittings on the Monday and the Tuesday. A procession of witnesses, consisting of the officers and warders and convicts, told their stories of the outbreak and the killing. Though they must have realized the result was foregone, the prisoners fought vigorously for their lives and cross-examined at length.

When the case for the Crown was closed, the accused were asked by the trial judge if they had any observations to offer to the jury. As the law then stood (and as it remained in Victoria until 1891)[15] an accused person was not a competent witness and could not give sworn evidence in his own defence. He could call witnesses, however, and he was allowed to tell his own story in a statement to the jury. Throughout the trial the prisoners sought to bring out the appalling treatment of men on the hulks, but accounts of their sufferings and the frauds practised by the officials made little impression on the judge. The prisoner Williams now spoke with desperate eloquence. He told how in the four years and five months since he began his sentence, he had been confined to his cell in the hulks for four years and two months, at first in the *President* for three years, and then in the *Success,* where he had not been allowed ashore until not long before Price's death. He said:

The blood that has been shed on those hulks is now crying for vengeance. The officers and warders are all picked men by the late Inspector-General; picked by him because they would suit his purposes, and so long as Mr. Blachford, Holles and Hyland are on board the hulks so long will prisoners be sent to this Court to be tried.

Henry Smith followed, and insisted he had never struck a blow, and that there was not one particle of evidence that showed he was even aiding or abetting in the murder. 'I have put my trust in God on this occasion', he said, 'and He has succoured me, and I have Him to thank for never having imbrued my hands in any man's blood.' Moloney told how he had been 231 days in solitary confinement out of two years and ten months on the hulks. He claimed that the cause of disturbances on the hulk was bad and insufficient rations, and that his complaints about these conditions had aroused the animosity of the officers. He said:

What I have stated is the truth, as I shall have to answer before my Judge for the ragged and dirty life I have led . . . as the God before whom I am going is my Judge, I took neither hand, act, or part in aiding or abetting the murder.

After the prisoners had called a number of convict witnesses, Mr Justice Barry summed up. He directed the jury that if they found that Williams and Moloney were active agents in the death of Mr Price, and that Smith was engaged with them in one common intention (the evidence of which they must look for in his actions) he was equally responsible in the first degree, even though he had not struck the Inspector-General. He said the prisoner Smith had relied in his defence on that circumstance, but if the jury came to the conclusion that the intention was a common one, all concerned in the result were equally

Williamstown in the 1850s — the third vessel from the left is a hulk

The Assassination of the Inspector-General

An artist's impression of the murder from Gibb, *Thrilling Incidents of the Convict System in Australasia* (1895)

guilty, for in cases of organized resistance against constituted authorities all parties concerned were responsible for the consequences, even if such results followed as were not at first contemplated or premeditated. It was for the jury to say if in the case of Smith he was so far acting in concert with the other two prisoners as to render him responsible for the consequences which followed. The deadliness of the summing-up was shown by the brevity of the jury's deliberations. They retired at 6.30 p.m. and at 7 o'clock returned with a verdict of guilty against all three prisoners. They strongly recommended Smith to mercy on the ground that it had not been proved he had struck any blows. Asked if they had anything to say why sentence of death should not be passed upon them, the prisoners made their last desperate efforts to escape the gallows.

Williams asked that sentence should be deferred until the cases of the prisoners who had been removed for later trial had been heard, because evidence exculpating him might emerge in those cases. If they had had money to employ counsel, he said, the result might have been different, but if it was the will of God that he should die he was content to die, for during the past four years and a half, he had lived a miserable life and therefore would as soon die as not. Smith again asserted his innocence, and asked the judge to act on the jury's recommendation. Moloney said that enough evidence had been given against him to hang any man or twenty men, but when he looked at the persecution which the Saviour had suffered, what could a wretch like him expect? He denied lifting a hand against Price. If His Honour would grant that his execution might be public he would be very glad, that the public might hear, at the last moment, his confession.

Before the judge could pronounce sentence, Williams spoke again. A young man named Brown, he said, was in the gaol charged with taking a spade out of his (Williams') hand and striking Price with it. He declared to God that Brown had never done so.

It had long been the custom in British criminal courts for the judge to accompany a sentence of death or of long imprisonment with a sanctimonious homily and an exhortation to repentance. Mr Justice Barry took full advantage of the usage. Addressing the doomed wretches, he spoke on and on in a fashion that showed no pity or charity or imagination. He reminded them of their past offences, of the opportunities for honest labour that had surrounded them that would have 'enriched them beyond the dreams of such poverty as that which you were originally acquainted with.' He brushed aside their grievances as trivial; he did not believe their complaints, which, he said, were unsubstantiated by proof. He begged them to use the little space of time now allotted to them to make the reparation not only to the society whose laws they had outraged, but to a higher being. Public executions had been abolished in Victoria by Act 18 Victoria No. 44, passed in November 1854, and he rebuked Moloney for impiety of language in asking to be executed publicly. 'Your life, unfortunate man, can afford no sufficient atonement for your crime.' He told Smith that he held out no hope to him for mercy. Without qualm he pronounced the death sentence, concluding with the traditional pious invocation, 'and may the Lord have mercy upon your souls.'

On the next day, Wednesday, John Williams, Henry Smith (No. 1222), James Kelly, Richard Jones, and William Jones were arraigned, with Mr Justice Barry again the trial judge, as he was in the two trials that were to follow. James Kelly asked for counsel to defend them, but the judge refused to depart from the unhelpful attitude he had adopted at the first trial, remarking virtuously that to be assisted by counsel would relieve him of a very great responsibility he had to assume when prisoners were left undefended, but from that responsibility he would not shrink. Despite his efforts to repeat the performance of the previous two days, the atmosphere of this trial was different. With considerable skill the prisoners cross-examined the witnesses about the events surrounding Price's murder, and the shocking manner in which prisoners were dealt with on the hulks. Even the judge was startled when the prisoner, William Jones, extracted from Superintendent Holles an admission that when they came aboard prisoners were stripped and their ears, noses, mouths and private parts searched for tobacco. There was a vivid exchange between overseer Hyland and the prisoner, Henry Smith:

PRISONER: Was there anything said to Mr. Price during the rush?
WITNESS: I cannot say there was. There was a yell—a howl like wild
beasts.
PRISONER: Just so; that is the name you have for us—'wild beasts'.
You speak of us and treat us as wild beasts. We are not much better,
certainly.

The trial proceeded during Wednesday, Thursday and Friday,
and was concluded on Saturday. During Saturday's sitting Mr
Milner Stephen announced he had been instructed to appear for
Henry Smith, and at the close of the Crown case he addressed
the jury. The men who struck the blows by which Mr Price was
killed were guilty of a barbarous murder, counsel said, but the
jury must be satisfied beyond the possibility of doubt that murder
was the common intention before they could find persons who
were merely present at the time guilty of the offence. He said it
did not appear that there was any original intention of commit-
ting the crime of murder, but only of making complaints; but
things went from bad to worse, till one man, with passions more
excited than others, struck the fatal blow. Counsel then analysed
the evidence and displayed the inconsistencies in the witnesses'
versions. Three of the prisoners also addressed the jury. One of
them, William Jones, observed that

there had been fifteen men committed for this unfortunate affair, and
out of that number not more than two or three were probably
guilty of the offence. The guilty men were just as likely to be among
those who went on board voluntarily as among those who stayed out.

The witnesses for the defence were then called, and late at night
the judge began his charge to the jury. He spoke for an hour
and a half. His charge was more balanced than at the trial of the
three prisoners whom he had sentenced to death, lending some
point to the bitter assertion by the condemned man Williams
that if they had had the money to employ counsel the first trial
might have been different. The jury retired at 11.30 p.m., the
judge having hinted broadly that, as he could not legally receive
a verdict on Sunday, they should agree before midnight. The
jury took the hint and were back at ten minutes to midnight
with a verdict that all five prisoners were not guilty.

On the following Monday, 20 April, Francis Branigan, William Brown and Richard Bryant were presented for Price's murder. Branigan told Mr Justice Barry that none of them could read the depositions. No counsel appeared for the defence when the trial began, but later Mr Milner Stephen announced he appeared for the prisoner Bryant. The evidence followed the pattern made familiar during the previous trials. The judge's attitude had hardened over the week-end, and the summing-up left no doubt of his opinion. After retiring for a quarter of an hour at 7 p.m. the jury returned to Court with its verdict: 'We find the prisoner Branigan guilty, most strongly recommending him to mercy. The other two prisoners guilty.' The judge asked what was the ground of the jury's recommendation to mercy, and the foreman replied that they understood from His Honour that the law required them to bring Branigan in guilty, but they believed he had not struck a blow.

The prisoner Bryant said he considered himself murdered; that he was not within thirty-five yards of Price when he was knocked down.

Mr Justice Barry then delivered a homily that was even more unworthy than his performance at the first trial. He said he had no doubt of the correctness of the verdict; they had all been engaged in the commission of an illegal act, and they were amenable for all its consequences, even though they did not originally contemplate that these should proceed to the length that they ultimately reached. He hoped Mr Price's successor would be equally considerate and humane. Public time had been wasted at a previous trial in investigating charges that were unfounded and fabricated. He hoped they would not abuse the privileges of the interval now afforded to them, but would make such preparations as it might be in their power to make for that awful change that awaited them. He then pronounced sentence of death upon the prisoners.

On the next day, Wednesday, 22 April, the remaining four prisoners, Daniel Donovan, John Chesley, James Anderson, and John Young, were presented for trial. The Attorney-General had led for the prosecution in the previous trials, but the final trial was left in the hands of Mr Sewell, junior counsel for the Crown. Mr Milner Stephen appeared for James Anderson, who was Australian-born, of good family. He came from Van Diemen's Land,

and was a first offender serving a sentence of five years' imprisonment for horse-stealing. Chief Warder Hyland gave damning
evidence against Chesley, who claimed that because of ulcerated
varicose veins he could not have played the active part ascribed
to him. When he heard of Chesley's bad legs, Mr Justice Barry
with ominous politeness asked him if he would like to sit down,
and Chesley replied, with equal courtesy, that he would later.
Chesley was well known to Price who, in his evidence to the
Legislative Assembly committee, had described his career in
crime.[16] Indeed, Chesley had escaped from Pentridge on one of
Price's horses, risking the fire of the sentries as he galloped between them, but his liberty was shortlived; he was recaptured
after a few hours. Chesley fought for his life, but the evidence
against him, which he vehemently insisted was false and fabricated in malice, was deadly. The Crown witnesses told their
stories again, and the prisoners called their fellow convicts and
made their piteous pleas to the jury. Mr Justice Barry summed
up, and the jury retired at 6.30 p.m. At seven o'clock the judge
sent for the jury and informed them that he could not receive
their verdict after midnight, but he would be available until
then. This was a broad hint that if the jury did not agree before
midnight, they would be locked up for the night. At half past
ten the jury returned to court with their verdict, finding Chesley
guilty, and the other three accused not guilty. In a moving
speech Chesley protested that he was as innocent of the murder
of John Price as any man breathing. Eager always to spread himself on such an occasion (his last and best remembered effort
was at the trial of Ned Kelly in October 1880),[17] Mr Justice
Barry delivered the third of his homilies. It was a great relief, he
said, that at the end of these protracted sittings he had to pass
the last sentence of the law on only one of the four accused. He
hoped the trials had done good. Only one influence could be
used in the management of the prisoners, that influence being
severity accompanied with unremitting vigilance. Still, severity
without justice would be cruelty, and to tolerate cruelty would
be abhorrent to the feelings of a British community. Price was
just, though severe. He told Chesley that he did not feel disposed to put his case favourably to the Executive. He then sentenced Chesley to death. After he had done so, the prisoner

Anderson thanked the jury and the judge and his counsel. The prisoner Young said, 'And so say I, John Young', and Donovan followed, 'And I, Daniel Donovan'.

It is tempting to discuss the trials, but it would serve no good purpose to do so. Mr Justice Barry's performance was that of a hanging judge, and his comments in sentencing the prisoners to death reveal that he entered upon the trials convinced of the guilt of the prisoners and of the desirability of hanging them by way of deterrent example. The verdicts of the different juries are hard to reconcile. It is very likely that some of the men who were acquitted were guilty, and that some of the men convicted were innocent, and that some of Price's assailants were not brought to trial at all. The trials were a demonstration of the authorities' determination to exact vengeance, and to instil fear by a dreadful example of retribution. In such circumstances, nicety of judgment is hardly to be expected.

Victoria had not yet achieved political stability, but there was no delay by the O'Shanassy government in deciding the sentences should be carried out. There were good reasons for discriminating between the prisoners, for Brown was a mere youth, and there was at least room for doubt that he had taken part in the mortal assault. Two of the condemned men, Henry Smith (No. 1794) and Branigan, had been strongly recommended to mercy. But within a week of the ending of the fourth and final trial, the hangman was busy in the most hideous week of hangings Victoria has known. The executions followed the order of the convictions. At 8 a.m. on 28 April Thomas Williams, aged 32, Henry Smith (alias Brennan), aged 37, and Thomas Maloney, aged 32, were hanged together at the Melbourne gaol. The next morning, Branigan, Bryant and Brown were hanged. The *Argus* reported that Branigan made a confession before he was hanged. He said he was the first man to attack the Inspector-General, whom he caught in his arms, and threw to the ground in the 'rush'; that Thomas Williams, executed the previous day, was the man who struck Price on the head with a shovel, and that the prisoner Brown and some others of the condemned men were innocent of any act of violence. Brown, described as a 'young and slight-made man', took longer to die than his companions. Chesley (whose name is given as Chisley in the official record of the executions) went alone to the gallows on 30 April, and the *Argus* noted that 'after an unusually protracted struggle the law was satisfied'.[18] According to the records in the Penal Department there had been another hanging, not connected with Price's murder, on 27 April, and thus eight men had met their deaths on the gallows within four days.[19] The tally was enough to glut the appetite of even the most fervent advocate of retributive justice.

This, then, is the appalling story of the slaying of John Price and the retribution exacted by the law. On any reasonable view, it appears fairly clear that the killing was not premeditated, but resulted from a mob impulse when, perhaps for the first and only time in his life, John Price showed irresolution before a group of convicts. Dr Wilkins, who performed the post-mortem examination, considered it was a blow that fractured the base of the skull that caused death, and this fracture was 'more likely to have been done by a blow from a stone' than from a shovel, so the actual killing was the horrible fruit of one man's violence. None of the other injuries, grave though they were, was of a kind likely to cause death. The events happened very quickly, and it is probable that each prisoner who struck Price, caught up in the contagious passion of the herd, was acting for himself and satisfying a personal grudge. It is clear, too, that initially the convicts' hatred was not directed against Price, but against the officials who actually had charge of them, and that the purpose in seeing Price was to have their grievances rectified. Despite later stories, such as the version by a notorious criminal, Henry Beresford Garrett, everything suggests that the attack on the Inspector-General was done on a sudden impulse and without prior arrangement, and that if he had not fallen he would not have been beaten to death.

There can be no doubt that among the men on the hulks were creatures who were capable of deeds of shocking violence and appalling cruelty. It was inevitable that few citizens should trouble whether these criminal proclivities were part of their make-up or were the product of brutalizing treatment; in a raw and unstable frontier society, law-abiding persons had ample reason to fear them, and fear begets hatred. Many of the convicts were not brutes. Indeed, apart from about sixty men who were not allowed ashore but were confined in similar fashion to the men on the *President,* the men from the *Success,* from whom Price's murderers were drawn, were regarded officially as much less dangerous than the convicts chained, day in and day out, in the fetid cells of the *President.* But in such a climate of feeling, there was little disposition to assess degrees of worthlessness; the men convicted of Price's murder were all wrongdoers who came from the hulks, and to the respectable citizen were all tarred with the same brush. The hangings were a naked assertion of the community's power, satisfying the lust for vengeance and providing an appalling example by way of deterrence, and in the ritual of deterrence it is the fate of the offender, and not the degree of his guilt, that is important. Furthermore, the killing of the head of the penal system challenged essential authority in a society where authority's hold was tenuous and insecure, and the challenge had to be met promptly and resolutely. The trial judge, bred in Ireland and all too familiar with the use of the criminal law as an instrument of swift coercion, accepted unquestioningly the theory of maximum severity. It is plain he entertained no doubts that public safety required that all the convicted men should be hanged by way of deterrent example, and it is equally plain the government was of the same mind. It is highly probable that Henry Kingsley, who came to Australia in 1853 and remained until the end of 1857, knew Price personally. He disclosed the extent of the public detestation of Price's murderers in a passage in *Ravenshoe,*[20] written in 1863, that reflects the general attitude to the felons charged with the murder. It runs, 'The incarnate devils who beat out poor Price's brains with their shovels, when they had the gallows before them, consistently perjured themselves in favour of the youngest of the seven, the young fiend who had hounded them on.' Kingsley's statement finds little support in the record of the trials; it derives from an emotional reaction of a kind that was inevitable in the circumstances and is easy to understand. The slaying of the Inspector-General by felons and the manner in which it was done were shocking and terrifying, intensifying every man's sense of insecurity. A dispassionate and impartial examination of the evidence and of the conditions that accounted for the outbreak (though, of course, they did not excuse it), could hardly be expected. Neither is it a matter for surprise that a century later, when the incident has become part of history and John Price a figure of legend, the version commonly accepted should be the story that society preferred in 1857.

Years earlier, when Price was still in command of Norfolk Island, the Rev. Thomas Rogers commented that Price had

comparatively more soldiers to overawe or coerce his 500 men than were formerly granted to Major Childs to overawe or coerce 18 or 1900 men . . . So exasperating was the conduct of the convict constables—so galling the manner in which Mr. Price thought fit to exercise his authority—so much was he abhorred by the prisoners in the gangs, that, unsupported, he could not have held them in subjection for forty-eight hours; he and the constables would have been massacred by the infuriated mob.[21]

It is doubtful if Rogers was right. In a sense, Price's death was an accident, the product of an unexpected and uncharacteristic irresolution on his part. It is not common for the keeper of dangerous animals to be killed by his charges, and so it is, too, with the keeper of desperate men. So long as the creatures subject to him are convinced of his mastery, he is invulnerable. He is protected, of course, by the mysterious psychological inhibitions that operate effectively to hold in check human beings who are subjected to the punitive mechanisms of society, but he will remain dominant only so long as he shows no weakness and no fear. Price's fatal error was that he turned his back on the mob and ran for safety. Once he lost his head in the face of an unexpected and unnerving situation, the group's mood changed in a flash from resentful submission to reckless savagery. Before authority could reassert itself, the more frenzied of the convicts had fallen upon the man who, though not the immediate object of their hatred, was nevertheless the symbol of the system that treated them as brutes. The really remarkable feature of the dreadful happening is that it was so soon over, and that Price's was the only death.

III   *The Bereaved*

Though the odds were in his favour until the fatal day in March, in a sense each day John Price lived dangerously. There was always a chance, remote but nevertheless real, that a crazed convict, goaded beyond endurance, would attempt to kill him. Price was arrogantly confident of his own ability to handle such a situation, and he had, too, the protection of his armed warders. But Mary Price must have gone in constant dread that he would die violently, and the children must have sensed the possibility, though perhaps familiarity with prison life throughout their impressionable years, and the fatalism of childhood, blunted the edge of a subconsciously-felt insecurity. The circumstances of their upbringing brought them early knowledge of evil things; men loaded with chains, working under the harshest conditions, were familiar sights, and within the narrow limits of Norfolk Island there could be no concealment of the horrible facts of the gallows and the lash. Yet two of the sons achieved careers of merit; like his father, the other met a violent death. One daughter elected to remain single, but the other two married well.

When she was widowed Mary Price was in her early forties. Her eldest son, John Frederick, was aged seventeen and a half; James Franklin had turned sixteen only the week before; Thomas Caradoc was fourteen and a half. Emily Mary was not yet thirteen; Anna Clara was approaching eleven and Jane de Winton was five. The prospect was frightening. During her marriage Mary Price had known the limited but comforting security that belongs to the wife of a senior government official, and her husband's position as a head of the penal system in Victoria assured her in Melbourne (though perhaps on a lesser scale) of the advantages of the free quarters, unpaid servants, and foodstuffs and services from convict labour, to which she had been used on Norfolk Island. Now all was changed. Price was not a man greatly concerned with money, and he left no property of consequence. He had not made a will, and on 11 June 1857 the Supreme Court of Victoria granted Letters of Administration of his meagre estate to Mrs Price. She deposed that it did not exceed in value £700.[22] Apparently Price had no estate in Tasmania, for a search of the records of the Supreme Court of Tasmania discloses no grant of administration in that colony. There was a fund created by a modest marriage settlement, and during her widowhood Mrs Price received the income. When she died her will, dated 13 July 1892, directed that the daughter, Emily Mary, should receive the income and that on Emily Mary's death, the fund should go equally to Anna Clara Hayward and Jane de Winton Knox, her two married daughters. Fortunately, the Victorian government recognized its moral obligation to make some provision for the widow of the Inspector-General; in 1857 she was paid £8,000, though there was no legislation authorizing the payment and no debate about it in Parliament.[23]

The children promised well, however, and except for James Franklin, fulfilled the promise. John Frederick was a diligent scholar; he was among the early students at the newly founded University of Melbourne, and in the 1861-2 calendar he is recorded in the list of officers and members of the university, which indicates he had taken out his Arts degree. He passed the Indian Civil Service examination in 1861, being probably the first from an Australian colony to do so. This determined his career; during thirty-five years he progressed through the civil service at Madras until he achieved the key position of Chief Secretary, which he held under various Governors for nine years. It is tempting but fruitless to speculate why he decided to serve in India; why, after gaining a C.S.I. in 1893, and a K.C.S.I. on retirement in 1898, he elected to be known as Sir Frederick instead of Sir John Price; and why he spent the long years of his retirement (he died in his eighty-eighth year) in England instead of Australia. He was a man of culture, editing the private diary of Ananda Ranga Pillai and writing a history of Ootamachund. He achieved what his father hoped for but had never managed; he spent his declining years in Trengwainton, amid constant reminders of the former glories of his eccentric grandfather, Sir Rose Price. There he died on 12 June 1927. He was buried in the family mausoleum at Madron.[24]

The bonds between the three Price boys must have been close, for both James Franklin and Thomas Caradoc made their way to India, possibly at the suggestion of their brother. James Franklin served in the Royal Indian Navy, but his path in life was far different from the decorous course followed by John Frederick. He returned to Australia, and linked up with Captain Francis Cadell. The latter's constructive work in pioneering the use of the River Murray and its tributaries for inland transportation was behind him, and he was in the dubious final phase of his adventurous career.[25] The schooner *Gem,* with Cadell as captain and James Franklin Price as second in command, presumably, put in for water at Badoo (or Mulgrave) Island late in July or early in August 1878. The *Gem* had been engaged, ostensibly, in pearl fishing. Price was in charge of a boatload of aborigines (some of them with their lubras), who had been engaged as divers. According to one account, the aborigines killed Price, and also 'a Chinaman, a Manilla man and a Kanaka' and made off with the boat. The full story was never ascertained, but one fact was certain; James Franklin Price, unmarried, died of violence at the age of thirty-seven.[26] Cadell did not long survive him; in the next year he was slain by his native crew.

Thomas Caradoc was an agreeable character, though he is best remembered for his direction to his troops, during the Melbourne maritime strike in 1890, that if they were given the command to fire on the strikers it would be their duty to do so, but they should 'fire low and lay them out'.[27] His claim that his order was intended to avoid fatal consequences is credible and in character. He entered a British military college in 1861 and served in India. Retiring in 1883 with the rank of Lieutenant-Colonel, he returned to Victoria, and was there employed to reorganize the colony's military forces. He founded the Victorian Mounted Rifles, thus providing the basis for the famous Australian Light Horse. In the Boer War he served with distinction, receiving a C.B. and the Queen's Medal, with five clasps. When he returned to Australia he was appointed to the command of the Victorian, and later the Queensland, military districts. He lived in retirement from 1904 until his death at Warrnambool, Victoria, on 3 July 1911. Preferring to be known as 'Tom' Price (his will, dated 25 July 1902, in which, amongst other things, he dealt with the disposal of his portion of his father's presentation silver dinner service, is signed 'Tom Price'), he was popular with his men, and was a competent and energetic officer. He was twice married, and though John Frederick had children the male descendants of John Price who carry the family name stem from Colonel Tom's first marriage.[28]

Emily Mary did not marry; she died, aged 77, on 27 June 1922. Anna Clara married a clergyman, the Rev. Ronald Hayward, in 1866. Her husband was the chaplain at the model prison at Port Arthur on Tasman's Peninsula, from 1869 until the Tasmanian government closed it in 1877. She and her husband then came to Victoria, where he was Anglican vicar at Inglewood for twenty-three years. Anna Clara lived on until 16 March 1941, when she died at the age of 95. In 1934, when she was in her eighty-eighth year, she was interviewed by the press, and gave an account of conditions on Norfolk Island when Price and his family arrived there in 1846, but she must have been speaking from family hearsay and not from genuine recollection, for she was then six months old and aged only seven years when the family left the island.[29]

The youngest daughter, Jane de Winton, married George Knox of Sydney on 5 July 1876. Her husband, who was an older brother of Sir Adrian Knox, Chief Justice of the High Court of Australia from 1919 to 1930, died in 1888. She survived him for almost fifty years, dying at Sidmouth, England, on 4 February 1937, in her eighty-fifth year.[30]

Mary Price died on 2 October 1894 at her home, Lindisfarne, Manning Road, Malvern.[31] She rests with her husband under the massive granite monument in the Melbourne General Cemetery. There, too, lie Emily Mary and Colonel Tom, and Colonel Tom's wife, Emmeline. The stone also bears an inscription in memory of one of Colonel Tom's sons, Vivian Franklin Lyon Price, Lieutenant-Commander, R.N., late Royal Indian Marines, who died on 5 November 1915, aged thirty-four, at Alexandria of illness contracted while serving on Anzac Beach.

Chapter Six

LEGEND

The stories told of John Price made him a legendary figure, even in his own lifetime. He knew it and gloried in it. It was at once satisfying to his vanity and useful in his daily affairs to be reputed omniscient and invulnerable. Over six feet tall and of magnificent physique, wearing a monocle in his left eye, clean-shaven except for side whiskers, and with his abundant reddish hair whitening along the parting on the right-hand side, his appearance commanded instant attention. He had, too, the easy authority of one accustomed to prompt obedience. Beneath a superficial urbanity there was a steely arrogance, and his affectations of manner gave no impression of weakness but had themselves an ominous quality. He was known to be ready to use any means, however merciless, to break a convict's spirit. Knowledgeable in every form of human wickedness and depravity, he possessed a strange fascination for many people, though more sensitive natures recoiled from him. The Legislative Assembly's Select Committee noted his 'singularly extensive and minute knowledge of individual criminals'. It was a knowledge gained during nearly twenty years of close contact with the corrupted and the debased. But his understanding of the degraded creatures over whom he held absolute sway was not merely professional; it was penetratingly intuitive, the result of a strange affinity between his warped and tigerish nature and the evil his convict charges personified. The fascination of his personality was not confined to the respectable elements in society; despite their hatred of him, the objects of his tyrannical discipline and his sardonic humour conceded 'John', as they called him out of his hearing, an unwilling but genuine admiration. He was a 'fly' man, and wherever criminals gathered, in the gaols or the stockades or the grog shanties, the man who had 'done time' under John could be sure of respectful attention; to have passed through the harsh

128

finishing schools of Norfolk Island and the hulks were creden-
tials that commanded the regard of the toughest among the
criminal class. In such company tales were told of his caprices, of
his terrifying rages, of his savage humour, of his merciless punishments, of the artfulness with which he exposed convict
stratagems, and of his relentless determination that no convict
should best or outwit him. Human love of the marvellous ensured that the tales lost nothing in the telling, but imaginative
embellishments usually found confirmation in incidents that had
actually happened.

Even if it were possible, it is doubtful whether it would be
worth the trouble to track down all the ephemeral material in
which Price finds a place. Hack writers short of a subject, jour-
nalists pandering to readers wth a taste for the sensational, story-
tellers seeking to shock or startle under the guise of moralizings,
have found the horrors of Norfolk Island and of the Victorian
hulks and the tragic retribution of Price's death rich in ready-
made material. There is little attempt in these writings to analyse
the man; he is depicted as a stern but just disciplinarian who
held vile creatures in subjection, or as a monster who wantonly
indulged his lust for cruelty. Much of the material is historically
worthless and misleading. The *Biographical Memoir of the late
Mr. John Price,* a compilation made in 1857 shortly after Price's
death by 'T.L.B.', a journalist whose identity cannot now be
ascertained, is an exception. The primary source of information
(extracted from the Melbourne *Argus*) about the circumstances
of Price's murder and the trials of the convicts, it is, too, the only
work purporting to give a complete biography of Price. It was
hastily put together to catch a market, however, and the author
relied mainly on hearsay and did not seem to have had access
to family material; its 'Life of Mr. John Price' is sketchy, adu-
latory and padded, and sometimes inaccurate. Of the personal
narratives, written after Price's death and ascribed to men who
knew Price, the most valuable is J. Lester Burke's *Martin Cash.*[1]
Cash was on Norfolk Island during the whole of the time Price
was there, and the account given in the two concluding chapters
of his 'ghosted' autobiography rings true, the more so because it
displays some insight into Price's character, and is told without
apparent bitterness. It differs in this respect from Henry Beres-

ford Garrett's recollections of Price.[2] Garrett, a confined criminal whose brazen exploits gave him some notoriety, had suffered under Price on Norfolk Island, and was serving a sentence on the *Success* when Price was murdered. In a 'portrait' called 'The Demon', written towards the end of his life (he died about 1885) while imprisoned in New Zealand, he gave his version of events connected with the murder. He claimed it was planned, but the manner of Price's death was different from what was intended; the plot was to hang him in a noose passed over the ridge-pole of a quarry tent. Garrett's story was not new, except in the details. On the Tuesday after Price's death, while the inquest was proceeding, the *Argus* carried a story that the murder was 'premeditated and planned', and that Price was to have been hanged from the cross-spars of a signal flagstaff, outside a shelter tent used by the convicts from the *Success,* at the upper end of the works tramway at Gellibrand Point. The report asserted that the police had possession of the rope it was intended to use. But the threat to hang officials was no novelty; Captain Blachford, superintendent of the *Lysander,* mentioned it at the inquest; he said, 'We—it is rumoured—were to have been hung up at the tent of the "Success"' if Melville and the convicts tried in the previous November for the murder of the warder Owen Owens had not been reprieved.[3] If Blachford knew of this wild threat, it is certain Price did too. It is not unlikely that some such harebrained scheme had been discussed among the convicts sustaining themselves with fantasies of revenge on their oppressors, but it is unbelievable that the sudden and spontaneous outbreak on 26 March was the fulfilment of such a plot, and no proof nor, indeed, any suggestion, was offered at the trials that it was.

From the standpoint of Australian literature, however, the enduring interest in Price lies elsewhere than in such concoctions. Price is important because two writers of stature freely used material relating to him in their works of fiction. In the first really great Australian novel, *For the Term of His Natural Life,* John Price was taken by Marcus Clarke as the prototype of the repulsive but unforgettable Maurice Frere, the merciless prison commandant. William Astley ('Price Warung') used him, too, in his short stories, once by name in 'John Price's Bar of Steel' (*Tales of the Old Regime* (Melbourne, 1897)), and elsewhere as the model for his fictional character, Mr Scragge, the Civil Commandant of Norfolk Island, in stories in *Tales of the Convict System* (Sydney, 1892) and *Tales of the Isle of Death* (Melbourne, 1898).

There are, of course, two versions of Marcus Clarke's novel. The novel as it appeared in serial form became available in 1929 as a book, published by Angus and Robertson, Sydney, but the text of the novel familiar to most readers is an abridged and recast version of the serial. It is from the original serial that it appears most clearly that Clarke based Captain Frere on John Price, though there is ample evidence, too, in the abridged version. As he himself claimed,[4] Clarke prepared himself by extensive research to write *His Natural Life,* as the novel was known until, after his death, the longer title was adopted in 1885.[5] The appendix of source references in the abridged version, though Clarke's biographer, Brian Elliott, regards it as a 'sketchy statement of his authorities', represents extensive and precisely relevant reading. These references, Clarke's two pages of notes for *His Natural Life,* the text itself and the page footnotes in the unabridged version, establish beyond doubt Clarke's use of Price as a model. Clarke's notes contain the entry, '1841 Norfolk for life—Horrors there, brutalities (see parson's book P.L. and Price).'[6] The 'parson's book' is the *Correspondence relating to the Dismissal of the Rev. T. Rogers from His Chaplaincy at Norfolk Island,* mentioned in footnotes in the 1929 Angus and Robertson edition and in the appendix of the abridged edition.[7] 'P.L.' in the note presumably means 'Public Library', where Clarke would have seen a copy of that rare publication. Moreover, in the unabridged version, Captain Maurice Frere's career parallels Price's in significant respects. When Frere leaves Norfolk Island he comes to Victoria as Inspector-General of Penal Establishments. At Pentridge, he uses the punishment of the stone—'a punishment which consisted simply of making a prisoner sit chained and handcuffed, on a big stone, doing nothing, and eating nothing until he gave in'.[8] He is 'rushed' (though at Pentridge stockade and not at Williamstown) by a mob of convicts and so severely beaten with shovels, stones and kicked with iron-shod heels, that he dies of his injuries.[9]

The material for the diary of the Rev. James North in the

Norfolk Island section is drawn partly from Robert Pringle Stewart's report, made in June 1846, but mainly from Rogers' *Correspondence*. For example, the incident in which the blind prisoner Mooney* is gagged with a piece of iron-wood and chained upright to a post, is narrated in the fictional diary of the Rev. James North, under 4 November, in almost the same language as Rogers uses.[10] Indeed, many of the horrible incidents in the portion of the novel dealing with Norfolk Island are taken almost word for word from Rogers, as may be seen by comparing Book IV of the usual edition (or Book Five of the 1929 edition) with the extracts from Rogers' book quoted in chapter 3 of this work. The characters in Clarke's book are thinly disguised; for example, Earle, the stipendiary magistrate, is Samuel Barrow, and Eastwood, the berserk convict, is 'Jacky-Jacky' Westwood. Incidentally, a mysterious feature is the absence of any known reaction by Rogers to Clarke's novel, in which the Rev. James North is depicted as a periodic dipsomaniac, which Rogers certainly was not. When the novel was appearing in serial form it is probable that both Clarke and Rogers were living in Melbourne; undoubtedly Rogers was when later editions of the book were published. Clarke died on 2 August 1881, and Rogers almost twenty-two years later. Though they lived in the same city, there is nothing to suggest that Clarke knew Rogers, but Rogers must have recognized the use Clarke had made of his detailed indictment of Price; he must have seen that the clash of personalities between Frere and North was an adaptation of the conflict between Price and himself. His silence is strange, particularly as he was himself engaged in journalism. It is remarkable, too, that, so far as can now be discovered, neither Price's widow nor any of his children made any public utterance about the novel.

Like Price, Frere is 'celebrated for his knowledge of convict tricks and wickednesses' and he, too, is disappointed in his ex-

---

*'Blind' (or 'Black') Mooney finished his days in an asylum for criminal lunatics in Macquarie Street, Hobart (see 'The Captain' (T. G. Ford), *Inhumanity, Historical Tales of the Convict Days* (Hobart, 1932), p. 39). He was a lunatic at Port Arthur when Marcus Clarke visited the prison in 1870. See Bill Wannan (ed.), *A Marcus Clarke Reader* (Melbourne, 1963), pp. 142-3; Marcus Clarke, *Stories of Australia* (London, 1897), p. 195.

pectation of a substantial legacy.[11] The description in North's diary of Frere also fits Price neatly:

His face is ruddy, his eyes bright, his voice firm and ringing. He must be a man of considerable strength and—I should say—of more than ordinary animal courage and animal appetite. There is not a nerve in his body that does not twang like a piano wire. In appearance he is tall, broad and bluff, with red whiskers and reddish hair slightly touched with grey. His manner is loud, coarse, and imperious; his talk of dogs, horses, cocks, and convicts.[12]

Of the many stories about Price, two are given in differing versions by various writers. Clarke uses both of them. He introduces the first when Frere visits Sydney, which, as a matter of history, Price never did.[13]

One anecdote concerning the method by which he shepherded his flock will suffice to show his character and his value. It was his custom to visit the prison-yard at Hyde Park Barracks twice a week. Visitors to convicts were, of course, armed, and the two pistol-butts that peeped from Frere's waistcoat attracted many a longing eye. How easy would it be for some fellow to pluck one forth and shatter the smiling, hateful face of the noted disciplinarian! Frere, however, brave to rashness, never would bestow his weapons more safely, but lounged through the yards with his hands in the pockets of his shooting-coat, and the deadly butts ready to the hand of anyone bold enough to take them.

One day a man named Kavanagh, a captured absconder, who had openly sworn in the dock the death of the magistrate, walked quickly up to him as he was passing through the yard, and snatched a pistol from his belt. The yard caught its breath, and the attendant warder, hearing the click of the lock, instinctively turned his head away, so that he might not be blinded by the flash. But Kavanagh did not fire. At the instant when his hand was on the pistol, he looked up and met the magnetic glance of Frere's imperious eyes. An effort, and the spell would have been broken. A twitch of the finger, and his enemy would have fallen dead. There was an instant when that twitch of the finger could have been given, but Kavanagh let that instant pass. The dauntless eye fascinated him. He played with the pistol nervously, while all remained stupefied. Frere stood, without withdrawing his hands from the pockets into which they were plunged.

'That's a fine pistol, Jack', he said at last.

Kavanagh, down whose white face the sweat was pouring, burst into a hideous laugh of relieved terror, and thrust the weapon, cocked as it was, back again into the magistrate's belt.

Frere slowly drew one hand from his pocket, took the cocked pistol and levelled it at his recent assailant. 'That's the best chance *you'll* ever get, Jack', said he.

Kavanagh fell on his knees. 'For God's sake, Captain Frere!'

Frere looked down on the trembling wretch, and then uncocked the pistol, with a laugh of ferocious contempt. 'Get up, you dog,' he said. 'It takes a better man than you to best me. Bring him up in the morning, Hawkins, and we'll give him five-and-twenty.'

As he went out—so great is the admiration for power—the poor devils in the yard cheered him.[14]

Price's friend Major de Winton told a similar story in his reminiscences. In his account, published long after both Price and Clarke were dead, the incident happened on Norfolk Island. Against warnings, Price enters the cell of a prisoner who has sworn to kill him. The prisoner seizes a pistol from Price's belt and aims it at him. As de Winton described it,

Price drew another pistol from the back of his coat, and fixing the prisoner with his eye, calmly said: 'drop it—this pistol is loaded, that is not'. The prisoner dropped his pistol and slunk back in his cell. Questioning Price afterwards as to which pistol was loaded, he smiled and I did not pursue the inquiry. I believe both were.[15]

Such stories about harsh prison commandants are not uncommon; even so sceptical an observer as Alexis de Tocqueville narrates a similar incident about Elam Lynds, the dreaded superintendent of Sing Sing. In that story Lynds requires a convict who has boasted he would murder him to shave him with an open-bladed razor. The convict does so, and when he fails to seize the chance to cut Lynds' exposed throat, he is dismissed with the contemptuous remark, 'Single and unarmed, I am always stronger than you are.'[16] Legends (and history) are made of such stuff. Probably the genesis of the story about Price is supplied by the author of the *Biographical Memoir of the late Mr. John Price.* In that version, on an occasion on Norfolk Island when Price appears with a brace of pistols in his belt, a 'new hand' urges that prisoners should rush him and seize them. The suggestion is turned down with the comment, 'Don't you believe Price is such a fool as that. They are only dummies outside; the real things are in his pocket.'[17]

Clarke used the other story for an incident where Frere taunts a recalcitrant and starving prisoner, 'Ha, Jack, wouldn't you like a nice beefsteak now? A brown juicy fellow, hey? with onions, hey?'[18] Major de Winton described (with doubtful veracity) an incident on Norfolk Island concerning Price's treatment of a violent prisoner who went on a hunger-strike on instructions from 'On High'. To prevent him from starving himself to death (though why the Commandant should have been perturbed about such a possibility is not made clear), Price prepares 'a juicy beef steak, well garnished with onions'. Taking it to the prisoner in his cell, he says, 'I have a message for you. The ban is off—you may eat—and, see, here is something sent to you to begin with.' The stratagem is successful.[19] Curiously, the steak and onions story figured in the accusation made by the Citizens' Committee against Price, but the incident was located at Pentridge. At the public meeting on 29 December 1856 at which the Citizens' Committee's Report to the Citizens of Melbourne was read, Mr Kerr spoke of the case of Thomas Porter, 'who after being chained for nine weeks to a stone had been brutally taunted by Mr Price, being asked how he would like some beef steaks and onions and some porter and tobacco . . . Mr. Price was represented to have stated to a prisoner named Whitmarsh that it was no use his praying to his God, for he (Price) was God of Pentridge.'[20] It is likely that the true story of the incident was told by the Rev. Dean O'Hea, who was the Catholic chaplain at Pentridge.

'One morning', said the rev. gentleman, 'I met Mr. Price going to make his daily visit to the "Palace". He said, 'Come with me I want to speak to these prisoners in your presence.' When we arrived at the place where a notorious prisoner was chained to one of the wheels of the hut, Mr. Price said, 'Now, Father O'Hea, I wish to speak to this man before you as a clergyman.' Then, turning to the man, he said, 'Will you promise before Father O'Hea, to go to work and conduct yourself properly for the future? If so, I will have you released immediately; for would it not be advisable to complete your sentence as soon as possible, and so be your own master again? Then you could have good beefsteak and onions for breakfast, instead of being chained to that wheel.' This advice was declined by the prisoner, who used most insulting language to Mr. Price, when the latter said, 'Now, Father O'Hea, what am I to do with prisoners of this kind; it is not my wish to be unnecessarily severe with them, but in my position as head of the department, I must not allow any of them to conquer me?'[21]

The sparse prison diet did not include steak and onions for breakfast, and doubtless the prisoner's intransigence was confirmed rather than lessened by the extraordinary suggestion, the more so if he understood the breakfast was to await his release.

Undoubtedly Price Warung was well versed in the official documents of the convict system as well as in the legends, true or fabricated, that clustered around it. In the preface to his first volume, *Tales of the Convict System,* he described the stories as 'the first fruits, in literary form, of nearly twenty years' study and investigation of the sources of Australian history'. He admits intentional anachronisms, which is, to say the least, an understatement. His method was to take some incident, actual or legendary, and build his story around it. Mr Scragge, the Civil Commandant of Norfolk Island, first appears as a leading character in 'The Commandant's Picnic Party' and 'The Special Commission'. The latter story is based on the trial of 'Jacky-Jacky' Westwood and others in 1846, just after Price had come to the island. Mr Scragge's mannerisms are a caricature of Price's, but his heartlessness accords with Price's reputation. Scragge appears in all the stories in *Tales of the Isle of Death.* Two of them, 'The Crime of Convict Cunliffe' and 'The Consequence of Cunliffe's Crime', revolve around the third visit to the island by Bishop Willson (who is named in the stories) in 1852, and the clash that led him to tell Price he would recommend the removal of all prisoners from the island. However, the most penetrating study of Price is in 'John Price's Bar of Steel', in *Tales of the Old Regime.* The characters are Price, the Comptroller-General of Convicts, Dr J. S. Hampton, a convict house-servant, Daniel (Danny) Duncan, and Price's son, a toddler at the prattling stage. The anachronisms are obvious; Hampton first visited the island in 1848, the youngest boy, Gustavus Lambart, who was three when he died in July 1853, was not born until 1849 or 1850, and none of Price's other sons was then a toddler. The convict has taught the child a new 'prayer' which he is to say only to his father. In Hampton's presence, the child, as he kneels before his father, repeats the 'prayer'. It is, 'God, p'ease damn John Price'. Hampton is curious to know how Price will

revenge himself on the prisoner. He has not long to wait. At a
muster three days later, Price discovers Duncan (so he asserts) is
in possession of 'a bar of steel, a dangerous weapon specially
prohibited by regulation to be in the possession of pris'ners'. In
truth, the 'bar of steel' is a common sewing needle stuck in
Duncan's coat. Price had contrived to have the child take the
needle to the convict, who was making sails for the toddler's toy
boat. Duncan is summarily charged with the offence of carrying
a dangerous weapon, and Price sentences him to fifty lashes and
the most dreaded of punishments, work in the wet quarry for
six months. The story is artificial and unconvincing but it contains, in the following passage,[22] 'Price Warung's' judgment upon
John Price:

A born captain of men, and knowing the seamy side of human
nature, as (to the evil Deities' sorrow) few men who have visited
these colonies have done, he was so constituted as to intensely enjoy
every form of physical beauty. In the midst of any scenic splendour,
or in the presence of finely-proportioned man, convicted or not, or
beautiful women, he would forget even to fix his eyeglass; and the
hard grey of his eyes would lose that dreadful faculty of penetration
in which consisted the main source of his power over the convict
creature and the newer penal official. And when John Price's face
lost the use of the stony stare of the crystal disc, and the metallic
keenness of the unveiled eye, then John Price was not himself.
    There were frequent moments when he was not himself. Take
any of the sparse convict survivors of the Old Régime, or any of the
scarcely more numerous representatives of the subordinate Penal
Officialdom, and they would deny this. They would assert that John
Price was never aught but himself—that is to say, the sternest of
disciplinarians, the most sceptical of moralists, the most saturnine of
humorists, and the most exquisite of torturers. That drawing of him
is about as true in perspective as that other picture limned by the
partial hand of superior officers and of personal friends, in which the
figure of the Commandant stands clothed with a majesty of character
little short, considering his temptations, of saintliness. John Price
was neither a saint, nor yet of that high degree among demons
which would entitle him to a shout of 'Hail, brother!' from the
sovereign and princes of the damned on his entrance into the
Nether World. He was, truly, a many-sided man, the majority of
whose facets were, unfortunately for himself, shaped by the planing-
steel of the System. The System put under its knife the material
which, under other conditions, wielded as a sword against the
nation's enemies, would have formed a general of inspired audacity,

a leader of dauntless courage, and an administrator of unerring prescience. But—the Fates were just! If there was scarcely a convict whom the System and the Régime did not spoil more or less, neither did they spare the officials. And as John Price, from his varied service in three colonies, was the instrument of contamination to more destinies than was any other administrator, it was only to be expected that the loss he personally suffered should have exceeded that of all other servants of the System. The life which might have ended at the doors of Westminster Abbey was miserably let out by a felon's hand on Williamstown Pier. He whom the System created, died by the System. Which was justice according to the System.[22]

Chapter Seven

ON CRUELTY

John Price was truly a complex character, and his story is worth telling, if only because of the notoriety that surrounded him in the dying days of the convict system. But his life has a deeper interest. St Paul remarked that whatsoever a man soweth, that shall he also reap. Doubtless the *Age* leader-writer had this grim prediction in mind when, commenting on Price's murder, he asserted bluntly, 'The whole affair lies in a nutshell. He was a cruel man, and his cruelty came back to him.' Was this a fair assessment? Was John Price in truth a cruel man? Certainly he did not think of himself in that way. A firm disciplinarian, yes; severe, perhaps, and at times even harsh. Yet his letter justifying what even the Hobart Town authorities regarded as the excessive use of the lash, and the explanations he gave when he was a witness before the Select Committees in 1857, show he would have angrily denied any charge that he was cruel. That, of course, does not dispose of the matter; to be stigmatized as cruel is the gravest of human condemnations, and it is hardly to be expected Price would admit he was cruel, even if, privately, he recognized he was.

It is worthwhile pausing to examine what is meant by an accusation of cruelty and what lies behind this peculiarly human characteristic. 'Cruel' and 'cruelty' are used loosely in daily speech. In matrimonial law, a married person whose conduct causes misery and injury to the other spouse's health may be adjudged guilty of cruelty, even though there was no intention to behave cruelly.[1] But this is an artificial meaning, a judicial extension which equates cruelty with ill-treatment. Even the dictionary is misleading when it defines cruel as 'indifferent to, delighting in, another's pain'. To delight in another's suffering is the hall-mark of cruelty; but while indifference to another's pain is reprehensible, it does not constitute cruelty, though it may be a strong indication of a propensity to it.

An event involving the infliction of physical cruelty requires at least two participants, a human being who is the agent, or, more specifically, the aggressor, and another sentient creature who is the patient, or victim. It requires, too, that the aggressor should actually carry into effect an intention to use physical violence designed to produce a sensation of pain in the victim, and that he should desire the victim's suffering. He may do so by personally inflicting pain on the victim, or he may use the services of one or more human beings (or even animals) to do so. His action must be gratuitous in the sense that there must be no legitimate purpose or justification for the imposition of the suffering, or, if there is a colour of justification, the occasion must be used primarily for the gratification of the aggressor, and not genuinely for a permissible purpose, such as domestic or magisterial correction, or the exaction of a legal sentence. The school teacher who seizes upon a minor dereliction as a pretext to thrash a pupil unmercifully, or the person with authority to award corporal punishment who directs, capriciously or arbitrarily, a flogging or other form of physical agony, misuses power for his own gratification, and is properly regarded as acting cruelly. Furthermore, a person who holds a position of authority, as, for instance, a judge or a headmaster or a superintendent of a correctional or penal institution, and who gets pleasure from ordering the infliction of pain is rightly described as cruel, even when the order is lawfully made, and so is the person who administers the punishment if he derives personal satisfaction from inflicting it. In correct language, there is no such thing as unconscious cruelty; the phrase is a contradiction in terms, for cruelty requires a positive mental state, a decision made deliberately and intentionally, and without reasonable justification, to inflict suffering upon another sentient creature, or, if there is justification, to derive a personal gratification from doing so.

With poetic insight, William Blake said cruelty has a human heart.[2] The capacity for cruelty is found only in the human being and of all human failings it is the most evil. Only the human mind can conceive cruelty; none but the human being is capable of deriving conscious satisfaction from the infliction of intellectually conceived suffering on other beings, including his own kind. It has been remarked acutely that wild animals never kill for sport; that man is the only one in whom the torture and death of his fellow creatures is amusing in itself.[3] A cat with a mouse, and sometimes a wild beast with its prey, may seem to inflict suffering wantonly upon their victims. But the conduct of the so-called lower animals is either instinctive or conditioned. There is no intellectual awareness of the agonies of the victim. Empathy, or the capacity for identifying oneself with another person in such a fashion as to comprehend that person's feelings, is peculiar to man; it finds no counterpart in other animal creatures. Why is it that man, alone among sentient beings, derives conscious satisfaction and enjoyment from performing or witnessing cruel acts? What are the physiological and psychological factors producing this uniquely human trait?

The only reliable measure of mankind's improvement is the growth and enlargement of compassion; human progress and happiness depend upon confining the expression of cruelty within the narrowest limits, in the wistful hope that ultimately it may be eliminated. Non-violent cruelty, resulting in the deliberate imposition of mental suffering without physical pain, will probably always feature in human relationships where there is an element of dependency. This chapter, however, is not directed to that deplorable aspect of man's nature; it is concerned with cruelty involving the infliction of physical agony.

In every generation in every community there are authenticated tales of appalling cruelty by individuals to one another, but it is when one is confronted with the record of torture and of agonized death, inflicted by direction of Church or State as officially approved means of interrogation and of community vengeance, that one comes close to despairing of the human race. When force takes the place of persuasion, human suffering is looked on with indifference, and soon the short step from indifference to enjoyment is taken. There is a passage in Lea's *History of the Inquisition of the Middle Ages* that is a sufficient reminder of European experience before the twentieth century:

We have only to look upon the atrocities of the criminal law of the Middle Ages to see how pitiless men were in their dealings with each other. The wheel, the caldron of boiling oil, burning alive, burying alive, flaying alive, tearing apart with wild horses, were the ordinary expedients by which the criminal jurist sought to deter crime by frightful examples which would make a profound impression on a not over-sensitive population. An Anglo-Saxon law punishes a female slave convicted of theft by making eighty other female slaves each bring three pieces of wood and burn her to death, while each contributes a fine besides; and in mediaeval England burning was the customary penalty for attempts on the life of the feudal lord. In the Customs of Arques, granted by the Abbey of St. Bertin in 1231, there is a provision that, if a thief have a concubine who is his accomplice, she is to be buried alive; though, if pregnant, a respite is given till after childbirth. Frederic II, the most enlightened prince of his time, burned captive rebels to death in his presence, and is even said to have encased them in lead in order to roast them slowly. In 1261 St. Louis humanely abolished a custom of Touraine by which the theft of a loaf of bread or a pot of wine by a servant from his master was punished by the loss of a limb. In Frisia arson committed at night was visited with burning alive; and, by the old German law, the penalty of both murder and arson was breaking on the wheel. In France women were customarily burned or buried alive for simple felonies, and Jews were hung by the feet between two savage dogs, while men were boiled to death for coining. In Milan Italian ingenuity exhausted itself in devising deaths of lingering torture for criminals of all descriptions. The *Carolina,* or criminal code of Charles V., issued in 1530, is a hideous catalogue of blinding, mutilation, tearing with hot pincers, burning alive, and breaking on the wheel. In England poisoners were boiled to death even as lately as 1542, as in the cases of Rouse and Margaret Davie; the barbarous penalty for high treason—of hanging, drawing, and quartering—is well known, while that for petty treason was enforced no longer ago than 1726, on Catharine Hayes, who was burned at Tyburn for murdering her husband. By the laws of Christian V. of Denmark, in 1683, blasphemers were beheaded after having the tongue cut out. As recently as 1706, in Hanover, a pastor named Zacharie Georg Flagge was burned alive for coining. Modern tenderness for the criminal is evidently a matter of very recent date. So careless were legislators of human suffering in general that, in England, to cut out a man's tongue, or to pluck out his eyes with malice prepense, was not made a felony until the fifteenth century, in a criminal law so severe that, even in the reign of Elizabeth, the robbing of a hawk's nest was similarly a felony; and as recently as 1833 a child of nine was sentenced to be hanged for breaking a patched pane of glass and stealing twopence worth of paint.[4]

The literature describing physical cruelty in all its dreadful manifestations began when man learned to record what he observed, and its extent is immense and its substance horrifying.[5] In particular the last four decades of human history have produced additions, appalling in their number and shocking in their content, to the melancholy history of man's inhumanity to man. But this literature is mainly descriptive; even the specialized works about human monsters and psychopathological aspects of sexuality content themselves in the main with connecting the atrocious conduct with clinically established psychoses or mental abnormalities.

Cruelty is so constant in human history that it has about it an aspect almost of naturalness and inevitability. But is cruelty a natural and inevitable attribute of man? Here it is possible only to speculate about the answer, and the question is posed largely in the hope that others better qualified may undertake the enquiry, for it is surprising that in all the literature about cruelty so little attention has been paid to this basic problem. This is so, perhaps, because it is only in relatively recent times we have begun painstakingly to gather together verified information about man's evolution and the most mysterious of his organs, his brain. If it be true that fear and rage originate in the primitive brain, but are under the control of the cortex,[6] it may be that the enigma can be profitably investigated. The primary and fundamental aggressive drives of the individual organism are towards survival and the perpetuation of the species. The expression of these urges involves an attempt to achieve mastery, whether of environment or of other creatures, and thus the will to power is biologically necessary. Havelock Ellis noted that the impulse to exert power is one of man's primary and fundamental urges, which tends to manifest itself in the attitude of the human male towards the woman he loves; and, it may be added, if circumstances are favourable, towards the enemy he fears and hates. Ellis concluded that the morbid infliction of pain upon a sexual partner and terrible and repugnant acts of sexual perversion, though themselves abnormal and sometimes grossly so, are linked to phenomena that are fundamentally normal.[7]

The verifiable fact that intense satisfaction is gained through practices that inflict pain upon the sexual partner has resulted in a theory that cruelty is to be explained as a manifestation of morbid aberrations of the normal sexual impulse. Unless the sexual act is a simple exercise in lust, however, there are usually present other elements that redeem the conduct and deprive it of the characteristic of cruelty. Havelock Ellis rightly stresses this aspect:

'Sadism' and 'masochism' are simply convenient clinical terms for classes of manifestations which quite commonly occur in the same person . . . it is scarcely correct to use the word 'cruelty' in connection with the phenomena we have been considering. The persons who experience these impulses usually show no love of cruelty outside the sphere of sexual emotion; they may even be very intolerant of cruelty. Even when their sexual impulses come into play they may still desire to secure the pleasure of the persons who arouse their sexual emotions, even though it may not be often true that those who desire to inflict pain at these moments identify themselves with the feelings of those on whom they inflict it . . . Our conclusion . . . must be that under certain abnormal circumstances pain, more especially the mental representation of pain, acts as a powerful sexual stimulant.[8]

The lively curiosity of H. G. Wells led him to speculate upon the connection between cruelty and the desire for sexual mastery, and to reject the theory that the satisfaction of sexual appetites was a sufficient explanation. In one of his last essays, *'42 to '44*, he wrote:

One has to distinguish between a simple form of sexual perversion and a deeper craving to be cruel for cruelty's own sake. The two things may have a psychological inter-relation, but I am doubtful about that. In what we should call a normal sexual affair there seems to be a desire, which is typically but not necessarily on the feminine side, to have a resistance overpowered, to be 'taken', as the phrase goes. There is no aversion from a certain rough masterfulness. As people go on with intercourse, especially if it does not discharge its energy normally in offspring, the reaction becomes jaded and demands elaboration. Odd attitudes, strange costumes and methods of approach are tried, and among others there is whipping, to whip the excitement. That is the end in view, and most of this stuff about sadism, masochism and so forth, as one may learn from the writings of the Marquis de Sade, is merely such elaboration. The reality of human cruelty and torture lies much deeper than that.[9]

Plainly he was right in his broad conclusion, but the theory he proffered that cruelty was a product of human 'congestion' is also inadequate. He considered that when human beings ceased to be nomads and became agriculturalists, the increase in the means of subsistence led to an increase in human numbers, bringing individuals into a closeness of contact for which their past had not prepared them. With urban life, human communities became

jostling *crowds* in which quite unprecedented reactions were possible. They were 'masses' whose enslavement by masterful groups and individuals was inevitable . . . [Cruelty] may have been latent in the Hominidae before the congestion of mankind by agriculture, or, what I think is more probable, it may have been produced by the incessant irritation of jostling in a confused *slum of unassimilated individuals* . . . *Cruelty is the human response to cruelty, and that is all our mental constitution will allow it to produce.*[10]

The suggestion that cruelty derives from 'congestion' is, however, no explanation. It leaves unanswered the central question, why does a human being find it agreeable to express, by the deliberate infliction of pain, the irritation caused by congestion? It would seem, too, that mere congestion (if it really existed except in over-crowded cities at a relatively late stage of human development) is not sufficient to produce irritation. The irritating factor is surely the competition to survive in conditions that imperilled survival. With animals it is true that the normal consequence of a sudden intrusion upon physical integrity (even if accidental) is prompt retaliation by violent measures. The caged bird will respond by an intentional peck to an accidental jostling from a companion on the perch, the dog suddenly disturbed by unintended violence from a stranger with a snarl and a snap. Indeed, animals seem normally to treat any unexpected physical violence as hostile in intent. This, presumably, is because violence is a threat to survival. The aggressive reaction is instinctive, and the immediate awakening and assertion of the instinct of self-preservation is primarily a response to fear engendered by an event that threatens (or appears to threaten) the individual. Fear begets violent measures where the individual organism has the capacity to respond by violence, and it has been truly said that there is nothing that man fears more than the touch of the unknown.[11] The vigour of the response will be roughly proportionate to the fear excited and the capacity to retaliate; if the fear is intense, there will be no moderation in retaliation, but a savage attempt to destroy. The reaction is biological and originates in the primitive brain, and man shares with the rest of the animal world the primeval impulse to respond violently by way of self-protection. If the reaction is successful, there is relief from tension and a sense of satisfaction, and in man it may result in intellectual consciousness of mastery over the intruder. This feeling is pleasurable, and once enjoyed, may be sought again even when there is no provocation. The human tendency is towards excess in situations from which pleasure is derived, and, as with sexual perversions, the emotional satisfaction gained from the infliction of intellectually conceived cruelty may in truth be a depraved aberration of a normal biological impulse. And, unfortunately, once an aberration is established the desire to satisfy the impulse frequently exhibits greater urgency and intensity than does the normal impulse.

Successful cruelty is always a manifestation of power, for it can be inflicted only by an aggressor with power or mastery over the victim. Probably it has an origin different from the impulse to inflict pain in achieving sexual satisfacton, but in each the urge to hurt is a manifestation of the desire for mastery, of the wish to exert power over another creature. The factors that operate to pervert a normal biological impulse so that it expresses itself in torturing a victim are all associated with fear and its misshapen offspring, anxiety, but the association is frequently difficult to recognize.[12] However arrogantly he may carry himself, the oppressor walks in fear, and it has been truly said that fear is the parent of cruelty.[13] This is so whether the oppressor be a paranoiac tyrant whose power enables him to torment and slaughter thousands, or a prison commandant who can exercise despotic power over his outcast charges without significant risk of being called to account for his conduct.

We exalt ourselves by debasing others, and the corrupting effects of despotic authority ('naked power', as Bertrand Russell has called it)[14] are peculiarly likely to manifest themselves in the capricious infliction of physical torment. Archbishop Ullathorne, with extensive experience of the convict system in Australia, remarked, 'It grows natural in men who have to control bodies of criminals, and who are often provoked, to prefer a sharp and decisive instrument like the lash . . . A discretion of this sort is liable to throw off its restraints.'[15] But the appalling happenings in the prisons of the secret police, and in the concentration camps that have polluted the earth's surface since a power-crazed tyrant, Napoleon, first used them, have shown that for the most horrifying inhumanities to occur it is not essential that the victims should bear the social stigma of criminality determined by legal processes. All that is required is a propensity to enjoy the infliction of pain (an appetite that will grow by what it feeds on), coupled with the opportunity for gratifying it that arises from unconstrained authority over an outcast and helpless minority, whether the outcasts be criminals, or lunatics, or children in institutions, or Jews, or prisoners of war, or political or religious dissidents.

The descriptions given by the Rev. Thomas Rogers and by Bishop Willson, the excessive use of the lash during the closing years of his command of Norfolk Island, and the conditions on the hulks (particularly the *President*) which he refused to ameliorate, establish that John Price was constantly guilty of cruelty. The measures he used to inflict grievous physical suffering upon convicts subjected to his discipline went beyond what was reasonably necessary to maintain control, and were designed to serve another and more sinister end. The Rev. Rogers, Bishop Willson, and Dr Singleton all noted Price's overbearing manner if his authority was challenged. His determination to achieve and maintain mastery is clearly revealed by a multiplicity of instances in Norfolk Island and in Victoria. Rogers and Singleton noted that 'old lags' appeared to receive preferential treatment. That was consistent with Price's domineering nature, for, made wise by harsh experience, they accepted his dominance. Their obsequiousness was incense to his nostrils, constant proof of the reality of his power, and when it was lacking there was always the proof positive that cruel punishments provided. An historian of penal methods, George Ives, commented,

In some respects [Price] was a man of good parts; he had a light, easy way with him, and an eye-glass; he was a man of courage and quick resolve; but he was also one of those human tigers who, if they cannot obtain some uniform to cover their crimes, are apt to get hanged for them, or at any rate to come to a violent end . . .[16]

This judgment may seem harsh, but there is enough justification to make it uncomfortably close to the truth. On the whole of the record, John Price was a cruel man.

APPENDIX A

COMMENTS ON HENRY BERESFORD GARRETT'S
'THE DEMON'

Although I had seen what purported to be extracts from the unpublished manuscript of 'The Demon', the full text did not become available to me until after I had completed revising the typescript of this book. After reading it critically, I think Garrett's essay deserves to be published in full, but only in a context that would enable the reader to form a judgment upon its reliability. Garrett's hatred of Price comes through every page, and for this reason, as well as others that are obvious, his account must be received with great caution.

The secondary sources containing information about Garrett are mostly of little worth, and none can be regarded as accurate. The story of his New Zealand activities, told by Robert Gilkison in *Early Days in Central Otago,* contains mistakes, and the account he gives of Garrett's early life cannot be relied on. After describing Garrett's bushranging exploits in New Zealand, Gilkison devotes a chapter to 'Garrett, the Maungatua Bushranger'. According to this version, Garrett was born in Leicestershire in 1813, and entered the army as a youth; he stabbed an officer in a fit of passion and was transported when a 'mere boy' to Norfolk Island. An account by another writer tells the tale differently; it states that during a voyage to New South Wales to join the New South Wales Corps, maddened by constant taunting, he seized a sword and killed a lieutenant. These stories are fanciful, and the assertion that he was sent to Norfolk Island when a youth cannot be true. On Garrett's own story he was not there when Alexander Maconochie was in charge of the penal settlement, and he must have arrived at some time after Major Childs became Commandant in February 1844. A note in the files of the New Zealand Department of Justice states he was born in 1819, which would make him then at least twenty-five years old, and if Gilkison is right in giving the year of his birth at 1813, he was thirty-two.

Mr John P. Kennedy, by whose foresight copies of Garrett's manuscripts have been preserved, says that Garrett, then a soldier, broke into a military commissariat, and that this was the offence for

148

which he was transported. When he was charged in the Melbourne Police Court with the robbery of the Ballarat branch of the Bank of Victoria, the account of the proceedings in the Melbourne *Argus* of 3 August 1855 stated he 'was transported from Nottingham for ten years in 1845, for a burglary', which fits in with the probable date of his arrival on the island.

He was removed from Norfolk Island to Van Diemen's Land towards the end of Price's command, and made his way to Victoria during the gold rush. He is said to have been one of the gang that robbed the *Nelson* in Hobson's Bay in 1852, but at his trial in 1855 for the Ballarat robbery he claimed, probably truly, he was not in Victoria in 1852. Though he asserted his innocence, there seems little doubt he was one of the four men who robbed the Bank of Victoria at Ballarat in October 1854. He went back to London with his share of the plunder, but was promptly apprehended. According to one account (Charles Finger, *Bushrangers,* pp. 127-59) Garrett was betrayed to the police by a man he had employed as a valet and was arrested while at ease in luxurious lodgings. Another story (told by Cronin and Russell in *Bushranging Silhouettes,* p.88) is that he was followed to London by Detective Webb. Garrett was living under an assumed name as a man of fashion. Uncertain if his suspicions were well-founded, Webb followed Garrett in the street, and called out suddenly 'Garrett!'. The suspect stopped and looked around, and Webb then arrested him. Contemporary reports in the *Argus* are less dramatic. On 27 June 1855 the *Argus* published an account of the proceedings, on 23 March 1855, at the Marlborough Street, London, police court. Henry Beresford Garratt (as the surname was spelled) was described as a 'powerfully built man, with an immense quantity of hair on his face'. He was charged with 'having, with others, armed with pistols, entered the Bank of Victoria, Ballarat, on 6 October 1854 and stolen therefrom £14,300 sterling and 250 ounces of gold.' Henry Webb, 'city detective', deposed that he assisted in apprehending the prisoner at the corner of John and Oxford Streets, London, on 22 March. The witness's evidence continued,

Previously to taking him into custody he stepped up to him and said, 'How do you do, Mr. Garratt? I believe you have just arrived by the Dawstone from Melbourne.' The prisoner said, 'Yes; but I don't remember you.' Witness said 'The fact is we are officers, and I hold in my possession a warrant for your apprehension for being one of the parties concerned in a robbery, in October last, at the Victoria Bank, Australia.'

Garratt was found to be carrying two revolvers and a dagger. He had in his possession two receipts from Coutts' Bank for £1975 and £300, respectively, and thirteen sovereigns in gold and a gold watch and chain. When his lodgings were searched two revolvers were found, one capped and loaded. There was a woman at the lodgings who said she was Mrs Garratt. Garratt refused to say anything in reply to this evidence for the prosecution, and was remanded for a week. He arrived in Melbourne in August 1855. The *Argus* of 2 August carried the following report:

Arrival of Garratt, the Bank Robber.—Our English correspondent, in a recent communication, announced, as our readers will remember, that Garratt, implicated in the robbery of the Ballarat branch of the Bank of Victoria, had been apprehended in London. The particulars of the capture showed an amount of professional cleverness and tact on the part of the London detectives which may serve as a model to our own with considerable advantage to them and the colonists. A large amount of money, more, indeed, than £2000, was said to have been recovered, and as the apprehension of the robber was effected without loss of time after the receipt of the intelligence of the robbery and details by the Argo, it is supposed that nearly all the booty which fell to his share has been recovered. Garratt arrived in Melbourne yesterday by the Waratah from Sydney, in the custody of Captain Hampton, the Inspector of a force of one hundred English police, who have been despatched for police duty in Sydney, and Serjeants Black, Doyle, Smith, and Healey, of the same detachment. He was committed into the custody of these officers at Liverpool, and sailed under their charge in the Exodus, bound for Sydney, which left on the 21st of April, and arrived at her destination on the 26th ult. The whole of the property recovered from Garratt has, of course, been brought with him. He was in close confinement the whole of the voyage out, and has also been kept under the strictest surveillance during the passage from Sydney. His custodians describe his conduct as evincing those traits of ruffianism which a long and complete acquaintance with crime, as taught in the penal schools of Port Arthur, would be sure to inculcate. He was, immediately on his arrival, locked up at the City Police station, and will, no doubt, be brought up this morning.

Garrett was convicted under the name of Henry Garratt on 21 November in the Supreme Court at Melbourne, and was sentenced to ten years' hard labour on the roads or other public works. In passing sentence Mr Justice Barry offered him strange and dubious comfort when he told him, 'If you are really innocent, the thought that you are so will be some consolation to you during the term of your punishment' (Melbourne *Argus*, 22 November 1855). Sent to the hulks, he was ashore in the gang from the *Sacramento* when Price was murdered.

After his release Garrett went to New Zealand in 1861, where he specialized in 'sticking up' wayfarers crossing Mount Maungatua on the journey to Dunedin. He fled to Sydney, but was arrested and extradited. In the Supreme Court at Dunedin on 15 May 1862 he was sentenced to eight years' imprisonment for robbery under arms, the first four years at hard labour, and the next four years at penal servitude. While serving his sentence in the Dunedin gaol he feigned a conversion to religion, a pretence he carried on when released on 9 February 1868. However, he was not long at liberty; discovered stealing from a seedsman's shop in the same year, a search of quarters disclosed he had a supply of strychnine, chloroform, arsenic, henbane, foxglove and other chemicals. The police theory was that Garrett intended to use these to poison people he hated, including Mr Justice Gresson, who had sentenced him for his bush-ranging crimes. On 3 December 1868 he was presented on two charges of shop-breaking and pleaded guilt. He gave his age as fifty-five. The trial judge, Mr Justice Ward, sentenced him to ten years' penal servitude on each charge, the second sentence being cumulative on the first, and his remarks indicated he accepted the police theory. Facing what was virtually a life sentence, as the judge intended it to be, Garrett became reconciled to his fate, and was an exemplary prisoner, spending his spare time writing and reading widely.

It was during this period he wrote 'The Demon' and various other pieces. There is nothing in the official records to show when he was released, but on 18 January 1883, in the Supreme Court at Christchurch, a Henry Garrett was sentenced to imprisonment for seven years for housebreaking. This Henry Garrett died in Wellington Prison on 3 September 1885, of chronic bronchitis. His age was entered as seventy-four years, and as there is no record of the death of any other Henry Garrett between 1885 and 1890, it is fairly certain he was Henry Beresford Garrett, and that Gilkison is mistaken in stating that he died in freedom in 1888.

The quotations from 'The Demon' in this note are taken from a typescript made by Mr John P. Kennedy, at one time a journalist in New Zealand, and now on the staff of the Melbourne *Herald*. While Garrett was a prisoner in the old Lyttelton Gaol, he became friendly with a Methodist lay preacher named Hall, who was a prison visitor. On Garrett's release after serving a considerable part of the twenty-years' sentence, Hall befriended him and gave him employment.

When he was again convicted and sentenced to seven years' imprisonment (presumably in 1883) Garrett gave his manuscripts to Mr Hall, saying that at his age he would never come out of prison again. This was the story told by Hall's son, who, in 1948, brought two exercise books containing the manuscripts to Mr Kennedy. In addition to 'The Demon', the manuscripts contained 'Portrait 2, Champ' and 'Portrait 3, George Duncan'. Recognizing their historical significance, Mr Kennedy copied them before returning them. Whether they still exist is not known, but so far (May 1964) efforts to trace them have not been successful. The manuscripts were written in a phonetic spelling which Garrett had himself devised (he used as a pen-name 'Klodopr', for 'Clodhopper'), and in transcribing 'The Demon' Mr Kennedy made an exact copy of the first page. He converted the rest of the text into normal spelling, preserving unaltered the language, grammar and punctuation, though in a few instances it was necessary to supply an indecipherable word. The Mitchell Library, Sydney, and the State Library of Victoria have photocopies of Mr Kennedy's transcript. The quotations below have been taken from a copy revised by Mr Kennedy, and there are some slight textual divergences from the photocopies in the Libraries, but there is no difference in sense.

'The Demon' is a document of about 25,000 words, far too long for publication in full as an appendix. A well-organized and vigorously written composition consisting of an introduction and thirteen chapters, it is Garrett's biography of his hated enemy, Price. It contains, too, descriptions of conditions and events on Norfolk Island and on the Hobson's Bay hulks, interspersed with Garrett's reflections on freewill and destiny and other philosophical notions. Garrett wrote it after reading *For the Term of His Natural Life*. He identifies Marcus Clarke's characters, Maurice Frere and his wife and the Rev. James North, as Price, Mrs Price, and the Rev. Thomas Rogers. He takes no exception to Clarke's depiction of Price, but he censures him for implying there was an illicit passion between 'the island's parson and the Demon's wife', who were 'the cream of amiability and goodness'. The style is vivid. Here is his description of Price:

John's features were not ill-formed. They were as far from ugly as beautiful. They were not what is called strongly marked, yet to those about him they had a most repellent effect. His cold grey eyes had a ferocious glitter. On one of them he wore a glass, not from any defect of vision, but from what he in another would have termed flashness. It became him about as much as a frilled shirt would have a sweep as his working dress.

To the disposition of a Nero he joined the frame of a Hercules. Over six feet in height, he had a round bullet head of the true Legree type, a light complexion and hair, the last almost sandy and slightly inclined to curl, a rather large but well-shaped mouth, a thick bull neck, square massive shoulders, no waist but ribbed down to the hips like an Atlas, legs strong and slightly bowed, his whole frame as indicative of immense strength as his face was of ferocity. How his presence would affect others unacquainted with his name and deeds I know not, but to all who knew him it was most unpleasant. Prisoners, warders and his own children felt and spoke of him alike, and from prisoner servants we learnt that his wife feared him worst of all. The same sternness ruled the home as the barracks.

Later he tells of the muster of prisoners when Price first arrived on Norfolk Island:

The yell of defiance from 500 throats rather startled him. He turned tail. It may have been either fear or anger. He stepped back a couple of paces, looked round at his attendants and up at the soldiers in the gallery and nodded. The soldiers brought their rifles to the ready and the snick of the locks was audible. Every man around him drew his cutlass and pistol and things began to look ugly.

Let me describe him as he then stood. He was dressed something after the style of a flash gentleman. On his round bullet head a small straw hat was jauntily stuck, the broad blue ribbon of which reached down between his shoulders, a glass stuck in one eye, a black silk kerchief tied sailor fashion round his bullneck, no vest but a bobtail or oxonian coat, or something like a cross between this and a stableman's jacket seemed to be bursting over his shoulders. A pair of rather tight pants completed his costume, except for a leather belt, six inches broad, buckled round the loins. In the belt two pepperbox revolvers were conspicuously stuck.

The yells subsided and, assured by the presence of the soldiers and the guard, he struck an attitude by placing his arms akimbo, and again spoke.

'You know me, don't you? I am come here to rule, and by God I'll do so and tame or kill you. I know you mean cowardly dogs, and I'll make you worry and eat each other.' What else he would have said was lost in another burst of yells . . .

His descriptions of floggings on Norfolk Island and the use of the gag, spread-eagling between ringbolts, and the 'gridiron', to which a man was fastened, lying on his back with his head projecting beyond the frame, leave little to the imagination. After mentioning the removal of the clergyman, Rogers, and the medical officer, Dr Graham, he continues:

The doctor's offence had been insisting on some little exemption from labour and a little medical treatment for those who had been flogged or who were suffering from dysentery. He was replaced by an old military doctor, Everett, as brutal and unfeeling as Price himself. There was no medical treatment under him except that of treating men's backs with a piece of ragged bluestone. For this he soon got the name from the men of 'Old Bluestone'.

Men's backs, ragged and bruised from the lash, were baked in the sun like crackling pork. They swarmed with flies and maggots, with not a drop of water to moisten them. They used to make poultices of lemon and lime pulp, and where these could not be got they poured their urine on to each other. Each was like a naked fire to their backs. Men ill with dysentery, their trousers wet with discharge and smothered with flies and maggots, and weak from disease, starvation and punishment, staggered to and from labour, until, no longer able to do so, they laid down and died, or committed suicide. The stench of their festering backs in those packed dormitories and their groans were horribly offensive to smell and pitiable to hear.

Under John flogging became an art. Men were trained to it as to a trade. Sheets of bark were stretched on the triangles and the novices made to practice on them. It became a task, too, as rigidly enforced as the task of field labour, and woe to the flogger whose victim's back did not show the desired amount of mutilation. He was sure of the same number of lashes as the other had received, laid on, too, by the severest floggers.

Conditions on the hulks are described with horrifying explicitness:

At this time there was in full play that atrocious hulk system which brought disgrace to the Government, misery to thousands and death to himself. Five of these swung at their moorings in Hobson's Bay and to these dens were sent all men sentenced to more than five years.

As all who have seen them might know and as all who have worn them can testify a pair of irons riveted round the ankles and worn day and night for years is no small punishment, and intended as a secondary one only to be inflicted by a Magistrate for some grave offence, yet every man sent to those hulks was placed in irons weighing from 14 to 40 lb.

This could not be for safety for aboard or in the quarries the men were guarded by warders armed with double-barrelled rifles and had there been none of these the clean-shaven faces and close-cropped heads and the branded prison dress would have made escape all but impossible, and though there could be shown a necessity for ironing those at work, there could be none for ever fettering those who never quitted the hulks. It was sheer love of cruelty which did this.

The course through these hulk dens varied from two years to any period the Demon chose to make it. The diet was of the worst possible description and barely possible to keep men alive, the contract price for each being 4d or 4½d per head.

One pound of bread, 4 oz. of maize meal, 4 oz. of meat with bone, and 8 oz. of turnips, tops and roots with dirt. The liquor the meat and turnips were boiled in was thrown away. This was the diet for those not at labour. That for those in the quarries was but little better—12 oz. of meat and bone, 8 oz. of maize meal and 12 oz. of potatoes. Religious and medical attention there was none, except the leaving of a paternoster tract by one dubbed a Scripture reader devoid of culture, charity or common sense or civility even could be called one, and a dose of salts the other. The first was not needed, but medical aid was . . .

The only other remedies were a change of diet, the stoppage of all other food for two pints of thin arrowroot a day. A month or six weeks of this was a cure for the most chronic diseases. Only like the horse trained to live without eating just as he got used to it it died, so did his [the hulk doctor's] patients.

In revenge for this the ingrates used to say the medicines and medical comforts which he should have supplied to us, he expended, the first in private practice on free patients, and the second on himself, but I never believed it, and, though it had been true, had we not the Epsoms, the glaubers, the arrowroot and the whip. Some people are never satisfied.

On the breaking up of these floating hulks on John's death many had the opportunity of seeing what they were like. One enterprising fellow bought one and exhibited it at a shilling a head, but for the information of those who did not see I may describe it. There were 42 separate cells on each of the two decks. The floor of the lower one being 5 ft. below the water, the only light and ventilation to which was through a hole of 4 in. by 8 in. covered with perforated iron and within 2 ft. of the water.

Through this in rough weather the water used to wash and make sleeping on the floor impossible. To sit on the night tub was the only remedy.

The bedding was one small blanket or rug, never washed, aired or changed till worn out, and so loathsome from dirt and vermin.

Along the seawalls of the cells about 3 ft. from the floor was a row of massive ringbolts. To these men were handcuffed with their hands behind their backs for punishment. To sit or lie down was impossible, the crime which caused this being a word or reply to some taunt or threat, other crimes being all but impossible. The time of punishment varied from one day to a week and to reply while on this ringbolt was to ensure bludgeoning and gagging often into insensibility and beyond it.

The bludgeoning they called warming you and then the cooling

down came in the shape of sundry buckets of cold sea water to wash
the blood off you, leaving you hanging on the ringbolt to dry.

While thus suspended your food, a pound of bread, would be
flung in on the floor among salt water, urine, blood and excrement.
To reach it except with your foot was impossible and any entreaty
to have it held while you gnawed it was jeered at. If gagged they
would not even remove it, but ten minutes after flinging the bread
in would fling it out again, saying, 'You haven't eaten it and don't
want it'. A word of expostulation ensured the warming and etceteras.
Often for a week, night and day, men have been thus suspended and
treated. Complaints but continued it.

One fellow did complain to John who said: 'Ah, you don't like it.
Can't meet it. You're not half a pebble. Keep him on it.'

From complaining the man protested, was bludgeoned and
gagged. The men heard the blows and shouts, and yelled their
detestation.

'Just go round', he said, 'and mark the doors of the most noisy of
those fellows, and when we have done with this one we'll have this
one out and a dozen or more one by one served the same way.' Still
the rest yelled cursed and groaned.

As at Norfolk I kept myself still but it did not save me from the
bludgeoning and the ringbolt. He shouted out that he sentenced
the whole ship to a month's bread and water and no beds and they
yelled louder than before and at the end of the month on his next
visit they greeted him with a storm of yells. All that month at certain
hours the men kept up these yells, night and day at intervals they
burst out. The river and bay steamers used to pass regularly by.
Ever as they did so a chorus of yells would greet them with cries of
'Murder', 'Starvation' etc.

They covered up our ventilation holes to stop the sound. Still the
cries arose and some who had heard them wrote to the Press, saying
something wrong must be going on and urging visitations and inquiries.

John replied that the prisoners were mutinous and dangerous and
that the guards feared an outbreak and massacre, and the Government moored the old guard ship, Sir Harry Smith, opposite, loaded
and double-shotted the guns with orders to sink us if the officers
gave the signal by flight.

It was very cheerful to starve and see the guns looking at you
which any moment a treacherous and cowardly flight might open
upon and sink us. We fully expected that this would have been
done and learnt that fear of trusting each other alone prevented it.

To me and to most the worst punishment of those hulks was the
bugs. They literally swarmed in every crevice of the wooden par-
titions. To sleep at night was impossible. They attacked you by
myriads.

The clothing was miserable as the diet. Low shoes, no socks, duck trousers open at the sides, grey jacket, no vest, check shirt, no flannels, drawers or necktie. Just sufficient to hide nakedness but not to keep warm.

On removing from the *President* to the labour hulks the 40 lbs. irons were replaced by 14 lb. ones, and, as in Dunedin, so in these hulks, scarcely any weather stopped labour. The few rags of clothes, sodden with rain and salt water were each night flung in a heap outside each cell door and back in the morning. From the day of arrest to that of discharge, a period of ten or twelve years, a change of diet or the warmth of a fire was unknown.

As a final quotation, here is Garrett's account of Price's murder:

Both gangs knew he had been sent for and were on the watch for his appearance. His fate had already been decided. Several of the men knew what awaited them aboard—the ringbolt, gag and bludgeon and flung back into the *President* during his pleasure. Death was preferable. They had nothing but life to lose, but he had much to lose. Death to them was an escape from misery. To him it was the loss of everything that makes life desirable. His death was no impulsive act but the calculation and determination of hours of cool thought. Only the manner of it was different to what they meant it should be.

In each quarry was a large tent formed of the sails and spars of the dismantled hulks and over the yard forming the ridge pole his executioners had passed a well-greased rope with a noose. He should die the death of a dog or of capitally sentenced criminals. He was to be inveigled or dragged into the tent and hung.

What must have been the misery these men suffered and anticipated to make them thus coolly throw their lives away? Let all ask themselves what amount would induce them to do a similar act.

The whole quarry of 100 men knew what was going to be done, saw the rope and knew its purpose. All were not to take a part but all approved. But out of that 100 men surely there is one traitor who for a hope of pardon will warn and save him? Not one. All had such a thorough hatred that his death was preferable to pardon. Not one would whisper to the officers the warning which would have saved. Perhaps one reason for this was his deceit to those who had served him and been cheated again and again of a promised reward. Nothing is more certain than that had he had the goodwill or confidence of one man he must have been warned.

About two o'clock he was seen coming up the raised tramway leading from the quarry to the jetty. With him were three or four hulk officers. The men were gathered in a crowd near the tent. All work in our gang was immediately suspended, the men mounting the quarry bank and walls so as to have a view of the others.

I and four others were employed dragging stones from the top of the quarry to the top of the embankment midway between the two quarries and commanding a good view of both.

On descending into the quarry he ordered the men to fall in. They refused and surrounded him, crying 'To the tent, to the tent', and fifty hands were raised aloft with the day's allowance of offensive bread, the owners shouting 'Look at this', and some who could not get near flung them at him.

'To the tent, to the tent', cried others and began to hustle him towards it, but as if smelling danger there, or he may have got a glimpse of the rope and guessed its purpose, he began to struggle and elbow his way from it.

He is surrounded by seven officers who are surrounded by 100 men, twelve to one, fearful odds, but many men more unequally matched have fought their way to safety, and the odds are not so great as appears. Not more than 20 of the 100 will do aught but shout and so the odds are reduced to 2½ to 1, and armed as some of them were with pistols and all with life preservers, well fed, with the law on their side the 8 men ought to be able to resist 12 unarmed men, fettered and weak from starvation.

As soon as he felt himself being borne towards the tent he began with his immense muscular strength to elbow and push his way from it and he finally succeeded in clearing the surging mass, flinging them aside as a vessel dashes aside the water from her bows.

He rushes up the embankment not 40 yards from where my cart party are looking on. He is alone. His seven dastardly officers have already turned tail and fled. After him rush about a dozen infuriated men who have snatched up shovels, picks, hammers and stones.

On gaining the top of the embankment he paused a moment to look where he should run. He had a wild frightened look. How one would like to know his thoughts and feelings at that moment? Men drowning are said to have a lightning-like view of their past lives. Had he aught of this? Did he even think of one of his many crimes and which? Did he feel the presentiment he had uttered not three hours previously? One thing at least he saw—that like a nobler man, all his friends and servants had deserted at the first sniff of danger.

Had he run into our gang he might have escaped, but seeing them all looking on and my party direct in the way he may have thought we were only waiting to bar his passage.

Some of his pursuers have cut off his retreat down the tramway. The rest are mounting close to him and he dashes down the other side towards the bay. He has hardly reached the bottom when a stone flung from the top strikes him between the shoulders and knocks him on his face in a shallow water hole. He never rises again. Before he can do so his enemies are upon him and we lose sight of him. All we can see is a confused scramble, blows of shovels, pick handles and hammers and it put one in mind of the hounds worrying a fox.

Yes, the strongman is down in the crush of his self-made foes who will show him the same mercy he showed them. He had no time to ask for other mercy. Whether he would have done so I have often wondered but what no plea on his part could have done (saved him) a little effort on the part of his seven cowardly officers must.

I have often heard John spoken of as brave and fearless. He may have been so but I never knew one act of his life which would have entitled him to be thought so. To bully and torture the defenceless is generally held a trait of cowardice as well as cruelty. If, as is said, the brave are ever humane, and again, if as is said, cowards are cruel, then judging him by his acts he has written his own epitaph by his own acts.

When backed by armed force as he was it needs not a brave man to bully, strike and swagger. The veriest coward that crawls can and none but such do it.

If his life was cowardly his death was still more so. A brave man would have died with his face to his foes and fighting. He fled from them and fell as a fool and coward falls.

[Accounts of or references to Garrett appear in the following: Anon., *Catalogue of the Convict Ship 'Success'* (Sydney, 1891), p. 9; Anon., *History of the British Convict Ship 'Success'* (n.d., no publisher's imprint), p. 124; Anon., 'Bushranger with an Oxford accent', Byways of History Series, Melbourne *Herald*, 4 June 1958, substantially reproduced as 'The First N.Z. Bushranger' in *True Stories of Australian Crime* (Melbourne, n.d.), pp. 18-19; Melbourne *Argus*, 27 June, 2 and 3 August, 22 November 1855; *Australian Encyclopaedia* (Sydney, 2nd ed., 1958), vol. 2, p. 217; George Boxall, *History of Australian Bushrangers* (Sydney, 1935), pp. 156-8, 310; Bernard Cronin and Arthur Russell, *Bushranging Silhouettes* (Sydney, 1932), pp. 86-8; Charles J. Finger, *Bushrangers* (London, n.d.), pp. 127-60; Robert Gilkison, *Early Days in Central Otago* Christchurch, 3rd ed., 1958, pp. 72-5, 82-91; W. Joy and T. Prior, *The Bushrangers* (Sydney, 1963), pp. 62-3; J. P. Kennedy, 'Convicts of Victoria's Hell-Hulks Took Revenge', Melbourne *Herald*, 3 September 1955.]

STANDING INSTRUCTIONS FOR THE REGULATION OF THE PENAL SETTLEMENT ON TASMAN'S PENINSULA*

Colonial Secretary's Office,
25th January 1833.

His Excellency the Lieutenant Governor has been pleased to direct that Tasman's Peninsula shall be established as a Penal Settlement, for the reception—

1st.—Of convicts under colonial sentence of transportation, or imprisonment and hard labour.

2nd.—Of convicts on their arrival, whose crimes in Great Britain may be notified by His Majesty's Government to have been of a nature peculiarly atrocious.

3rd.—Of convicts who may be convicted of violence or outrage during the voyage from England.

4th.—Of that class of offenders denominated, in familiar language, gentlemen convicts.

The situation and local advantages of this peninsula adapt it in an especial manner, for the confinement and discipline of such convicts. It is a natural penitentiary, from which ordinary precaution will render escape impossible, and it includes within its boundaries, a sufficient variety of soil and of products, to supply work of every degree of severity. It is cut off from any secret means of communication with the cultivated districts, and yet it is so near Head Quarters, that the local Government may exercise the strictest surveillance over it.

These criminals, when placed upon it, will be quite apart from the rest of the community, and the educated convicts, whom it is desired by His Majesty's Government especially to sequestrate, will have no victims upon whom their superior cunning will enable them to prey, and that intelligence which they have so miserably abused and mis-directed, will not avail them.

It is distinctly to be kept in view by the Commandant and the several public officers employed on Tasman's Peninsula, that the design of this Establishment, is the severe punishment of the vicious

*From James Ross, *The Van Diemen's Land Annual and Hobart Town Almanac for the Year 1833* (Hobart), pp. 105-15.

part of the community, as the means of deterring others from the
commission of crime, as well as the reformation of the criminals
themselves; and to this end, the most unceasing labour is to be
exacted from the convicts, and the most harrassing vigilance over
them is to be observed, together with such a minute system of
classification as may be best calculated to develop their characters,
habits, and dispositions.

On the faithful and zealous discharge of the duties assigned to
the officers in charge, will greatly depend the result of this important
penal institution; therefore, although no orders in writing can meet
the exigency of every case, and much must rest upon that individual
effort which previous instruction cannot reach, the following outline
of duties is laid down for the information and guidance of all classes
of persons upon the peninsula, and the strictest attention to them is
enjoined.

THE COMMANDANT

He is responsible for his acts to the local Government only, and
he is absolute with reference to all under his jurisdiction, which
shall include the whole peninsula.

He shall regulate his measures according to the instructions he
may receive from the Government, and by the laws in force within
the territory of Van Diemen's Land.

He shall keep a register of every exertion of authority, which is
not of the most ordinary routine, so as to be enabled, at any time, to
assign to the local Government good and sufficient reasons for each
act of his command.

He shall issue written instructions to each person in any charge
under his command.

He shall take care, by frequent inspection and constant supervision, that every officer or person in charge under his command
shall perform with diligence the duties assigned to him.

He shall cause periodical reports in duplicate to be made to him
regularly by the several officers in the settlement; and upon one set
of these reports he shall make his remarks, add such directions as may
be suggested by any thing contained in it, and return it to the party
from whom it was received; on the other set he shall cause such
observations &c. to be copied, and he shall transmit it quarterly to
the Colonial Secretary for the information of the Government.

He shall once every week, independent of his daily ordinary visit,
make a formal inspection of the various buildings and works on the
settlement, and on every such occasion, note in a visiting book, to
be kept by the persons in charge respectively, whether he is satisfied

with the condition of the several buildings and works, and with the manner in which the duties of every kind connected with them are discharged, and he shall assign his reasons for the opinions he may then express.

He shall once a week at least, attended by the surgeon, cause the gangs to be mustered in his presence, in order that he may ascertain whether the men are clean, orderly, and in good health; and he shall enter his remarks in a memorandum book to be kept by the superintendent, and to be presented by him on every such occasion.

He shall not commence any new building until after the plan and estimate have received the sanction of the Lieutenant Governor.

He shall not, without the previous consent of the local Government, remove any individual from the settlement.

He shall take care that the convicts under his charge do not hold any communication whatsoever with any person or persons, not specially authorised.

But he shall always forward communications of every description, however incorrect, in manner or matter from whomsoever received, provided they be addressed to any member of the local Government.

He shall take care that strangers not having the license of the Government shall not enter upon or remain in the settlement.

He shall take care that no articles not included in the manifest shall either be landed from or taken on board of any vessel.

He shall be allowed 2 acres of ground for his own garden, and have 2 prisoners out of the appropriate gang to cultivate it.

He shall not employ any other convict for his private convenience or comfort without making the circumstance the subject of an especial report.

He shall make the following returns:—

1. Annual returns of buildings and other permanent works.
2. Annual return of stores (not perishable) received and issued.
3. Annual return of all free persons, with dates of arrival, and nature of occupations.
4. Quarterly return of all convicts, with their names, ships, numbers, date of arrival on the settlement, occupations, conduct, merits or demerits.
5. Monthly return of work of every description.
6. Manifests of all articles shipped for Hobart Town or elsewhere.
7. Lists of all persons visiting the settlement or departing from it.
8. A return enclosing all the reports &c., he may receive from the officers under his command and copies of his official correspondence.

He is a Justice of the Peace, and shall sit with the Police Magistrate in all cases in which two Magistrates are required.

He is to support the Chaplain in the discharge of his duties, and more particularly he is to take care that the Sabbath be not profaned, but be in every respect kept holy and rendered available, as a day of moral and religious instruction.

POLICE MAGISTRATE

He is a Justice of the Peace of the Territory and has jurisdiction accordingly.

His duties making allowance for difference of situation shall be the same with those of the District Police Magistrates.

But he shall personally inspect and when necessary, punish offences upon 'view'.

He is, when the accusers are able to give their evidence coolly, and are not under excitement from recent irritation, to make the trial and punishment follow the offence as closely as possible, so that crime and its consequences may be associated in the convicts' mind as cause and effect, and form parts as it were of the same idea.

It will be expedient for him on each occasion to admonish the convicts whom he has sentenced to punishment, and to assign to them temperately and firmly, the reasons for their punishment and then to have it carried into effect, promptly and effectually.

He is generally to assign such punishments as will inflict the requisite amount of pain or misery, within the shortest period of time.

He shall make himself acquainted with the habits, ideas and characters of the convicts, so that he may assign the punishment, indicated by the constitution of each man's mind.

He shall order flagellation in every case in which from blunted sensibility, it is impossible to punish effectually through the mind.

He shall take care that, when flagellation is ordered, it is executed with due severity, in the presence of the Surgeon who shall attend for the usual purposes.

He is to remember that to order punishments and to permit their infliction to be either uncertain or imperfect, is to invite the repetition of offences and to increase the necessity for punishments, and is therefore cruelty rather than clemency.

He shall request the assistance of the Commandant at his convenience to act with him, when two Magistrates are required by law.

He shall make reports of his decisions and judgments to the Commandant, who may suspend the execution of them until the pleasure of the Lieutenant Governor, upon a full report, is known.

He shall transmit to the Commandant, quarterly Reports of the cases brought before him.

He shall transmit a quarterly Specification of the character of each convict under his jurisdiction, of the effect of the labour and discipline of the settlement upon his mind and feelings,—how far they are appropriate and in what respects deficient. He shall give his reasons succinctly yet minutely for the particular punishment he may have assigned in each case, he shall state the manner in which it appears to have affected the individual on whom it was inflicted, and his companions, and he shall recommend in writing, to the Commandant, any indulgences or other measures that may appear to him to be expedient.

THE SURGEON

He has an hospital under his charge and he is responsible for the manner in which it is kept in every respect, as is customary.

His most difficult duty is the distinguishing of feigned from real illness.

He shall not exempt any individual from labour, or receive him into the hospital, without taking down for subsequent report, a minute detail of the symptoms of his case, to which must be added the reasons which induced him to conceive the disease not to be feigned but real.

He shall inspect daily every building in which the men sleep or work, and report whether it be clean and healthy, or otherwise.

He shall inspect the clothing and bedding of the men weekly, and report upon them so far as relates to his department.

He shall ascertain the effect of the food, labour, and discipline of the settlement, upon each of the convicts as respects his health and strength, and he shall report the same to the Commandant monthly.

It is his duty to report upon any and every circumstance which may appear to him to affect or to have affected the health of the convicts under his medical charge either beneficially or injuriously.

He is from time to time to make such recommendations relating to his department to the Commandant as to himself may appear necessary and desirable, and these recommendations shall be inscribed in his journal, and transmitted quarterly to the Colonial Surgeon for the information of the Government.

THE CHAPLAIN

He is to take care that the Sabbath be not profaned by any individual, either free or bond, but that it be solemnly observed, and in every respect improved to the utmost as a day of moral and religious instruction, and he is to pray with and for the convicts at morning and evening muster, and he is not to omit any opportunity of giving advice and exhortation.

He is to send quarterly reports of the manner in which the Sabbath has been kept, and to particularise offenders, whether free or bond, of whatever class or rank.

He is to make himself acquainted with the temper and disposition of the persons under his charge, and he is to treat each accordingly.

He is to transmit quarterly reports, stating the particulars of the impression made upon the convicts by his own teaching, as well as by the general discipline.

He is to establish Schools and anxiously to superintend them.

He is to make such recommendations connected with his duty monthly to the Commandant, as may from time to time appear to be necessary.

SUPERINTENDENT

His principal duty is to carry into effect the daily instructions of the Commandant.

He is to see that the men go to bed and rise at the regulated hours —that they are clean in their persons—that they do, each, a man's work daily—that they are all present at the morning and evening muster—that they be not allowed to absent themselves from duty— and that they do not escape from the settlement.

In the event of disobedience, insubordination, or impropriety of conduct of any description, he is to have the Police Magistrate instantly informed of it, and to have the necessary witnesses at hand, so that not a moment may be unnecessarily interposed betwixt the commission of an offence and its punishment.

He is to take care that the men have their rations regularly, and that they do not in any way receive or use any luxury or comfort other than is specially authorised—that they do not get any letters conveyed from the settlement irregularly, and that they never under any pretext approach the wharf when strangers may be at work landing goods or taking them on board of any vessel.

His duty combines that usually assigned to a Superintendent of Convicts as well as that of an Inspector of Works.

COMMISSARIAT OFFICER

He shall have charge and be responsible for the receipts and issues of all stores of whatsoever description within the settlement, and shall issue rations to every person entitled to receive them, according to regulation, the 'Returns' being signed by the Commandant.

He shall conduct the business of his office in the customary manner, receiving instructions from, and making his reports to, the head of his department at Hobart Town, but, although he must obey any order he may receive from the Commandant in writing, he nevertheless shall not fail to bring the same under the consideration of his superior officer, when such order is at variance with his general instructions.

He shall make to the Commandant such recommendations from time to time, as may appear to him to be calculated to facilitate or improve the mode of conducting the business of his office, and shall transmit quarterly to the head of his department, the correspondence which takes place.

OFFICERS GENERALLY

They shall obey such directions as they may receive.

They will be called to account if any offence is committed with their privity, whether they assist in its perpetration or not, unless they actually endeavour to prevent it, and inform the authorities thereof.

Officers in charge of branch departments shall furnish the Commandant with a copy in duplicate of every instruction they may receive from their superiors in Hobart Town, and they shall not act upon any such instructions, until they have received the approbation of the Commandant, who will treat the instruction so forwarded as an ordinary report.

They shall not cultivate any portions of land for their own advantage except as gardens for the exclusive use of their own families.

They shall not employ any convict or convicts under any pretext whatever, for their own benefit, unless specially authorized by the Commandant so to do.

They shall not leave the settlement without the written authority of the Commandant.

Should the Commandant direct any work to be done for the comfort of a public officer, he (the public officer) shall not give the mechanic or other convict who does the same, any remuneration whatever.

All trading and trafficking between the free and bond are expressly prohibited.

CONVICTS GENERALLY

The convicts shall be employed in hard labour from sunrise to sunset, with one hour's intermission for breakfast and the like time for dinner.

They shall cut timber and draw it to the water's edge—they shall make roads, erect buildings, break up new land, and cultivate the old, but the infirm shall be employed in the settlement garden.

They shall all, with the exceptions hereafter mentioned, wear the coarse yellow dress, the imposition of which has been found to be a severe punishment.

They shall perform every description of labour required at the settlement, and shall not be assisted by beasts of burthen of any sort.

No convict females (except as servants of officers) and no wives of convicts shall ever be admitted into the settlement.

They shall receive bedding, clothing and rations as established by regulation.

They shall not barter or sell any articles amongst themselves.

FIRST CLASS

All convicts, except educated convicts, arriving at the settlement, shall be placed in this class, unless the order received with them shall direct otherwise.

They shall be employed in hewing and cutting timber, and drawing it to the water's edge, or in any other hard labour which may be specially required.

They shall wear the yellow dress.

They shall not be put to task work, neither shall they be allowed to labour lazily, or to reserve their strength.

They shall never, under any pretence, be allowed to use the hoe, or the spade, or the rake, or any other agricultural implement, neither shall they ever be permitted to enter into the garden of the settlement, except under circumstances of the most pressing necessity, which shall form the subject of a special report.

Agriculture and horticulture are employments not to be committed to felons twice convicted, who have not as yet shewn any disposition to reform their conduct.

CHAIN GANG

Shall consist principally of convicts who have been sentenced to the gang by the Police Magistrate, or have been specially sent to the settlement to be worked in chains.

They are to wear chains and the yellow dress, with the word 'Felon' stamped upon it in several places—they are to sleep in separate cells—they are to go out to work one by one in Indian file, and no conversation is to be allowed among them—they are to be put to the heaviest and most degrading labour that can be found on the settlement.

No sentence to this gang shall ever exceed 3 months in duration, without a special report being made to the Government.

RELIEF GANG

Men who have conducted themselves properly after long probation, may by direction of the Commandant be removed to this gang.

The dress of this class shall be grey or blue.

They shall be regarded in the light of probationers, acquiring habits fitting them to be useful in society.

Their labour shall not be less continuous, but it shall be less severe, and less degrading than that of the first class.

They may be employed in agriculture and horticulture, the use of the hoe and spade is not prohibited to them.

Out of this class the Commandant may occasionally, with the approbation of the Lieutenant Governor, appoint Constables, Messengers, &c. for the settlement.

EDUCATED CONVICTS

They form a distinct class.

They wear the grey dress.

They are employed in gardening, fencing and farming.

They are kept under the strictest surveillance and the labour done by each daily is carefully ascertained.

They may be punished by removal to the first class, and to the chain gang, and by flagellation, or in any other way that may appear best suited to the particular circumstances of each case.

They are deprived of every article whether of comfort or convenience they may have about them on their arrival and are to be in every respect restricted to such provisions and clothing as are specially authorized.

By command of the Lieutenant Governor,

J. BURNETT.

Colonial Secretary.

REGULATIONS AND INSTRUCTIONS FOR HULKS, VICTORIA*

REGULATIONS FOR THE CONTROL OF PRISONERS
ON BOARD THE HULKS
1853

Each prisoner on arrival will be taken separately to the searching room, where he will be strictly searched by a warder in the presence of the Chief Warder or an Overseer and every article taken from him, his description will then be taken and his hair closely cut, and whiskers shaved completely off. He will then wash and all the clothing he may bring with him will be destroyed and a suit of the Hulk clothing furnished him, which will consist of

1 Jacket or Frock
1 Pair of trowsers
2 Shirts
1 Pair of Shoes
1 Hat or Cap

(2)

If not ironed on arrival he will then be placed in irons which will never under any circumstances be removed except by the Special direction of His Excellency the Lieutenant Governor.

(3)

He will immediately be placed in a cell where he will be kept in close confinement during the period he remains on board.

(4)

Each prisoner will be supplied with the following articles, 1 Rug, 2 Blankets, Plate, Pannecan and spoon, comb and towel, which he will be required to keep clean.

(5)

They will rise every morning at 6 o'clock in summer and 7 in winter when they will wash, fold up their bedding and each clean out his own cell, the bedding will then be removed.

* From original MS. in possession of Royal Historical Society of Victoria, Item 23798.

(6)

The breakfast will be served out at 8 o'clock and the dinner at 12, the supper will be issued at 5 P.M. in summer and 4 in winter.

(7)

The bedding will be returned at 5 P.M. in winter and 6 in summer and they will be required to be in bed by 6 in winter and 7 in summer.

(8)

They will be strictly searched every morning and evening and will not be permitted to have in their possession any Article whatever beyond that issued to them by the Government.

(9)

Strict silence upon all occasions whether in the cells or at exercise will be enforced.

(10)

Should a prisoner require anything while in his cell he will apply to the warden on duty.

(11)

They will be allowed on deck for exercise at such periods as may be convenient but never to exceed ten (10) at one time, and in marching round the deck they will never approach each other nearer than 7 paces.

(12)

Each prisoner who can read will be supplied with a Bible and Prayer Book and allowed the constant use of them as long as they are kept without being damaged.

(13)

A record of each prisoner's crime sentence and character with the period he may serve on board the Hulk will be hung up in his cell on which also will be monthly entered his character and conduct during the past month.

(14)

No person will at any time be permitted to see a prisoner except the officers of the Hulk neither will any communication either by letter or otherwise be permitted to take place.

(15)

Any prisoner moving from his allotted place in the rank when at exercise or making the slightest movement at any time indicative of an attempt to escape will render himself liable to be shot by the warder or other person in whose charge he may be and each prisoner is hereby duly warned and cautioned that if he infringes or departs from this rule he does so at his own risk and peril.

(16)

They must bear in mind that it is by the most exemplary conduct alone during the whole time they are on board that they will be allowed to emerge into the 2nd stage at the expiration of their allotted periods—the slightest irregularity, want of cleanliness, insolence, riotous or disorderly conduct, attempting to hold communication with a fellow prisoner or any other person except the Officers of the Hulk on matters of discipline, disobedience of any order, damaging or destroying any article and any other act of misconduct will not only subject them to immediate punishment but their allotted period of service on board the Hulk will recommence from the date of such punishment.

(17)

At frequent uncertain periods during the month they will have an opportunity of making complaints to the Superintendent of any grievance under which they may consider themselves to be labouring.

INSTRUCTIONS FOR THE GUIDANCE OF THE OFFICERS ON BOARD THE HULKS
(1st)

The Assistant Superintendent will have sole charge of the Hulk, upon him will rest the responsibility of carrying out all the regulations he may from time to time receive from the Superintendent for the safety and good order of the vessel.

(2)

The other officers will be

1 Overseer of Stores
1 Overseer and coxswain
1 Chief Warder
1 Assistant Warder
18 Ordinary Warders

who will all take their orders from him and he will take care by constant and frequent inspection that their respective duties are correctly and efficiently performed.

(3)

The safe custody of the prisoners being the primary consideration he will report to the Superintendent immediately any alteration or improvement in the vessel or regulations which may appear to him desirable to ensure this object.

(4)

He will see that the accompanying regulations for the control of the prisoners are strictly carried out.

(5)

He will muster the prisoners in their cells every night and morning taking care that the Chief Warder and overseers are also in attendance.

(6)

He will daily visit the cells and enquire if the prisoners have any complaints to make of their treatment which it will be his duty to regulate bearing in mind that while humanity is not lost [sight] of yet the punishment of the prisoner must be rigidly enforced.

(7)

He will not remove the irons of any prisoner without the directions of the Superintendent.

(8)

He will regulate the employment of the prisoners according to their character and conduct and will not permit any of them to be employed at other than Government work except by the special authority of the Superintendent.

(9)

He will also regulate the exercise of the prisoners and will allow them as much time as practicable but never allow on deck a greater number than 10 (ten) at one time.

(10)

He will take care that no prisoner under his charge holds communication by letter or otherwise with any person whatever except the officers of the Hulk and then only on matters of duty.

(11)

He will have authority to confine any prisoner for misconduct in a dark cell on half rations for any period not exceeding 5 days reporting the same to the Medical officer within 24 hours thereafter and will forward to the Superintendent a weekly return of offences and punishments, and any case requiring more severe discipline he will bring before the visiting Justice and also report the same to the Superintendent.

(12)

He will keep a daily register of the character and conduct of every prisoner, and will furnish the Superintendent with a monthly nominal return of the same with his remarks thereon.

(13)

He will take care that the prisoners rations are of good wholesome quality and are regularly issued and that they do not in any manner use or receive any article of luxury or indulgence except medicinally by order of the Medical Officer.

(14)

It will be his duty to inspect weekly the clothing and bedding of the prisoners and to ascertain how far their health may be affected by the discipline and food and make a monthly report of the same and of any other circumstance which may be desirable to the Superintendent.

(15)

He will never permit a prisoner to be removed from the Hulk without the authority of the Superintendent.

(16)

He will be held responsible for the receipt and issue of all stores and that the material supplied for the employment of the prisoners is properly accounted for.

(17)

He will make a monthly muster of all stores, tools, utensils, bedding clothing, &c. on board the Hulk and will furnish to the Superintendent's office a report of the state in which he may find them.
He will take that everything received on board is strictly examined and will on no account permit the introduction of spirits or anything not absolutely necessary for the officers of the Hulk.

(19)

He will have a boat placed at his disposal for the service of the Hulk which will be employed bringing rations, stores etc. from the shore to the Hulk, and he will employ three of the warders as boatmen and one of the overseers as coxswain who will have charge of the boat and without whom it will never leave the vessel.

(20)

He will take care that no other boat is allowed to approach the Hulk without an authority from the Lieutenant Governor in which case they will be provided with a distinguishing signal and no boat whatever will be permitted to approach or leave the vessel between sunset and sunrise.

(21)

He will never permit any person except the officers of the Hulk to come on board the Hulk without the special permission of the Superintendent to whom written application for that purpose must be made to be laid before His Excellency the Lieutenant Governor.

(22)

Leave of absence will not be allowed to any officer or warder without the special authority of the Superintendent.

(23)

He will not permit any person to leave the Hulk without his personal knowledge.

(24)

He will issue such instructions from time to time to the various officers as may appear to him desirable for maintaining the safe custody of the prisoners and the discipline and good order of the Hulk generally and in writing as far as practicable and will enter such instructions in a book which he will keep for that purpose for the inspection of the Superintendent.

(25)

He will keep a daily diary in which it will be his especial duty to note his remarks upon the conduct and efficiency of the officers under his charge, a copy of which he will forward monthly to the Superintendent.

(26)

He will forward any application he may receive from any officer or warder to the Superintendent.

(27)

He will report any irregularity of whatever description to the Superintendent.

(28)

He will have authority to suspend any officer or warder for misconduct reporting the circumstances immediately to the Superintendent to be laid before His Excellency the Lieutenant Governor for his decision thereon.

(29)

He will make out and furnish to the Superintendent's office periodically the returns and accounts mentioned in the accompanying list and will keep all necessary books for that purpose.

(30)

It will be his duty to impress upon the minds of all officers placed under his authority that firmness, determination and temper are absolutely necessary in maintaining discipline and he will on no account permit any violence either of language or address to be used, for whilst it is essential for the due and effective discipline of the prisoners that they should be compelled to be obedient and respectful it is equally necessary that the officers should enforce the same by judicious and temperate conduct.

(31)

A Guard will be kept up each night beside those actually on sentry and the 2 (two) overseers, the Chief and Assistant Warders will each in his turn, as an officer of the guard remain up all night.

(32)

The officer of the guard will constantly at uncertain times at intervals of not more than one hour visit the sentries on their posts and particularly examine the bows and gangway of the vessel and assure himself of the general security of the Hulk.

(33)

If more convenient to those officers they may divide the night into watches but it will be the duty of the Assistant Superintendent to see that one of them is always on duty.

The Overseer of Stores
(34)

The overseer of Stores will have charge of every article received on board for the use or employment of the prisoners which he will issue only on requisition approved by the Assistant Superintendent to whom he will be responsible for their proper expenditure.

(35)

He will attend every morning to issue the materials for the employment of the prisoners and will be held responsible that every thing is properly and fairly used and returned to store when completed.

(36)

He will keep a store receipt and store issue Book, and general store account which he will regularly balance every half year to enable the Assistant Superintendent to furnish the regular half yearly return.

(37)

He will generally superintend the employment of the prisoners as may be directed by the Assistant Superintendent.

(38)

He will when the prisoners are on deck read the regulations to them and so arrange that they may all hear them at least once every week.

(38a)

He will issue all rations, stores etc. and will regularly and upon all occasions attend at the distribution of the meals to each prisoner at his cell.

The Overseer and Coxswain

(39)

The overseer and coxswain will have charge of the board and it will be his duty to proceed to the shore for stores and rations and otherwise as directed by the Assistant Superintendent.

(40)

He will never permit the boat to leave the Hulk unless in his charge and he will be responsible to the Assistant Superintendent that nothing is brought on board without his authority.

(41)

He will take care that when on board the Hulk the boat is properly secured so that no unauthorized person can have access thereto.

(42)

He will not take off or bring on shore any person beyond his crew without the express authority of the Assistant Superintendent.

(43)

He will daily inspect every cell and see that they are properly cleaned and will be responsible to the Assistant Superintendent for the general cleanliness of the Hulk and perform such other duties as may be required of him by the Assistant Superintendent.

The Chief Warder

(44)

The Chief Warder will be held responsible to the Assistant Superintendent both night and day for the safe custody of the prisoners to secure which he will have placed under his immediate authority 1 Assistant and 18 ordinary warders and he will carry out any instructions he may receive from the Assistant Superintendent having this object in view.

(45)

He will be responsible that the duties allotted to the warders are properly and efficiently performed.

(46)

He will also be responsible that no trafficking or communication of any kind is carried on by or with the prisoners, and that no person is allowed on board the Hulk without the written authority of the Superintendent which it will be his duty to receive and hand to the Assistant Superintendent prior to admitting any person on board the Hulk.

(47)

He will not permit any person to leave the Hulk without the authority of the Assistant Superintendent.

(48)

Should any boat or other vessel approach the Hulk or come within the boundary marked out by the buoys without the written authority of the Superintendent in which case they will be provided with a distinguishing signal, it will be his duty to warn them to depart, and in the event of their not immediately complying therewith he will (having previously assured himself that a notification authorising such a course has been published in the Gazette) fire on such boat or other vessel and compel its departure.

(49)

It will be his duty daily both morning and evening personally to examine minutely the irons of every prisoner and any one having them ovalled, the rings or links cut or broken or otherwise tampered with will be immediately brought before the Assistant Superintendent.

(50)

He will also morning and evening personally examine every cell, sound the boards etc. to see that have not been loosened or tampered with and his particular attention is directed to the scuttles.

(51)

He will likewise every morning and evening see that the prisoners are strictly searched and will take care that they retain no article whatever beyond that issued by the Government.

(52)

He will also daily inspect their plates, pannicans and spoons and will be careful that these articles are taken from them immediately after their meals so that no opportunity may be afforded of making an improper use of them.

(53)

He will have charge of the keys of the cells which he will never entrust to any person but the Assistant Warder, who will on all occasions lock and unlock the prisoners as may be required.

(54)

When the prisoners are let out for exercise they will be marched on deck separately, and a second prisoner will never be let out until the first is on deck so likewise on their return one only will be permitted to descend at a time.

(55)

He will never allow two cells to be unlocked at one time except when the prisoners are at exercise.

(56)

When the prisoners are on deck he will provide such guard as may be desirable in addition to the regular sentries but never less than 4 (four) warders together with the Chief or Assistant Warder will at such times be on guard on deck and the number will be irrespective of those on duty below.

(57)

Should any boat or vessel be seen approaching the Hulk when the prisoners are at exercise they will immediately be marched below and locked up in their cells.

(58)

He will see that the prisoners are all in bed at the proper hour in accordance with the regulations and he will at 8 p.m. report to the Assistant Superintendent that all is correct.

(59)

He will take care that the lights are kept properly burning throughout the night, he will also see that the prisoners sleep in such a position as at all times to be seen by the warder on duty, from the inspection holes.

(60)

He will constantly have two warders on guard on each deck whom he will visit as often as practicable throughout the day and night to see that they are properly on the alert.

(61)

The warders will be armed with a short carbine bayonet and cutlass at all times when on duty.

(62)

The night duty will be divided into two watches and he will take care that those warders not actually on guard do not go to bed—but remain in the guard room ready dressed with their arms ready for any emergency.

(63)

The firearms will require the utmost attention their cleanliness and careful loading will be his especial care and will hold each warder responsible for the good order and efficiency of his arms which he will daily inspect and discharge as often as may appear to him necessary, but never at longer intervals than one week when all the prisoners are locked up.

(64)

He will never permit more than one third of the arms to be unloaded at one time.

(65)

His particular attention is directed to the bows and gangway of the Hulk which he will frequently and strictly examine and to which points he will draw the particular attention of the warders on guard on the upper deck.

(66)

Should the slightest attempt to escape be made by any prisoner it will be his duty to instruct the warders to fire upon such prisoner first however challenging and to impress upon them the absolute necessity that such fire should be effective as to prevent the escape of these prisoners is their duty and must be effected at any sacrifice.

(67)

He will keep a daily duty book and diary in which he will record the duty performed by each warder and any breach of discipline or misconduct which may occur which he will also report to the Assistant Superintendent to be laid before the Superintendent on his visit.

(68)

He will have authority to suspend any warder from duty reporting the circumstances immediately to the Assistant Superintendent, who will report accordingly to the Superintendent.

(69)

In reference to the discipline management and conduct of the warders he will carry out as far as practicable the rules and regulations which prevail at the Penal Establishment, Pentridge.

(70)

He will upon all occasions when the prisoners are let out for exercise take care that they are securely handcuffed before they are permitted to leave their cells and also that their irons are strictly examined.

The Assistant Warder and Other Warders

(71)

The Assistant Warder will generally assist and carry out any instruc-tions he may receive from the Chief Warder.

(72)

The warders will never when under arms allow a prisoner on any pretence to approach them nearer than 10 paces.

(73)

They will never speak to a prisoner unless purely on a matter of duty and will by every means prevent communication of any kind being held with them.

(74)

They will enforce strict silence both above and below deck and will immediately report to the Chief Warder any prisoner who may attempt to infringe this rule.

(75)

When on duty on the upper deck they will keep a constant and vigilant look out that no boat or other vessel approaches the Hulk or comes within the buoys unless carrying the authorised signal.

(76)

He will report to the Chief Warder by means of a rattle with which they will be supplied, the approach of every boat whether authorised or not which they may observe.

(77)

They will challenge every boat or craft approaching and any vessel which does not show the authorised signal they will order to depart and if not immediately obeyed it will be their duty to fire on such vessel or other boat under the direction of the Chief Warder and compel its departure.

(78)

They will not under any pretence whatever permit any boat or vessel to approach the Hulk between sunset and sunrise but upon the slightest suspicious noise or circumstance they will alarm the guard and (first challenging in a loud voice) fire upon anything they may observe approaching the vessel.

(79)

The special attention of the warders on guard on the upper deck is directed to the bows and gangway of the vessel which they will constantly and vigilantly examine and upon the slightest occasion alarm the guard.

(80)

They will challenge every person approaching their posts after dark and will not be satisfied with the simple answer 'Friend' but will in every case ascertain who the party may be before they allow him to pass.

(81)

Should a prisoner at any time endeavour to escape it will be the duty of the warders to fire upon him (first challenging in a loud voice) and they will take care in firing it is effective for although the loss of life may be deplored yet the escape of any of these prisoners is of infinitely greater consequence and must be prevented at any sacrifice.

(82)

Three warders will be employed as boatmen but they will distinctly understand that they are also liable to perform any other duty which the exigencies of the service may demand.

(83)

They will be subject in reference to their discipline and control to the same rules and regulations as prevail at the Penal Establishment, Pentridge which as far as practicable will be strictly carried out.

SCALE OF PERIODS TO BE SERVED BY PRISONERS SENTENCED TO TERMS EXCEEDING SEVEN YEARS

Term of sentence	Period on board of the Punishment Hulk	Period on board of the Probationary Hulk	Period at Stockade for the indulgence of Ticket of Leave	Number of years to serve for indulgence of Ticket of Leave	Proportion of sentence unexpired on receiving Ticket of Leave
8 years	1 year	2 years	3 years	6 years	One fourth
10 ,,	1½ ,,	2½ ,,	3½ ,,	7½ ,,	do.
12 ,,	2 ,,	3 ,,	4 ,,	9 ,,	do.
15 ,,	3 ,,	5 ,,	4 ,,	12 ,,	One fifth

LIST OF BOOKS TO BE KEPT BY THE
ASSISTANT SUPERINTENDENT

Prisoners Register Book
Ration Register
Magisterial Record
Salary Abstract
Store Receipt
Store Issue
General Store
Requisition
Prisoners Labour Register
Prisoners daily Character Register
Clothing Issue Register
Register of Clothing etc. made by Prisoners
Daily Diary
General Report Book
Order Book
Visitors Book

LIST OF RETURNS TO BE FURNISHED BY THE
ASSISTANT SUPERINTENDENT TO THE SUPERINTENDENT'S OFFICE

Weekly

Return of employment of Prisoners and amount of work performed.
Return of Prisoners confined in a dark cell or otherwise punished.
Return of Stores received.

Monthly

Ration returns and vouchers.
Fuel and light returns and voucher.
Salary Abstract, Officers.
    do. Warders.
Nominal return of prisoners received and discharged.
Nominal return of character and conduct of prisoner.
Return of Magisterial duties performed.
Report of duties performed by Officers and Warders.
Quality of rations, health of prisoners, state of tools etc.
Nominal return of persons, not belonging to the vessel who have
    been on board during the month with their length of stay.
Copy of Daily Diary.

Quarterly

Return of clothing, bedding etc. issued to prisoners.
Return of stores and utensils issued for use of prisoners.

Half Yearly

General store return showing receipts issued and stores in hand and whether serviceable or unserviceable.

Return of the value of work performed by prisoners.

Requisitions (in triplicate) for every article required for the service of the Hulk during the succeeding six months.

Annual

General Report on state of Hulk.

Efficiency of officers and warders and upon any other subjects which may appear to him desirable.

THE PRECEEDING *[sic]* REGULATIONS AND INSTRUCTIONS
APPROVED OF BY THE LIEUTENANT GOVERNOR

ABBREVIATIONS

The following abbreviations are used in reference notes:

Biographical Memoir	*Biographical Memoir of the late Mr. John Price, Inspector-General of Penal Establishments for Victoria;* with an account of the Assassination, Inquest, and Funeral; also, a full report of the Trial of the Prisoners.
C.S.O.	Records of Colonial Secretary's Office, Tasmanian State Archives.
G.O.	Records of Governor's Office, Tasmanian State Archives.
H.R.A.	*Historical Records of Australia.*
P.P.	*Parliamentary Papers* (Great Britain).
Report of Legislative Assembly	Victoria, 1856-7, Report from the Select Committee upon Penal Discipline, together with the Proceedings of the Committee, Minutes of Evidence, and Appendices, ordered by the Legislative Assembly to be printed 11 September 1857 (*Votes and Proceedings of the Legislative Assembly of Victoria, 1856-7,* vol. 3). Pagination used is of the Report, not the sessional volume.
Report of Legislative Council	Victoria, 1856-7, Report of the Select Committee of the Legislative Council on the subject of Penal Establishments, together with the Proceedings of Committee, Minutes of Evidence and Appendices, ordered by the Council to be printed 30 July 1857 (*Votes and Proceedings of the Legislative Council of Victoria,* 1856-7). Pagination used is of the Report, not the sessional volume.
Rogers, *Correspondence*	T. Rogers, *Correspondence relating to the Dismissal of the Rev. T. Rogers from His Chaplaincy at Norfolk Island.*
Rogers, *Review*	T. Rogers, *Review of Dr. Hampton's First Report on Norfolk Island.*

NOTES

1 BACKGROUND

1 *Hobart Town Courier,* 27 May 1836.
2 *Burke's Peerage and Baronetcy* (London, 1869), p. 917; G. C. Boase and W. P. Courtney, *Bibliotheca Cornubiensis* (London, 1878), vol. 2, p. 526; G. C. Boase, *Collectanea Cornubiensia* (Truro, 1904), pp. 762-6.
3 *Dictionary of National Biography* (Oxford, 1921-2), vol. 15, p. 753.
4 Ibid., vol. 16, p. 323.
5 Boase and Courtney, op. cit., vol. 2, p. 526.
6 In heraldic terms, the crest was 'A dragon's head, vert, erased, gu., holding in the mouth, a sinister hand, erect, couped at the wrist, dropping blood, all ppr.'. The Arms were 'Sa., a chevron, erminois, between three spears' heads, arg., embrued at the points, ppr.' *(Burke's Peerage* (1869), p. 918).
7 Much of the information concerning Sir Rose Price is derived from a lengthy communication, dated 10 February 1960, from Lt-Col. R. C. R. Price, D.S.O., O.B.E., to Wilson Evans, Esq., of Williamstown, Victoria. Lt-Col. Price is a great grandson of John Price and a grandson of Colonel Tom Price. He gives the year of Sir Rose Price's marriage as 1798, not 1795 as stated in *Burke's Peerage.*
8 Joseph Foster, *Alumni Oxonienses, the members of the University of Oxford, 1715-1886* . . . (Oxford, 1891), vol. 1, p. 1148.
9 Report of Legislative Assembly, Evidence, p. 25.
10 *Biographical Memoir,* p. 7.
11 Record Keeper, Principal Probate Registry, Somerset House, London, to Chief Librarian, Public Library of Victoria, 11 May 1960.
12 Photostat copy in the State Library of Victoria.
13 Report of Legislative Assembly, Evidence (Edmund Wilson), p. 54.
14 *Biographical Memoir,* p. 7.

2 SETTLER AND MAGISTRATE, VAN DIEMEN'S LAND, 1836-1846

1 C. N. Hollinshed, 'The Nepean Peninsula in the 19th Century', *Victorian Historical Magazine,* vol. 28 (1962), p. 145; Hugh Anderson, *Out of the Shadow, The Career of John Pascoe Fawkner* (Melbourne, 1962), pp. 12-19, 69; James Backhouse Walker, 'The Expedition under Lieutenant-Governor Collins in 1803-4', *Early Tasmania* (Walker Memorial Volume, Hobart, 3rd impr., 1950); H.R.A., III. i. Introduction.
2 James Backhouse Walker, 'The Founding of Hobart by Lieutenant-Governor Collins', *Early Tasmania,* pp. 60-81.
3 H.R.A., I. vii. 618; M. H. Ellis, *Lachlan Macquarie* (Sydney, 1952), p. 208.
4 H.R.A., I. vii. 624; K. R. von Stieglitz, *A History of Local Government in Tasmania* (Launceston, 1958), pp. 15-16.
5 See G. C. Ingleton, *True Patriots All* (Sydney, 1952), p. 167, for a broadsheet calling for public rejoicing at Arthur's departure.
6 E. T. Emmett, *Short History of Tasmania* (Sydney, 1937), p. 69.
7 W. D. Forsyth, *Governor Arthur's Convict System* (London, 1935), p. 5.
8 Proclamation, July 1856, C.S.O. 24/137/4637.
9 Gunn Papers, A.316, Mitchell Library, Sydney; Harry O'May, *Hobart River Craft* (Hobart, n.d., but about 1958), p. 25; *Hobart Town Gazette,* 3 March 1843; *Launceston Examiner,* 27 May 1854.

[10] Report of Legislative Assembly, Evidence, p. 8.

[11] Murray's *Review*, 5 May 1843, p. 3.   [12] *Biographical Memoir*, p. 7.

[13] See Kathleen Fitzpatrick, *Sir John Franklin in Tasmania 1837-1843* (Melbourne, 1949); Frances J. Woodward, *Portrait of Jane, A Life of Lady Franklin* (London, 1951).

[14] Frances J. Woodward, op. cit., p. 209.

[15] A. H. Markham, *Life of Sir John Franklin* (London, 1891), p. 5.

[16] *Cornwall Chronicle*, 23 June 1838, p. 2.

[17] *Hobart Town Gazette*, 4 January 1839; C.S.O. 50/2. For abolition of position, see C.S.O. 22/106/2247; 22/34/1808.

[18] K. R. von Stieglitz, *A History of Local Government in Tasmania*, p. 26.

[19] See John Vincent Barry, *Alexander Maconochie of Norfolk Island* (Melbourne, 1958) pp. 46-56.

[20] Report of Legislative Assembly, Evidence, p. 13.

[21] N. Nixon, *The Pioneer Bishop in Van Diemen's Land, 1843-1863* (Hobart, 1953), p.10.

[22] *Adventures of a Griffin on a Voyage of Discovery (H.M.S. Fly)*, written by himself [H. S. Melville] (London, 1867), p. 52.

[23] Chief Police Magistrate to Colonial Secretary, 9 August 1838, C.S.O. 5/134/3227.   [24] C.S.O. 22/39/1245.

[25] Franklin to Stanley, 17 November 1842, no. 123, G.O. 33/43. The appointment as Coroner is in C.S.O. 22/106/2247.

[26] C.S.O. 5/241/6251.

[27] G.O. 33/52, C.S.O. 22/83/1804(b), C.S.O. 22/33/811.

[28] G.O. 33/51, G.O. 1/35, C.S.O. 22/23/499.

[29] H. F. Gurner to Sir Redmond Barry, 25 June 1876 (State Library of Victoria).   [30] Report of Legislative Assembly, Evidence, pp. 8-9.

[31] Report of Legislative Assembly, Evidence, p. 40.

[32] Rogers, *Correspondence*, p. 169.

[33] *Martin Cash, The Bushranger of Van Diemen's Land in 1843-4* (Hobart, 1929), pp. 98, 135, 161, 174. For Lester Burke's authorship of *Martin Cash*, see Frank Clune, *Martin Cash, The Last of the Tasmanian Bushrangers* Sydney, 1955), p. 329.

[34] Report of Legislative Council, Evidence (Dr Richard Youl), p. 103; Major de Winton, *Soldiering Fifty Years Ago, Australia in 'The Forties'* (London, 1898), p. 132; Rogers, *Correspondence*, pp. 168-9.

[35] See Louis Becke (ed.), *Old Convict Days* (London, 1899), pp. 37, 40.

[36] *Colonial Times*, 11 February 1840, p. 7.

[37] Denison to Grey, 12 June 1852, Confidential, G.O. 33/76; Report of Legislative Assembly, Evidence, p. 23.   [38] C.S.O. 20/29/637.

[39] Denison to Newcastle, 26 November 1853, no. 260, G.O. 33/79.

[40] L. Norman, *Sea Wolves and Bandits* (Hobart, 1946), p. 165.

[41] See Eris O'Brien, *The Foundation of Australia, 1786-1800* (Sydney, 2nd ed., 1950), pp. 84-8; John Vincent Barry, *Alexander Maconochie of Norfolk Island*, pp. 31-42; *Australian Encyclopaedia* (Sydney, 2nd ed., 1958), vol. 3, pp. 24-38; L. Radzinowicz, 'Changing Attitudes Towards Crime and Punishment', *Law Quarterly Review*, vol. 75 (1959), 388-90.

[42] See Charles Bateson, *The Convict Ships, 1787-1868* (Glasgow, 1959).

[43] John Vincent Barry, op. cit., p. 39.

[44] Report from the Select Committee . . . [on] Transportation, 3 August 1838, P.P. (H.L.), 1838, vol. 36, pp. xxi, xxxii, xli.

[45] Stanley to Franklin, 25 November 1842, *H.R.A.*, i. xx. 516; Acts 6 & 7 Victoria, c. 7.

[46] A. G. L. Shaw, 'Origins of the Probation System in Van Diemen's Land', *Historical Studies, Australia and New Zealand*, vol. 6 (1935), p. 16; A. G. L. Shaw, 'Sir John Eardley-Wilmott and the Probation System in Tasmania', *Papers & Proceedings*, Tasmanian Historical Research Association, no. 11 (1963), p. 5.

47 *Official Year Book of the Commonwealth of Australia,* no. 48 (1962), p. 124; *Australian Encyclopaedia* (2nd ed.), vol. 6, p. 349.
48 See John Vincent Barry, *Alexander Maconochie of Norfolk Island,* ch. 5; W. S. Hill-Reid, *John Grant's Journey* (London, 1957), p. 113; R. A. Daly, 'Archdeacon McEncroe on Norfolk Island 1838-1842', *Australian Catholic Record,* vol. 36 (October 1959); Colin Roderick, *John Knatchbull* (Sydney, 1963), pp. 85-102, 183-219.
49 See John Vincent Barry, op. cit., especially pp. 171-5, and the same author, 'Alexander Maconochie', *Pioneers in Criminology,* ed. H. Mannheim (London, 1960), p. 68.
50 Rev. John West, *The History of Tasmania* (Launceston, 1852), vol. 2, p. 295.
51 Report of Robert Pringle Stewart, Correspondence on the Subject of Convict Discipline and Transportation, *P.P.* (H.L.), 1847, vol. 8, pp. 80-97; Rev. John West, op. cit., vol. 2, pp. 296-8; John Vincent Barry, op. cit., pp. 97, 154-6.   52 Rogers, *Correspondence,* p. 58.
53 Rogers, *Correspondence,* p. 144; J. Lester Burke, *Martin Cash,* p. 151; Frank Clune, *Martin Cash,* pp. 281, 284, 294.
54 See Report of Commission on Murders of 1 July 1846, Correspondence on the Subject of Convict Discipline and Transportation, *P.P.* (H.L.), 1847, vol. 8, pp. 177-83; John Vincent Barry, op. cit., pp. 158-9; G. C. Ingleton, *True Patriots All* (Sydney, 1952), p. 241; J. Lester Burke, op. cit., p. 154.
55 *Biographical Memoir,* p. 11. For Price's appointment, see *Hobart Town Gazette,* 21 July 1846.

3   COMMANDANT OF NORFOLK ISLAND
1846-1853

1 Price gave the date of his arrival as 5 August (Rogers, *Correspondence,* p. 150), but Rogers asserted it was 3 August. Price reported to the Van Diemen's Land authorities that he assumed the duties of the office of Civil Commandant on 1 August (C.S.O. 20/31/753). For his appointment see *Hobart Town Gazette,* 21 July 1846.
2 See Alan Gross, *Charles Joseph La Trobe, Superintendent of the Port Phillip District 1839-1851, Lieutenant-Governor of Victoria 1851-1854* (Melbourne, 1956).
3 Melbourne *Age,* 10 February 1934, p. 24.
4 Deaths on Norfolk Island, 1849, p. 5; Tasmanian State Archives. Death certificate of Mrs Mary Price, Malvern, Victoria, 2 October 1894, records her as having borne eight children, six of whom were living when Price died, and five when she died.
5 Frank Clune, *Martin Cash, The Last of the Tasmanian Bushrangers* (Sydney, 1955), pp. 301-2.
6 Alexander Maconochie, *On Reformatory Discipline in County and Borough Prisons* (Birmingham, 1851), p. 26.
7 See opinion of Chief Justice Forbes, *H.R.A.,* I. xvii. 331-4, and compare *Quinn v. Hill* (1957) *Victorian Reports* 449-52, *Hall v. Whatmore* (1961) *Victorian Reports* 234.
8 Sir William Blackstone, *Commentaries on the Laws of England* (London, 1771), vol. 4, p. 297.
9 Cf. N.S.W. Act 3 William 4, no. 3 (24 August 1842); John Vincent Barry, *Alexander Maconochie of Norfolk Island* (Melbourne, 1958), pp. 93-4.
10 J. H. Cullen, Papers & Proceedings, Tasmanian Historical Research Association, no. 2 (1952), p. 6; W. B. Ullathorne, *Memoir of Bishop Willson* (London, 1887), pp. 57-61; Report of Robert Pringle Stewart, Correspondence on the Subject of Convict Discipline and Transportation, *P.P.* (H.L.), 1847, vol. 8, p. 80. For an account of the conduct of earlier commandants, James Morisett, Foster Fyans and Joseph Anderson, see Colin Roderick,

John Knatchbull, From Quarterdeck to Gallows (Sydney, 1963), pp. 83-102, 179-218.

11 J. Lester Burke, *Martin Cash, The Bushranger of Van Diemen's Land in 1843-4* (Hobart, 1929), p. 151.

12 Regulations for Penal Settlements, 1829, regulation 27, *H.R.A.*, I. xv. 105-13; Rogers, *Correspondence*, p. 143. For 'Instructions for the Superintendents of Iron Gang Stockades' see *H.R.A.*, I. xvii. 336-41.

13 J. Lester Burke, op. cit., p. 159. Childs died at Liskeard, England, on 2 January 1870, aged eighty-three, having attained the rank of Major-General in the Royal Marines.

14 Rogers, *Correspondence*, pp. 63-4. Lieutenant T. A. Butler, who was dismissed in December 1846 from the superintendency of the Cascades Station, allegedly for misappropriation of stores, made serious allegations against Price, but the latter's explanations were accepted by his superiors. See Denison to Grey, 14 October 1848, no. 207, G.O. 33/65, Grey to Denison, 7 June 1849, rec'd 28 October 1849, no. 94, G.O. 1/73.

15 Rogers, *Correspondence*, pp. 59-63.

16 Report of Legislative Assembly, Evidence, pp. 10-12. He gave the number executed during his first months as eighteen.

17 W. H. Barber, *Household Words*, ed. Charles Dickens (London, 1852), vol. 5, p. 486; Rogers, *Correspondence*, p. 163.

18 *H.R.A.*, I. xxii. 517; Rogers, *Correspondence*, p. 162; Rev. John West, *The History of Tasmania* (Launceston, 1852), vol. 2, p. 304.

19 *Hobart Town Courier*, 28 October 1846; Rev. E. Strickland, *The Australian Pastor, A Record of the Remarkable Changes in Mind and Outward Estate of Henry Elliott* (London, 1862), pp. 45-6; Eric Gibb, *Thrilling Incidents of the Convict System in Australasia* (London, 1895), pp. 66-7, a work on which not much reliance can generally be placed. For the trial, see letter of 13 October 1846, Fielding Browne to Colonial Secretary, V.D.L., Tasmanian State Archives, Wilmot Period, A series), no. A.590, vol. 27; Fielding Browne's report of 4 January 1847, *P.P.* (H.L.), 1847, vol. 8, p. 239.

20 Rogers, *Correspondence*, p. 105.   21 Ibid., p. 164.

22 *P.P.* (H.C.), 1847, vol. 7, p. 548; W. B. Ullathorne, *Memoir of Bishop Willson*, pp. 65-7; Rogers, *Correspondence*, pp. 164-5; Rev. John West, op. cit., vol. 2, p. 304.

23 Rogers, *Correspondence*, p. 120, where the date of Brown's execution is given as 18 October. Judge Fielding Browne gave it as 19 October (report, 4 January 1847).   24 Ibid., p. 63.

25 Matthew Arnold, 'Poor Mathias'.

26 Rogers, *Correspondence*, pp. 109, 168-70.

27 William Wills, *An Essay on Circumstantial Evidence*, ed. Sir Alfred Wills (London, 6th ed., 1912), p. 250.

28 Cf. Wills, op. cit., p. 12; W. M. Best, *The Principles of the Law of Evidence* (London, 12th ed., 1922), p. 14; Pitt Taylor, *A Treatise on the Law of Evidence* (London, 12th ed., 1931), vol. 1, pp. 335-7; Mr Justice Eggleston, 'Probabilities and Proof', *Melbourne University Law Review*, vol. 4 (1963), p. 180.

29 Anon., *The Story of the Life of Thomas Jones, an Escaped Norfolk Island Convict* (London, n.d.). The prison chaplain who prepared the story for publication was the Rev. W. Foster Rogers, a brother of the Rev. Thomas Rogers.

30 Mark Jeffrey, *A Burglar's Life* (Melbourne, n.d.), pp. 64-8.

31 Op. cit., pp. 160-76; Frank Clune, *Martin Cash*, p. 318.

32 Rogers, *Correspondence*, p. 2.

33 W. H. Barber, *The Case of Mr. W. H. Barber* (London, 7th ed., 1849), pp. 19-20, 100-1; J. B. Atlay, *Famous Trials* (London, 1899), pp. 64-90; see also J. A. Ferguson, *Bibliography of Australia* (Sydney, 1955), vol. 4, pp. 90-1.

34 W. Foster Rogers, 'Man's Inhumanity, Being A Chaplain's Chronicles of Norfolk Island in the 'Forties', p. 3 (typescript, C.214, Mitchell Library, Sydney; photocopy in State Library of Victoria).

35 Rogers, *Correspondence*, pp. 27, 149-62.

36 Rogers, *Correspondence*, pp. 7, 196.

37 *Statement of the Churchwardens of Windermere (Van Diemen's Land) relative to the case of the Rev. T. Rogers* (Launceston, n.d. but 1849), p. 5 (283-8/R, Mitchell Library, Sydney).

38 W. Foster Rogers, op. cit., pp. 5, 181-2; obituary in *Advocate*, Melbourne, 24 January 1903. W. Foster Rogers asserts his grandfather was appointed an Inspector of Charities, and was dismissed on 'Black Wednesday' (9 January 1878) but his name does not appear in the records. The *Chronicles* are inaccurate in some respects, but appear to be substantially reliable. Professor Douglas Pike informed me (letter, 1 July 1963) that, according to a family story, Rev. Thomas Rogers was an indifferent husband and father after he left for Norfolk Island. For Rogers' son, John William Foster Rogers, see P. Mennell, *Dictionary of Australian Biography* (London, 1892), p. 395.

39 John Vincent Barry, *Alexander Maconochie of Norfolk Island*, p. 162.

40 Reports of Committees during 1847, *P.P.* (H.C.), vol. 7, 21 June 1847.

41 Further Correspondence on the Subject of Convict Discipline and Transportation, presented 15 August 1850, *P.P.* (H.L.), 1850, vol. 11, p. 112.

42 *P.P.* (H.L.), 1852-3, vol. 18, p. 88. The letter is reproduced in Rev. Thomas Kelsh (comp.) '*Personal Recollections' of the Right Reverend Robert William Willson*, D.D. (Hobart, 1882), pp. 38-52. See also W. B. Ullathorne, *Memoir of Bishop Willson*, pp. 57-61.

43 Kelsh, op. cit., p. 38; J. G. Murtagh, *Australia, the Catholic Chapter* (Sydney, 2nd ed., 1959), p. 44.

44 J. G. Murtagh, op. cit., p. 45.

45 Sir William Denison, *Varieties of Vice-Regal Life* (London, 1870), vol. 1, p. 384, letter dated 3 April 1857.

46 J. F. Fairfax, *The Story of John Fairfax* (Sydney, 1941), p. 144; *Australian Encyclopaedia* (Sydney, 2nd ed., 1958), vol. 9, p. 244; P. Serle, *Dictionary of Australian Biography* (Sydney, 1949), vol. 2, p. 480.

47 Rev. John West, *The History of Tasmania*, vol. 2, pp. 299-302.

48 Denison to Earl Grey, 12 June 1852; Price to Comptroller-General, 15 March 1852, Further Correspondence on the Subject of Convict Discipline and Transportation, presented 18 July 1853, *P.P.* (H.L.), 1852-3, vol. 18.

49 Major de Winton, *Soldiering Fifty Years Ago, Australia in 'The Forties'* (London, 1898), pp. 148, 132 (cf. G. de Winton, 'Norfolk Island', *British Australasian*, 1 November 1894, p. 1472).

50 Bishop Willson's letter of 22 May 1852, para. 21, *P.P.* (H.L.), 1852-3, vol. 18, p. 88.

51 *Household Words*, vol. 5, p. 76.

52 W. H. Barber, *The Case of Mr. W. H. Barber*, pp. 19, 78.

53 Rogers, *Correspondence*, pp. 157-8.

54 H. G. Turner, *History of the Colony of Victoria* (London, 1904), vol. 2, p. 103.

55 G. W. Rusden, *History of Australia* (London, 1884), vol. 2, pp. 555, 591, 742. Frank Clune, writing much later, has much the same approach as Rusden; see *Martin Cash*, pp. 304-5, 315-19, *Captain Melville* (Sydney, 1957), pp. 197-212.

56 See A. G. Austin, *George William Rusden and National Education in Australia 1849-1862* (Melbourne, 1958), Preface, and p. 127.

57 Stanley to Franklin, 25 November 1842, *H.R.A.*, I. xxii. 514.

58 Cf. G. W. Rusden, op. cit., vol. 2, p. 557.

59 Report of Legislative Assembly, Evidence, pp. 11, 12.

60 Rogers, *Correspondence*, p. 60.

61 Op. cit., vol. 2, p. 742.

62 Proverbs xxx. 21-2.
63 Rogers, *Review*, p. 16.
64 Rogers, *Correspondence*, pp. 65-6.
65 Price to G. W. Walker, 8 June 1848, University of Tasmania Archives.
66 Rogers, *Review*, pp. 7-9, 17-19, and cf. Rogers, *Correspondence*, pp. 41-2.
67 Marcus Clarke, *For the Term of His Natural Life*, unabridged ed. (Sydney, 1929), p. 454 (Oxford World's Classics ed. (London, 1952), p. 532); Rogers, *Correspondence*, pp. 41-3.
68 Rogers, *Correspondence*, p. 43.
69 Ibid., p. 55.
70 Rev. John West, *The History of Tasmania*, vol. 2, p. 303.
71 C.S.O. 24/54/1914.
72 Rogers, *Correspondence*, pp. 96-100.
73 Ibid., p. 109.
74 Rogers, *Review*, p. 5.
75 Ibid., p. 1.
76 Ibid.
77 *Australian Encyclopaedia* (2nd ed.), vol. 4, p. 422; G. W. Rusden, *History of Australia*, vol. 2, pp. 398, 577, vol. 3, p. 629; H. A. White, *Crime and Criminals, or Reminiscences of the Penal Department in Victoria* (Ballarat, 1890), pp. 125-6.
78 Willson to Comptroller-General, 10 December 1849, Further Correspondence on the Subject of Convict Discipline and Transportation, presented 15 August 1850, *P.P.* (H.L.), 1850, vol. 11, pp. 88-95.
79 Willson to Denison, 22 May 1852, *P.P.* (H.L.), 1852-3, vol. 18, p. 88.
80 Price to Hampton, 20 April 1850, Further Correspondence on the Subject of Convict Discipline and Transportation, *P.P.* (H.C.), 1851, vol. 45, p. 51.
81 Hampton to Denison, 10 December 1852, Further Correspondence on the Subject of Convict Discipline and Transportation, *P.P.* (H.L.), 1852-3, vol. 18, p. 97.
82 Hampton to Denison, 11 November 1852, ibid., p. 95.
83 Newcastle to Denison, 26 June 1852, ibid., p. 122.
84 Quoted by Alfred Zimmern, *The Greek Commonwealth* (London, 5th ed., 1931), p. 127.
85 Denison to Grey, 6 February 1851, no. 21, G.O. 33/73.
86 G. de Winton, 'Norfolk Island', *British Australasian*, 1 November 1894, p. 1472.
87 Grey to Denison, 4 June 1851, no. 103, G.O. 1/81.
88 Denison to Grey, 10 February 1852, no. 31, G.O. 33/75; Pakington to Denison, 23 July 1852, no. 71, G.O. 1/85.
89 Sir William Denison, *Varieties of Vice-Regal Life* (London, 1870), vol. 1, p. 384, letter 3 April 1857.
90 Denison to Grey, 12 June 1852, G.O. 33/76.
91 Ibid.
92 Denison to Newcastle, 26 November 1853, no. 260, G.O. 33/79.
93 Report of Legislative Assembly, Evidence, p. 16.
94 *Launceston Examiner*, 27 May 1854.
95 Major de Winton, *Soldiering Fifty Years Ago*, pp. 141, 144.
96 Newcastle to Denison, 27 February 1854, no. 32, G.O. 1/91.
97 The first address is given in the register of Hutchins School, and the other in a To Let notice in the *Hobart Town Courier*, 6 April 1854, for a house as lately in the occupation of J. Price, Esq., Commandant, Norfolk Island.
98 *Hobart Town Courier*, 9 February 1853.

4 INSPECTOR-GENERAL OF PENAL ESTABLISHMENTS,
VICTORIA, 1854-1857

1 James Bonwick, *Port Phillip Settlement* (London, 1883), pp. 416-24; Edward Jenks, *The Government of Victoria (Australia)* (London, 1891), p. 28.
2 Geoffrey Serle, *The Golden Age, A History of the Colony of Victoria, 1851-1861* (Melbourne, 1963).
3 *Victoria, The First Century, an Historical Survey*, comp. by the Historical Sub-Committee of the Centenary Celebrations Council (Melbourne, 1934), p. 193; see also G. Serle, op. cit., Appendix 1.
4 Op. cit., p. 223.
5 Charlotte Haldane, *Daughter of Paris, The Life Story of Céleste Mogador* (London, 1961), pp. 146-51; W. Kelly, *Life in Victoria 1853 and 1858* (London, 1860), p. 41; T. McCombie, *The History of the Colony of Victoria from its Settlement to the Death of Sir Charles Hotham* (Melbourne, 1858), pp. 233-4; Mrs Clacy, *A Lady's Visit to the Gold Diggings 1852-53* (London, 1853; Melbourne, 1963), chs. 3 and 12.
6 Stanley to Gipps, 27 July 1844, *H.R.A.*, i. xxiii. 699; Grey to Fitzroy, 3 September 1847, *H.R.A.*, i. xxv. 735; Hepworth Dixon, *The London Prisons* (London, 1850), p. 163. For some unascertained reason, in Stanley's despatch of 27 July 1844 the prisoners to be sent from Parkhurst and Pentonville prisons are referred to as 'exciles'. For the *Randolph* incident see H. G. Turner, *History of the Colony of Victoria* (London, 1904), vol. 1, p. 274; and Margaret Kiddle, *Men of Yesterday* (Melbourne, 1961), pp. 152-62.
7 G. W. Rusden, *History of Australia* (London, 1884), vol. 2, p. 557n.; Hugh Anderson, *Out of the Shadow, The Career of John Pascoe Fawkner* (Melbourne, 1962), p. 169; Margaret Kiddle, op. cit., p. 150.
8 This account follows H. G. Turner's version (op. cit., vol. 1, p. 345) and that given in *Golden Years 1851-1951*, ed. E. A. Doyle (Melbourne, n.d., but 1951), pp. 137-8. See also Marcus Clarke, 'The "Nelson" Gold Robbery', *Stories of Australia* (London, 1897), p. 184. 'Garryowen' (E. Finn) differs (*The Chronicles of Early Melbourne* (Melbourne, 1888), vol. 2, p. 903). A compact account of crime in the wake of the gold discoveries is given in G. Serle, op. cit., pp. 129-38.
9 See Gipps to Stanley, *H.R.A.*, i. xxiv. 128.
10 Alan Gross, *Charles Joseph La Trobe, Superintendent of the Port Phillip District 1839-1851, Lieutenant-Governor of Victoria 1851-1854* (Melbourne, 1956), pp. 119-22; G. W. Rusden, op. cit., vol. 2, pp. 577-84; F. Sweetman, *Constitutional Development of Victoria, 1851-1861* (Melbourne, 1920), pp. 146-61; G. Serle, op. cit., pp. 126-30.
11 See *Ryall v. Kenealey* (1869) 6 Wyatt, Webb and à Beckett (L.) 193.
12 'Victorian Blue Book', 1854, p. 494 (State Library of Victoria).
13 Superintendent's Report, 1 May 1853, printed 1 September 1853; Inspector-General's Report (Price), 25 October 1854, ordered to be printed 30 January 1855, p. 1; Inspector-General's Report (Champ), 27 June 1857, p. 4 (*Parliamentary Papers* (Vic.)).
14 G.O. 33/41/467-71; C.S.O. 22/15/651, 20/1/8, 20/4/125; G.O. 33/71/317/51; Rogers, *Correspondence*, pp. 142-7. Barrow was the fifth son of Simon Barrow of Lansdowne Grove, Somersetshire (*Hobart Town Courier*, 1 and 21 July 1842).
15 For proclamation of Pentridge as a prison and Barrow's appointment see *Port Phillip Gazette*, no. 48, 13 November 1850, p. 962, and 'Victorian Blue Book', 1850, which states his appointment was from 1 September 1850. For accounts of his death see the Melbourne *Argus*, 6 and 9 May 1854; H. A. White, *Crime and Criminals, or Reminiscences of the Penal Department in Victoria* (Ballarat, 1890), p. 40; *Victoria, the First Century, An Historical Survey*, p. 177. White is wrong in giving the date of the drowning as 6 May.
16 Superintendent's Report, 1 May 1853, para. 18.

17 W. Branch-Johnson, *The English Prison Hulks* (London, 1957); M. Grünhut, *Penal Reform* (Oxford, 1948), p. 74; Hepworth Dixon, *The London Prisons* (London, 1850), p. 122.

18 H. A. White, 'The True History of the Hulk "Success" ', *Austral Light*, vol. 7 (1898), pp. 152, 205.

19 *Votes & Proceedings* (Legislative Council, Victoria), 1853-4, vol. 1, p. 682.

20 Report of Legislative Council, Appendices G and H.

21 Ibid., Evidence (Price), pp. 1-3, 10.   22 Ibid., p. 21.

23 Cf. Douglas Gordon, 'Sickness and Death at the Moreton Bay Convict Settlement', *Medical Journal of Australia*, vol. 2 (21 September 1963), pp. 478-80.

24 Report of Legislative Council, p. 2.

25 Ibid., Appendix F.

26 'Garryowen', *Chronicles of Early Melbourne*, vol. 1, p. 199; H. A. White, *Crime and Criminals*, p. 4. 'Garryowen' is mistaken in the dates. See note 15, above.

27 H. A. White, op. cit., pp. 51-129.

28 Ibid., p. 129.   29 Ibid., p. 52.

30 Report of Legislative Assembly, section 7; Report of Inspector-General Evans, 27 May 1895 (Prisons Division, Department of Social Welfare, Melbourne; *Parliamentary Paper* (Vic.), 1895-6).

31 Report of Legislative Assembly, Evidence, p. 21; H. A. White, op. cit., p. 64.

32 Report of the Commission appointed to Enquire into the State of the Police (Victoria), ordered to be printed 5 December 1855.

33 H. A. White, op. cit., pp. 38-9.

34 Inspector-General's Annual Report, 10 November 1855, p. 4 (Prisons Division, Department of Social Welfare, Melbourne).

35 Melbourne *Age*, 13 December 1856.

36 Melbourne *Argus*, 26 November 1856.

37 Report of Legislative Council, Evidence, pp. 20-1; Inspector-General's annual report, uncompleted and post-dated 21 May 1857, laid on table of Legislative Council 14 July 1857 (duplicate in Prisons Division, Department of Social Welfare, Melbourne); Frank Clune, *Captain Melville* (Sydney, 1956), p. 115; see also W. Joy and T. Prior, *The Bushrangers* (Sydney, 1963), p. 60.

38 Melbourne *Argus*, 24 October 1856; for first account of events of 22 October and for trials, see the daily issues of the *Argus*, 20-27 November 1856; cf. Frank Clune, *Murders on Maungatapu* (Sydney, 1959), pp. 30-2.

39 Glanville Williams, *Criminal Law* (London, 2nd ed., 1961), p. 397.

40 *R. v. Melville* (1856) 1 *Victorian Law Times* 209; *R. v. Templeton* (1956) *Victorian Reports* 709.

41 Frank Clune, *Captain Melville*, pp. ix-x, 214-15.

42 Report of Legislative Assembly, Evidence, p. 9.

43 Report of Legislative Assembly, Evidence, pp. 26, 31 (Price), 80 (R. C. F. Smith).

44 Act 17 Victoria No. 26, Section 6 (1854); Gaols Act 1958 (Victoria), Section 44.

45 Report of Legislative Council, Evidence, p. 5.

46 Report of Legislative Council, Evidence (A. Willis), p. 89.

47 Report of Legislative Assembly, Evidence (Price), pp. 23, 29; H. A. White, *Crime and Criminals*, pp. 59-60; Report of Legislative Council, Evidence (Dr Youl), p. 99.

48 Report of Legislative Council, Evidence, p. 62.

49 John Singleton, M.D., *A Narrative of Incidents in the Eventful Life of a Physician* (Melbourne, 1891), p. 160.

50 Annual report of Inspector-General, 10 November 1855, para. 14; *Coburg Courier*, 7 August 1962.

51 Report of Legislative Assembly, p. 47.

52 Report of Legislative Assembly, Evidence, p.25.

53 *Victorian Hansard,* 1856-7, vol. 1, p. 19.
54 Ibid., p. 21.
55 Ibid., p. 128.
56 Hugh Anderson, *Out of the Shadow,* p. 37.
57 Melbourne *Argus,* 2 December 1856.
58 For David Blair (1820-99) see P. Serle, *Dictionary of Australian Biography* (Sydney, 1949), vol. 1, p. 81.
59 H. A. White, op. cit., Table of Contents, ch. 3.
60 Melbourne *Argus,* 2 and 30 December 1856; Melbourne *Age,* 30 December 1856. For George Milner Stephen (1812-94) see P. Serle, op. cit., vol. 2, p. 357, and C. H. Fitts, 'Lines of Communication', *Proceedings of the Medico-Legal Society of Victoria during the Years 1953-1954* (Melbourne, 1955), vol. 6, p. 131; for William Westgarth, see P. Serle, op. cit., p. 482; for Dr Adam Cairns, see J. H. Heaton, *Australian Dictionary of Dates and Men of the Time* (Sydney, 1879), p. 31.
61 Melbourne *Argus,* 31 December 1856.
62 Ibid., 30 December 1856, Melbourne *Age,* same date.
63 Melbourne *Argus,* 26 November 1856.
64 Melbourne *Age,* 13, 18, 22-25 December 1856.
65 Report of Legislative Assembly, Evidence, pp. 50-2.
66 Mary Kent Hughes, *Pioneer Doctor, A Biography of John Singleton* (Melbourne, 1950); John Singleton, M.D., *A Narrative of Incidents in the Eventful Life of a Physician.* Singleton was born on 2 January 1808 and died on 30 September 1891.
67 For Singleton's version, see Report of Legislative Council, Evidence, p. 38, and John Singleton, op. cit., pp. 161-2; for Price's version, see Report of Legislative Assembly, Evidence, p. 43.
68 Report of Legislative Council, Evidence, pp. 38, 40.
69 Report of Legislative Council, Evidence, p. 41.
70 John Singleton, op. cit., pp. 155-6.
71 Ibid., pp. 158-9.
72 Annual report (Price), 26 October 1854, para. 12; annual report (Champ), 27 June 1857, para. 8.
73 Report of Legislative Council, Evidence, p. 8.
74 Ibid., Evidence (Duffy), pp. 25, 27.
75 Ibid., Evidence (Berkeley), pp. 54-5.
76 Ibid., Evidence (Tye), p. 43.
77 Ibid., Evidence (Webster), pp. 51-2.
78 Cf. C.R.D. Brothers, *Early Victorian Psychiatry 1855-1905* (Melbourne, n.d., but 1961), pp. 31-2. For an account of Dr Richard Youl (d. 6 August 1897) see *Australasian,* 25 April 1891.
79 Report of Legislative Council, Evidence, p. 79.
80 Ibid., p. 54.
81 Ibid., p. 29.
82 Ibid., p. 34.
83 Cf. W. L. Clay, *The Prison Chaplain, A Memoir of Rev. John Clay* (London, 1861), pp. 262-3.
84 *Victorian Hansard,* 1856-7, vol. 2, p. 1038.
85 Bishop Willson's letter, 22 May 1852, para. 47, P.P. (H.L.), 1852-3, vol. 18, p. 88.
86 H. A. White, *Crime and Criminals in Victoria,* pp. 132-3. See also P. Serle, *Dictionary of Australian Biography,* vol. 1, p. 157; *Australian Encyclopaedia* (Sydney, 2nd ed., 1958), vol. 2, p. 329; P. Mennell, *Dictionary of Australian Biography* (London, 1892), p. 87; F. C. Green (ed.), *A Century of Responsible Government 1856-1956* (Hobart, 1956), pp. 115-16.
87 Report of Inspector-General on the present state of the Penal Department and of his views as to its future management, 27 June 1857 (Prisons Division, Department of Social Welfare, Melbourne).

88 See Gilbert Geis, 'Jeremy Bentham', *Pioneers in Criminology,* ed. H. Mannheim (London, 1960), p. 63.

89 For the effect of solitary confinement, see John Vincent Barry, *Alexander Maconochie of Norfolk Island* (Melbourne, 1958), pp. 180, 185; Dr John Singleton's evidence, Report of Legislative Council, p. 40; Hepworth Dixon, *The London Prisons* (London, 1850), pp. 162-4; Right Rev. Bishop Ullathorne, *On the Management of Criminals* (London, 1866), pp. 39-44; and statement by South African psychiatrists, Melbourne *Herald,* 29 December 1963.

90 *Parliamentary Debates* (Victoria), 1870, vol. 10, pp. 210, 1205.

91 Progress Report of the Royal Commission on Penal and Prison Discipline, Pentridge Penal Establishment, 18 November 1870, *Parliamentary Papers* (Vic.), 1870, 2nd session, vol. 2, p. 533; Report (No. 2), Penal and Prison Discipline, 23 May 1871, *Parliamentary Papers* (Vic.), 1871, vol. 3, p. 327; Report (No. 3), Industrial and Reformatory Schools, 12 August 1872, *Parliamentary Papers* (Vic.), 1872, vol. 3, p. 521.

92 H. A. White, op. cit., pp. 172-6; *Parliamentary Debates* (Vic.), 1884, vol. 46, pp. 694, 740, 1297; 1885, vol. 49, pp. 1204-9.

5   THE MURDER OF JOHN PRICE AND THE TRIALS OF

THE MURDERERS

1 Unfinished annual report of late Inspector-General, posthumously dated 21 May 1857, and sent under cover of letter of that date from W. Snelling, Chief Clerk, Penal Department, to the Honourable the Chief Secretary. (Manuscript copy in possession of Prisons Division, Department of Social Welfare, Melbourne.)

2 Ibid.

3 The account given is compiled from the evidence at the inquest and the trials, as set out in *Biographical Memoir.*

4 *Biographical Memoir,* p. 58.

5 Ibid., p. 61.

6 Ibid., pp. 18, 29; p. 52, evidence of Christopher Farrell.

7 Ibid., pp. 36, 40.   8 Ibid., p. 22.

9 A. W. Grieg, 'The First Australian War-ship', *Victorian Historical Magazine,* vol. 9 (1923), p. 97.

10 Melbourne *Age,* 28 March 1857.

11 Original in possession of Mrs Nicholas, Warrandyte, Victoria; photographic copy in State Library of Victoria.

12 *Biographical Memoir,* p. 2.

13 *Plowden's Reports of Cases in the Reigns of King Edward VI, Queen Mary, King and Queen Philip and Mary, and Queen Elizabeth* (London, 1816), vol. 1, p. 100; H. F. Gurner, *The Practice of the Criminal Law of the Colony of Victoria* (Melbourne, 1871), p. 133.

14 *Biographical Memoir,* p. 81. The account of the trials given in this chapter, and the quotations, are taken from this publication.

15 See J. V. Barry, 'A Note on the Prisoner's Right to give Evidence in Victoria', *Res Judicatae* (Melbourne), vol. 6 (1952), p. 60.

16 Report of Legislative Assembly, Evidence (Price), pp. 45-6.

17 Frank Clune, *A Noose for Ned* (Melbourne, 1948), pp. 53-6.

18 Melbourne *Argus* 29 and 30 April, 1 May 1857; Melbourne *Age,* same dates.

19 For the official announcement of the eight executions, see *Victorian Government Gazette,* 5 May 1857, vol. 1, pp. 775-6. The hangman, 'Jack Harris', is said to have found the week's work too much for him and to have disappeared after the executions; see *Parliamentary Debates* (Vic.), 1962 session, 8 October, p. 559, and 'Knights of the Knot', *Tocsin,* 22 March 1900, an article probably written by Bernard O'Dowd.

20 Henry Kingsley, *Ravenshoe* (London, 1862), ch. 59 (coll. ed., p. 396).

21 Rogers, *Review*, pp. 9-10.

22 File, In the Goods of John Price, deceased, Intestate, Supreme Court of Victoria, Probate Jurisdiction. Mrs. Price's affidavit was sworn on 10 June 1857.

23 'Victorian Blue Book', 1857, Treasury Expenditure, Gratuities and Pensions (State Library of Victoria).

24 Obituary, *The Times*, 14 June 1927; Melbourne *Argus*, 23 August 1927.

25 A. Grenfell Price, *Founders and Pioneers of South Australia* (Adelaide, 1929), pp. 221-53; P. Serle, *Dictionary of Australian Biography* (Sydney, 1949), vol. 1, p. 138; *Australian Encyclopaedia* (Sydney, 2nd ed., 1958), vol. 2, p. 234; Ian Mudie, *River Boats* (Adelaide, 1961), pp. 36-59.

26 Melbourne *Argus*, 17 August 1878; *Queenslander*, 24 August 1878, p. 645.

27 P. Serle, op. cit., vol. 2, p. 253; *Australian Encyclopaedia* (2nd ed.), vol. 7, p. 274; Brian Fitzpatrick, *Short History of the Australian Labor Movement* (Melbourne, 1944), p. 73.

28 Obituary, Melbourne *Argus*, 4 June 1911; private communication, Lt-Col. R. C. R. Price, D.S.O., O.B.E., to Wilson Evans, Esq., Melbourne, 10 February 1960.

29 Melbourne *Age*, 10 February 1934, p. 24.

30 Death notice, *The Times*, 6 February 1937; *Burke's Peerage* (London, 1949), p. 1636.

31 Probate of Mrs Mary Price's will was granted by the Supreme Court of Victoria on 22 November 1894. She left about £800, £450 of which was represented by the house, Lindisfarne, in which she lived. (Probate file 56/189 of 1894, Supreme Court, Melbourne.)

6   LEGEND

1 *The Adventures of Martin Cash* (Hobart, 1870), abridged and reprinted as *Martin Cash, The Bushranger of Van Diemen's Land in 1843-4* (Hobart, 1929), pp. 159-76. See Frank Clune, *Martin Cash, The Last of the Tasmanian Bushrangers* (Sydney, 1955), pp. 329-32; John Alexander Ferguson, *Bibliography of Australia, 1851-1900* (Sydney, 1963), vol. 5, pp. 551-2.

2 'The Demon' (unpublished manuscript, Mitchell Library, Sydney); J. P. Kennedy, 'Convicts of Victoria's hell-hulks took revenge', Melbourne *Herald*, 3 September 1955; Anon., 'Bushranger with an Oxford Accent', ibid., 4 June 1958. See Appendix A.

3 *Biographical Memoir*, pp. 28, 31.

4 See Bill Wannan (ed.), *A Marcus Clarke Reader* (Melbourne, 1963), p. xviii.

5 Brian Elliott, *Marcus Clarke* (Oxford, 1958), p. 141n.; see also H. M. Green, *A History of Australian Literature* (Sydney, 1961), vol. 1, pp. 215-25.

6 Elliott, op. cit., pp. 142, 260. The article by L. L. Robson, 'The Historical Basis of *For the Term of His Natural Life*', *Australian Literary Studies*, vol. 1 (1963), p. 104, did not become available until after this chapter was completed.

7 See 1929 edition, p. 449, and also p. 467 where Rogers is mentioned in the text. In the appendix of the abridged edition (e.g. Home Entertainment Library (Sydney, 1935), p. 493, and Oxford World's Classics (London, 1952), p. 608) the year of publication of Rogers, *Correspondence*, is wrongly given as 1846, instead of 1849. Incidentally, Clarke did not 'lift' material from Lester Burke's *Martin Cash* without due acknowledgment, as Frank Clune alleges (*Martin Cash*, p. 330). He acknowledged *Martin Cash* as a source at p. 450 of the 1929 edition, and in the appendix to the abridged edition.

8 1929 ed., pp. 614, 632.

9 Ibid., pp. 634-8.

10 Ibid., pp. 454-5, under 12 November; World's Cl., p. 532; Rogers, *Correspondence*, p. 42.

11 World's Cl., p. 471.
12 1929 ed., p. 407; World's Cl., p. 474.
13 Report of Legislative Assembly, Evidence (Price), p. 50.
14 1929 ed., pp. 358-9; World's Cl., pp. 405-6. The version quoted is from the World's Cl. edition.
15 Major de Winton, *Soldiering Fifty Years Ago, Australia in 'The Forties'* (London, 1898), p. 132.
16 Gustave de Beaumont and Alexis de Tocqueville, *On the Penitentiary System in the United States* (Philadelphia, 1833), p. 203n.
17 *Biographical Memoir*, p. 15.
18 1929 ed., p. 632.
19 Major de Winton, op. cit., pp. 133-4.
20 Melbourne *Age*, 30 December 1856.
21 H. A. White, *Crime and Criminals, or Reminiscences of the Penal Department in Victoria* (Ballarat, 1890), pp. 59-60.
22 'John Price's Bar of Steel' is republished in a selection of Price Warung's stories, *Convict Days* (Sydney, 1960), p. 53, and (without acknowledgment of authorship) in 'The Captain' (T. G. Ford), *Inhumanity* (Hobart, 1932), p. 65. For accounts of 'Price Warung', see J. V. Barry, 'An Unacceptable Foreword', *Meanjin*, vol. 20 (1961), p. 96; H. M. Green, *A History of Australian Literature* (Sydney, 1961), vol. 1, p. 564; Vance Palmer, *The Legend of the Nineties* (Melbourne, 1954), pp. 96-100.

7   ON CRUELTY

1 See *Gollins v. Gollins* (1963) 3 *Weekly Law Reports* (Eng.) 176 (House of Lords).
2 William Blake, Appendix to *Songs of Innocence and Experience, A Divine Image*.
3 J. A. Froude, *Oceana* (London, 1886), p. 77.
4 H. C. Lea, *History of the Inquisition of the Middle Ages* (New York, 1887), vol. 1, pp. 234-6.
5 For two recent surveys from different standpoints, see S. A. Coblentz, *The Long Road to Humanity* (New York, 1959), and Christopher Hibbert, *The Roots of Evil* (London, 1963).
6 See A. T. W. Simeons, *Man's Presumptuous Brain* (London, 1960), pp. 35, 43-5.
7 Havelock Ellis, 'Love and Pain', *Studies in the Psychology of Sex* (New York, n.d.), vol. 1, pp. 82, 104.
8 Ellis, op. cit.; see also S. Freud, *An Outline of Psycho-analysis . . .* (London, 1949), p.6; Otto Fenichel, *The Psychoanalytic Theory of Neurosis* (New York, 1945), p. 354, and cf. Sigmund Freud, 'The Sexual Aberrations', *Basic Writings of Sigmund Freud* (New York, 1938), p. 570; 'Infantile Sexuality', ibid., pp. 593-4.
9 H. G. Wells, *'42 to '44, A Contemporary Memoir upon Human Behaviour during the Crisis of the World Revolution* (London, 1944), p. 18.
10 Ibid., pp. 14, 15, 17, 18.
11 Elias Canetti, *Crowds and Power* (London, 1962), p. 15.
12 See Charles Berg, *Madkind, The Origin and Development of the Mind* (London, 1962), p. 143.
13 J. A. Froude, 'Party Politics', *Short Studies on Great Subjects* (London, 1877), p. 326.
14 Bertrand Russell, *Power* (London, 1938), pp. 84-107.
15 Rt Rev. Bishop Ullathorne, *On the Management of Criminals* (London, 1866), p. 17.
16 George Ives, *History of Penal Methods* (London, 1914), p. 167.

BIBLIOGRAPHY

1 OFFICIAL PUBLICATIONS

Report from the Select Committee of the House of Commons appointed to inquire into the System of Transportation, its Efficacy as a Punishment, its Influence on the Moral State of Society in the Penal Colonies, and how far it is susceptible of Improvement; with Minutes of Evidence, &c., 3 August 1838, *P.P.* (H.L.), 1838, vol. 36, p. 1.

Correspondence on the Subject of Convict Discipline and Transportation, presented 16 February 1847; Further Correspondence, presented 15 April 1847; Further Correspondence, presented 14 May 1847, *P.P.* (H.L.), 1847, vol. 8, pp. 1, 205, 221.

Further Correspondence, presented 5 May 1848, *P.P.* (H.L.), 1847-8, vol. 9, p. 449.

Further Correspondence, presented February 1849; Further Correspondence, presented 30 July 1849, *P.P.* (H.L.), 1849, vol. 11, pp. 1, 289.

Further Correspondence, presented 31 January 1850; Further Correspondence, presented 15 August 1850, *P.P.* (H.L.), 1850, vol. 11, pp. 1, 145.

Further Correspondence, presented 14 May 1851; Further Correspondence, presented 4 August 1851, *P.P.* (H.L.), vol. 11, pp. 83, 347.

Further Correspondence, presented 30 April 1852, *P.P.* (H.L.), 1852, vol. 13, p. 417.

Further Correspondence, presented 13 December 1852; Further Correspondence, presented 18 July 1853, *P.P.* (H.L.), 1852-3, vol. 18, pp. 153, 409.

Further Correspondence, presented May 1854, *P.P.* (H.L.), 1854, vol. 15, p. 137.

Further Correspondence, presented February 1855, *P.P.* (H.L.), 1854-5, vol. 14, p. 105.

Further Correspondence, presented August 1855, *P.P.* (H.L), 1854-5, vol. 14, p. 339.

Hobart Town Gazette.

Tasmanian State Archives, documents including:
  Records of Governor's Office
  Records of Colonial Secretary's Office
  Records of Convict Office.

Victoria, Government Gazette.

Victorian Blue Book.

Victorian Hansard, 1856-7, vol. 1.

Victoria, 1856-7, Report of the Select Committee of the Legislative Council on the subject of Penal Establishments, together with the Proceedings of Committee, Minutes of Evidence and Appendices, ordered by the Council to be printed 30 July 1857, *Votes and Proceedings of Legislative Council of Victoria,* 1856-7.

Victoria, 1856-7, Report from the Select Committee upon Penal Discipline, together with the Proceedings of the Committee, Minutes of Evidence and Appendices, ordered by the Legislative Assembly to be printed 11 September 1857, *Votes and Proceedings of the Legislative Assembly of Victoria,* 1856-7, vol. 3.

Annual Report of Superintendent of Penal Establishments, 1 May 1853, and annual reports thereafter by successive Inspectors-General of Penal Establishments (1853-1921: Prisons Division, Department of Social Welfare, Melbourne; also in *Parliamentary Papers* (Vic.)).

Progress Report of the Royal Commission on Penal and Prison Discipline, Pentridge Penal Establishment, 18 November 1870, *Parliamentary Papers* (Vic.), 1870, 2nd session, vol. 2, p. 533; Report (No. 2), Penal and Prison Discipline, 23 May 1871, *Parliamentary Papers* (Vic.), 1871, vol. 3, p. 327; Report (No. 3), Industrial and Reformatory Schools, 12 August 1872, *Parliamentary Papers* (Vic.), 1872, vol. 3, p. 521.

Historical Records of Australia.

II BOOKS AND ARTICLES

Anon. (T.L.B.). *Biographical Memoir of the late Mr. John Price, Inspector-General of Penal Establishments for Victoria;* with an account of the Assassination, Inquest, & Funeral; also a full report of the trial of the Prisoners. Melbourne, n.d., but 1857.

Anon. [John Butler Cooper]. *History of Tasmania. Truth* newspaper, Melbourne, 1915.

Anon. *The History of the British Convict Ship 'Success'.* n.d., no publisher's imprint. [Possibly written by Joseph C. Harvie.]

Anon. *The Story of the Life of Thomas Jones, an Escaped Norfolk Island Convict.* London, n.d., prepared by Rev. W. Foster Rogers.

Australian Encyclopaedia. 2nd ed. vol. 7. Sydney, 1958.

Barber, W. H. *The Case of Mr. W. H. Barber,* 7th ed. London, 1849.

———— In *Household Words,* ed. Charles Dickens, vol. 5, 1852.

Barry, John Vincent. *Alexander Maconochie of Norfolk Island, A Study of a Pioneer in Penal Reform.* Melbourne, 1958.

Bateson, Charles. *The Convict Ships, 1787-1868.* Glasgow, 1959.

Becke, Louis (ed.). *Old Convict Days.* London, 1899.

Boase, G. C. *Collectanea Cornubiensia*. Truro, 1904.
———— and Courtney, W. P. *Bibliotheca Cornubiensis*. vol. 2. London, 1878.
Boxall, George E. *History of Australian Bushrangers*. Sydney, 1899; often reprinted.
Burke, J. Lester. *The Adventures of Martin Cash*. Hobart, 1870. Abridged and reprinted as *Martin Cash, The Bushranger of Van Diemen's Land in 1843-4*. Hobart, 1929.
Burke's Peerage and Baronetcy. London, 1869 and 1949.
'The Captain' (T. G. Ford). *Inhumanity*. Hobart, 1932.
Clune, Frank. *Martin Cash, The Last of the Tasmanian Bushrangers*. Sydney, 1955.
———— *Captain Melville*. Sydney, 1956.
———— *Murders on Maungatapu*. Sydney, 1959.
'Cygnet'. *The Story of the East India Merchantman 'Success'*. Swan River Booklet no. 11, Perth, n.d.
Denison, Sir William. *Varieties of Vice-Regal Life*. vol. 1. London, 1890.
de Winton, G. 'Norfolk Island', *British Australasian*, 1 November 1894.
———— *Soldiering Fifty Years Ago, Australia in 'The Forties'*. London, 1898.
Foster, Joseph. *Alumni Oxonienses, the members of the University of Oxford, 1715-1886* . . . vol. 1, later series. Oxford, 1891.
Gibb, Eric. *Thrilling Incidents of the Convict System in Australasia*. London, 1895.
Heaton, J. H. *Australian Dictionary of Dates and Men of the Time containing the History of Australasia from 1542 to May 1879*. Sydney, 1879.
Ingleton, G. C. *True Patriots All*. Sydney, 1952.
Ives, George. *History of Penal Methods*. London, 1914.
Jeffrey, Mark. *A Burglar's Life*. Melbourne, n.d.
Joy, W. and Prior, T. *The Bushrangers*. Sydney, 1963.
Kelsh, Rev. Thomas. *'Personal Recollections' of the Right Reverend Robert William Willson, D.D.* Hobart, 1882.
Kent-Hughes, Mary. *Pioneer Doctor, A Biography of John Singleton*. Melbourne, 1950.
Melville, H. S. *Adventures of a Griffin on a Voyage of Discovery*. London, 1867.
Mennell, P. *Dictionary of Australian Biography, 1855-1892*. London, 1892.
Murtagh, J. G. *Australia, the Catholic Chapter*. 1st ed., London, 1946; 2nd ed., Sydney, 1959.
Nixon, N. *The Pioneer Bishop of Van Diemen's Land, 1843-1863*. Hobart, 1953.
Norman, L. *Sea Wolves and Bandits*. Hobart, 1946.

Rogers, T. *Correspondence relating to the Dismissal of the Rev. T. Rogers from His Chaplaincy at Norfolk Island.* Launceston, 1849.

———— *Review of Dr. Hampton's First Report on Norfolk Island.* n.d., but published with *Correspondence,* above.

Rogers, W. Foster. 'Man's Inhumanity, Being a Chaplain's Chronicles of Norfolk Island in the 'Forties.' Typescript, C.214, Mitchell Library, Sydney; photo copy, State Library of Victoria.

Rusden, G. W. *History of Australia.* vol. 2. London, 1884.

Serle, G. *The Golden Age, A History of the Colony of Victoria, 1851-1861.* Melbourne, 1963.

Serle, P. *Dictionary of Australian Biography.* 2 vols. Sydney, 1949.

Singleton, John, M.D. *A Narrative of Incidents in the Eventful Life of a Physician.* Melbourne, 1891.

Smith, Coultman. *Shadow over Tasmania.* 13th ed. Hobart, 1961.

Strickland, Rev. E. *The Australian Pastor, A Record of the Remarkable Changes in Mind and Outward Estate of Henry Elliott.* London, 1862.

Turner, H. G. *History of the Colony of Victoria.* vol. 2. London, 1904.

Ullathorne, W. B. *Autobiography of Archbishop Ullathorne.* London, 1891.

———— *Memoir of Bishop Willson.* London, 1887.

Wannan, Bill. *Tell 'em I Died Game.* Melbourne, 1963.

West, Rev. John. *The History of Tasmania.* vol. 2. Launceston, 1852.

White, Henry A. *Crime and Criminals, or Reminiscences of the Penal Department in Victoria.* Ballarat, 1890. (English edition, entitled *Tales of Crime and Criminals in Australia.* London, 1894.)

———— 'The True History of the Hulk "Success"', *Austral Light,* vol. 7, 1898.

Woodward, Francis J. *Portrait of Jane, A Life of Lady Franklin.* London, 1951.

III NEWSPAPERS

Age, Melbourne
Argus, Melbourne
Colonial Times, Hobart Town
Cornwall Chronicle, Launceston
Hobart Town Courier
Launceston Examiner
The Times, London

INDEX